DOCUMENTED

FACTS

THE
WATCHTOWER
SOCIETY DOESN'T
WANT YOU TO

KNOW

Christina R. (Harvey) Darlington

First Edition Copyright ©1997
Published by Christina Harvey of
Witnesses for Jesus, CO 80949 USA

Second Edition Copyright ©2012
Christina R (Harvey) Darlington
All rights reserved.

Witnesses for Jesus Inc
PO Box 50911
Colorado Springs, CO 80949 USA
4witness.org * 4jehovah.org

ISBN: 1479193917
ISBN-13: 978-1479193912

DEDICATION

This book is dedicated to the millions of Jehovah's Witnesses who are deceived by the Watchtower Society into thinking they are serving God's organization when in fact they are serving an organization of mere men. Let's pray for God's Spirit to free them from this delusion to accept true eternal life in Christ alone.

TABLE OF CONTENTS

INTRODUCTION

Jehovah's Witnesses are some of the most devoted, religious people you can meet on the streets, actively preaching a message of a future Earthly Paradise under the rule of a Heavenly Kingdom led by Jehovah God and His Son Jesus Christ.

Incited with passion for this message, under the leadership of the Watchtower Society, Jehovah's Witnesses flock to the streets of businesses and neighborhoods, in hopes of gaining converts to their ever-growing organization.

Since they believe that they are the only people who know the real "Truth" about what God desires of humankind, they seek to persuade potential converts to join their religion before Jehovah God brings His wrath of judgment upon the wicked who do not follow His arrangement for salvation.

This book examines the history and doctrines of the Jehovah's Witness religion and reveals many facts the Watchtower Society tries to hide from Jehovah's Witnesses and investigators of this religion. Photocopied documentation for all of the claims made within the pages of this book are numbered, reproduced at the end of this book, and noted in the text by a "DP" (Documentation Page Number) in parenthesis.

CHAPTER ONE: A BUSY RELIGION

As of 2010, there are over 7 million active Jehovah's Witnesses worldwide, spending approximately one billion hours each year serving the Watchtower organization. The Jehovah's Witnesses are active in over 230 countries and are the fastest growing religion in the former USSR.

Claiming that people must "come to Jehovah's organization for salvation,"[1] the Watch Tower Society places great pressure on Jehovah's Witnesses to perform according to their guidelines.

In addition to attending several meetings each week, Jehovah's Witnesses are required to spend many hours each month distributing *Watchtower* articles, conducting Watchtower "Bible studies," and researching various topics in Watchtower literature for discussion during their meetings.

Witnesses are forbidden to serve in the military, salute the flag, say the pledge of allegiance, vote in elections, take blood transfusions, celebrate birthdays and holidays including Thanksgiving, Easter, and Christmas, and are forbidden to read literature critical of the organization. Over the years, Jehovah's

---

[1] *The Watchtower,* November 15, 1981, p. 21   (DP 1)

Witnesses have also been discouraged from associating with non-Jehovah's Witness friends, participating in after school activities such as sports, and furthering their education by going to college.[2]

All these restrictions and demands placed on Jehovah's Witnesses tend to isolate them from the rest of Society with the result that the organization becomes the "life" of the Jehovah's Witnesses who actively serve it. If a certain Jehovah's Witness fails to follow the guidelines set up by the organization, he is then subject to "disfellowshipping" in which the individual is shunned by all his friends and relatives in the organization.[3]

For many, this is a painful experience which leaves former Jehovah's Witnesses feeling hopeless and empty. Because of these policies and the overwhelming control this organization has over the physical and spiritual lives of so many people, it is of paramount importance that a person thoroughly examine the Society's claims and history before becoming involved with this organization.

> **"We need to examine**, not only what we personally believe, but also what is taught by any **religious organization** with which we may be associated. Are its teachings in full harmony with God's Word, or are they based on the traditions of men? **If we are lovers of the truth, there is nothing to fear from such an examination."**—*The Truth that Leads to Eternal Life*, Watch Tower Bible & Tract Society, 1968, p. 13 (DP 22)

---

[2] *United in Worship of the Only True God*, 1983, pp. 166-167; *Blood, Medicine and the Law of God*, 1961, pp. 54-55; *School and Jehovah's Witnesses*, 1983, pp. 13-21, 23; *The Watchtower*, March 15, 1962, pp. 178-179; *The Watchtower*, March 15, 1986, pp. 12, 19 (DP 2-18)

[3] *The Watchtower*, September 15, 1981, pp. 25, 29-30 (DP 19-21)

CHAPTER TWO: HISTORICAL BACKGROUND

In 1879, at the age of 27, Charles Taze Russell, founder of the Watch Tower Bible & Tract Society, began publishing *Zion's Watch Tower and Herald of Christ's Presence.* Born in Allegheny, Pennsylvania in 1852. He was raised a Presbyterian but later joined a liberal Congregational Church because he preferred its views.

For 10 years, prior to publishing his *Watch Tower* articles, Russell studied with a splinter group off of Second Adventists and was greatly influenced by their teachings against the bodily return of Christ and the immortality of the human soul.[4] Russell taught and published many doctrines that the current Watch Tower Society totally rejects and engaged in practices regarded by current Jehovah's Witnesses to be of pagan origin. In fact, if Russell were a Jehovah's Witness in the current Watchtower organization, he would have been disfellowshipped for his beliefs and practices! Among these are the following:

- Using the **symbol of the sun god Ra** on the cover of his books.[5]

---

[4] *Jehovah's Witnesses—Proclaimers of God's Kingdom,* 1993, pp. 45-46 (DP 23-24)
[5] *Studies in the Scriptures,* vol. 1-7 (DP 25-26)

- Using the **Masonic Knights Templar logo** of the Cross and Crown on his issues of *Zion's Watch Tower.*[6]
- Teaching that he was the "Faithful and Wise Servant" of Matt. 24:45-51, which resulted in many of his followers actually **worshipping** him.[7]
- Teaching that "the forming of a **visible organization**...would be out of harmony with the spirit of the divine plan." "Beware of 'organization.' It is wholly unnecessary."[8]
- Teaching that Christians "**are divine beings—hence all such are Gods**, thus we have a family of God....in the resurrection we will rise in our true character **as Gods**."[9]
- Teaching that "the **whole body of Christ the 'Mighty God'**...shall share in the work of restoring the life lost in Adam, and therefore be members of that company which **as a whole will be the *Everlasting Father*** to the restored race."[10]
- Teaching that the Lord Jesus should be **worshipped** and that He **is not Michael the archangel**.[11]
- Celebrating **birthdays and holidays** such as Christmas.[12]
- Teaching that one can **join the military** as long as he did "not shoot anybody."[13]

---

[6] *Jehovah's Witnesses—Proclaimers of God's Kingdom,* 1993, p. 200 (DP 27-28)

[7] *The Watch Tower,* April 15, 1904, p. 125; *The Divine Plan of the Ages, Studies,* vol. 1, 1925ed. Biography, p. 7; *1975 Yearbook of Jehovah's Witnesses,* p. 88 (DP 29-31)

[8] *Zion's Watch Tower,* December 1, 1894, p. 384; *Zion's Watch Tower,* September 15, 1895, p. 216 (DP 32-33)

[9] *Zion's Watch Tower,* December 1881, pp. 2-3 (Reprints p. 301) (DP 34)

[10] *Zion's Watch Tower,* November 1881, p. 10 (Reprints p. 298) (DP 35)

[11] *The Atonement Between God and Man, (Studies, vol. 5),* 1899, 1916ed, p. 85; *Watch Tower,* November 1879, p. 4 (Reprints p. 48); *The Plan of the Ages,* 1891, p. 178 (DP 36-38)

[12] *Jehovah's Witnesses—Proclaimers of God's Kingdom,* 1993, p. 201; *Zion's Watch Tower,* November 15, 1907, p. 351; *Zion's Watch Tower,* December 1, 1904, p. 364 (DP 39-41)

[13] *Zion's Watch Tower,* July 1, 1898, p. 204; *Zion's Watch Tower,* August 1, 1898, p. 231 (DP 42-43)

- Teaching that white skin is better than black skin and that "the **white race** exhibits some qualities of **superiority** over any other."[14]
- Teaching that the **shape of one's brain** determines his responsiveness to God.[15.]
- Teaching that Jehovah "governs his universe" from the star "Alcyone" in the **Pleiades** constellation.[16]
- Teaching that the "Great Pyramid of Gizeh" was "**God's stone witness**" which proved Russell's claims that "the time of the end" embraced a period from 1799-1914, with Jesus' invisible presence beginning in 1874, and the destruction of present government in 1914.[17]

In the 1954 *Douglas Walsh Trial* in Scotland, Fred Franz, who was Watchtower president from 1977-1992, was asked about the Society's changes in doctrine. Here is how he answered:

Q. So that what is published as the truth today by the Society may have to be admitted to be wrong in a few years?

A. We have to wait and see.

Q. **And in the meantime the body of Jehovah's** Witnesses **have been following error?**

A. They have been following misconstructions on the Scriptures.

Q. Error?

A. **Well, error**.

 —*Douglas Walsh Trial,* Pursuer's Proof, 1954, p. 114 (DP 50)

"**Satan attempted to use his** *influence* **in a subtle way**, and in this he was successful. How so? By

---

[14] *Zion's Watch Tower,* October 1, 1900, p. 296; *Zion's Watch Tower,* July 15, 1902, p. 216 (DP 44-45)

[15] *The Watch Tower,* March 15, 1913, p. 84; *Pennsylvania Superior Court Reports,* vol. 37, p. 351 (DP 46-47)

[16] *Thy Kingdom Come, (Studies, vol. 3)* p. 327 (DP 48)

[17] *Jehovah's Witnesses—Proclaimers of God's Kingdom,* 1993, p. 201; *Finished Mystery, (Studies, vol. 7)* 1917, p. 60 (DP 39, 49)

insinuation and falsehood. **He put forth error, under cover of a lie, as a substitute for truth. In other words, he put darkness for light**."—*The Watchtower,* May 15, 1976, p. 304 (DP 51)

"**If we were following *a man*** undoubtedly it would be different with us; undoubtedly one human idea would contradict another **and that which was light one or two or six years ago would be regarded as darkness now**: But with God there is no variableness, neither shadow of turning, **and so it is with *truth;* any knowledge or light coming from God must be like its author. A new view of truth never can contradict a former truth. *'New light'* never extinguished older *'light,'* but adds to it**....So is it with the light of truth; the true increase is by adding to, not by substituting one for another."—*Zion's Watch Tower,* February 1881, p. 3 (DP 52)

CHAPTER THREE: THE NEW WORLD TRANSLATION

In 1950, the Watch Tower Society came out with their own translation of the Bible, the *New World Translation.* Jehovah's Witnesses are told that this translation is the most accurate, unbiased translation available. The Society claims that the *New World Translation Committee* was made up of highly trained Greek scholars who did their best to "transmit his [God's] thoughts and declarations as accurately as possible."[18] However, when one endeavors to check into the credentials of these translators, one finds that the Society is unwilling to release this information, stating that the Committee desires that all the glory for this translation go to Jehovah God and therefore the translators desire to remain anonymous.

On the surface, this may sound quite noble and honorable; but one may wonder, is this the real reason why they desire to remain anonymous? Over the years, further investigation has revealed who the translators of the *New World Translation* were, and the facts show that they were totally unqualified for the task of translation. Five of the six Watchtower Governing Body members who were on the Translation Committee had no formal training whatsoever in the Biblical languages. The sixth

---

[18] *New World Translation,* 1984, p. 5   (DP 53)

one, Fred Franz, (former Governing Body member and Watchtower president from 1977-1992) claimed to have some education, but in the *Douglas Walsh Trial* in Scotland, he gave this testimony under oath:

Tuesday, 23rd November, 1954:
Frederick William Franz, Examined:

Q. **Have you also made yourself familiar with Hebrew?**

A. **Yes....**

Q. **So that you have a substantial linguistic apparatus at your command?**

A. **Yes, for use in my biblical work.**

Q. **I think you are able to read and follow the Bible in Hebrew**, Greek, Latin, Spanish, Portuguese, German, and French?

A. **Yes.**

Q. It is the case, is it not, that in 1950 there was **prepared** and issued what is called the New World Translation of the Christian Greek Scriptures?

A. Yes....

Q. **I think that it was your duty, was it not, before the issue of that New World Translation by your Society to check that translation for accuracy?**

A. **That is true.**

Q. In light of your studies and in light of your knowledge?

A. That is true.

Q. And did you do so?

A. I did so....

Q. **And was it your duty on behalf of the Society to check the translation into English from the original Hebrew of that first volume of the Old Testament Scriptures?**

A. **Yes....**

Q. **In so far as translation of the Bible itself isundertaken, are you responsible for that?**

A. **I have been authorised to examine a translation and determine its accuracy and recommend its acceptance in the form in which it is submitted.**

Q. Are the translators members of the Editorial Committee?

A. That is a question which I, as a member of the Board of Directors, am not authorised to disclose....

Q. When did you go to the University?....

Q. **Did you graduate?**

A. **No, I did not....**

Q. **Had you done any Hebrew in the course of your University work?**

A. **No, I had not, but in the course of my editorial work, my special research work for the president of the Society, I found it was very necessary to have knowledge of Hebrew, and so I undertook a personal study of that.**

ADJOURNED

Wednesday, 24th November, 1954:
Frederick William Franz, Cross Continued:

Q. **You, yourself, read and speak Hebrew, do you?**

A. **I do not speak Hebrew.**

Q. You do not?

A. No.

Q. **Can you, yourself, translate that into Hebrew?**

A. Which?

Q. That fourth verse of the Second Chapter of Genesis?

A. You mean here?

Q. Yes?

A. **No, I won't attempt to do that.**
   —*Douglas Walsh Trial,* Pursuer's Proof, 1954, pp. 7-9, 88, 91-92, 102-103 (DP 54-62)

This exercise that Franz was unable to do is something that the average first or second year Hebrew student could have accomplished without any difficulty. Is it any wonder the Society refuses to publicly reveal the people who were involved in the translation of their Bible? Would you put your trust in a doctor who refused to give his credentials? Yet, this is what many Jehovah's Witnesses are doing when it comes to vital Bible truth.

THE NEW WORLD TRANSLATION COMPARED WITH THE KINGDOM INTERLINEAR TRANSLATION OF THE GREEK SCRIPTURES:

In 1969, the Watch Tower Society produced *The Kingdom Interlinear Translation of the Greek Scriptures,* "Presenting a literal word-for-word translation into English under the Greek text as set out in 'The New Testament in the Original Greek—The Text Revised by Brooke Foss Westcott D.D. and Fenton John Anthony Hort D.D.' "—Title page of 1969 ed. (DP 63) The Watch Tower Society states:

> "The purpose behind the publishing of *The Kingdom Interlinear Translation of the Greek Scriptures* is to aid such seekers of truth and life. **Its literal interlinear English translation** is specially designed to open up to the student of the Sacred Scriptures **what the original *koi-ne'* Greek basically or literally says**.... The word-for-word interlinear translation and the *New World Translation* are arranged in parallel on the page, so that comparisons can be made between the two readings. **Thus, the accuracy of any modern translation can be determined**....We offer **no paraphrase** of the Scriptures....To each major word **we have assigned one meaning** and have held to that meaning as far as the context permitted."—*The Kingdom Interlinear Translation of the Greek Scriptures*, 1985 edition, pp. 5, 9-10 (DP 64-66)

The following is a comparison between the rendering of the Society's *Kingdom Interlinear Translation* and the *New World Translation*:

Verse	*Interlinear Translation*	*New World Translation*
Col. 2:9 (DP 67)	"all the fullness of the **divinity**" dwells in Christ.	"all the fullness of **divine quality**" dwells in Christ.

Note: Greek scholar Joseph Henry Thayer states that the Greek word used here *"Theotes"* literally means "deity i.e. the state of being God, Godhead"—*The New Thayer's Greek English Lexicon of the New Testament,* 1974 p. 288 (DP 68)

Verse	*Interlinear Translation*	*New World Translation*
Col 1:16-17 (DP 69)	Christ created **"all (things)."**	Christ created **"all [other] Things."**

Note: The Watch Tower Society inserts the word "other" four times into this passage, in order to make it compatible with their doctrine of Christ having been created. However, in John 1:3, we read that Christ created "all things"—not all other things.

Verse	*Interlinear Translation*	*New World Translation*
Gal. 2:20 & 2 Cor. 13:5 (DP 70-71)	Christ is living **"in me."**	Christ is living **"in union** with me."
Phil. 3:9 (DP 72)	"be found **in him**"	"be found **in union** with him"

Note: To be found "in Christ" means that one is trusting in Christ alone for his righteousness and is therefore positionally "in Christ." Thus, when God looks at this person who is "in Christ," He sees this person in the context of Christ's righteousness instead of his own (see Col. 3:3). There is a big difference between being "in union" with Christ and actually being positionally "in Christ."

Verse	*Interlinear Translation*	*New World Translation*
Phil. 2:9 (DP 73)	God gave Christ the name "over **every** name."	God gave Christ the name "above **every [other]** name."

Note: The Watch Tower Society teaches that Jehovah God has the name above every name and therefore, they had to insert the word "other" to justify their doctrine. However, according to John 17:11, Jesus has Jehovah's Name!

Verse	*Interlinear Translation*	*New World Translation*
John 1:1 (DP 74)	"**god** was the Word."	"the Word was **a god**."

Note: The Society argues that because the definite article "the" doesn't appear before God in this half of the verse, that justifies their insertion of the article "a" in their translation. However, the Society is inconsistent with their "rule" for if they were consistent, they would have to translate John 1:6 as, "there arose a man that was sent forth as a representative of **a** God." Since this translation wouldn't make sense, the Society picks and chooses how it wants to apply its "rule" in accord with its doctrine.

Verse	*Interlinear Translation*	*New World Translation*
John 8:58 (DP 75)	"Before Abraham to become **I am**."	"Before Abraham came into existence, **I have been**."

Note: The Greek words for "I am" are *"ego eimi"* (εγω ειμι). In every place where these words appear in the text of the Bible, the Society correctly translates them as "I am," EXCEPT in this verse.[19] Why the inconsistency in translation? Jesus was identifying

---

[19] See also John 9:5, 9 (DP 76)

Himself with the "I am" of Exodus 3:14 who is Jehovah God, and this is why the Jews tried to stone Him for blasphemy (see verse 59, compare with Leviticus 24:16). The Society mistranslated this verse because its correct translation contradicts their doctrine.

Verse	Interlinear Translation	New World Translation
John 14:10 (DP 77)	"Not you are believing that I **in** the Father and the Father **in** me is?"	"I am **in union** with the Father and the Father is **in union** with me?"
John 14:14 (DP 77)	"If ever anything you should **ask me**...."	If you ask anything...."

Note: Because the Society teaches that Jesus isn't God, they teach that one should not pray to Jesus. Since prayer is a form of worship, Jesus shouldn't be prayed to unless, of course, He is God (see Exodus 23:13). As one can clearly see, since Jesus asked his followers to request things of Him in prayer, the Society had to omit the words "ask Me" in their translation so that this verse would be compatible with their doctrine.

Does the Society's *New World Translation* pass the test of accuracy when measured by the Society's *Kingdom Interlinear Translation?* Could this be why no recognized Greek scholars support the Watch Tower Society's *New World Translation*, and instead, affirm along with Dr. Julius Mantey that the Society's translation is "a grossly misleading translation."? [20]

---

[20] In the 1969 edition of the Watch Tower Society's *Kingdom Interlinear Translation of the Greek Scriptures,* pp. 1158-1159, the Society misquoted Dana and Mantey's *A Manual Grammar of the Greek New Testament* to try to support their translation of "a god" at John 1:1. In response, Dr. Julius Robert Mantey, Professor of Greek and New Testament at Northern Baptist Theological Seminary of Chicago, Illinois wrote a two page report entitled, "A Grossly Misleading Translation." (DP 78-80)

CHAPTER FOUR: THE WATCHTOWER PROPHET

" **S** o, does Jehovah have a prophet to help them, to warn them of dangers and to declare things to come? These questions can be answered in the affirmative. Who is this prophet?...This 'prophet' was not one man, but was a body of men and women. It was the small group of footstep followers of Jesus Christ, known at that time as International Bible Students. Today they are know as Jehovah's Christian witnesses....Of course, it is easy to say that this group acts as a 'prophet' of God. **It is another thing to prove it. The only way that this can be done is to review the record. What does it show?**"
—*The Watchtower,* April 1, 1972, p. 197 (DP 81)

1914: "...the 'battle of the great day of God Almighty' (Rev. 16:14), which will end in **A.D. 1914** with the complete overthrow of earth's present rulership, is already commenced."—*The Time Is At Hand,* 1886, p. 101 (DP 82)

1915: "...the 'battle of the great day of God Almighty' (Rev. 16:14), which will end in **A.D. 1915**, with the

15

complete overthrow of earth's present rulership, is already commenced."—*The Time Is At Hand,* 1915 edition, p. 101 (DP 83)

1918: "Also, **in the year 1918, when God destroys the churches wholesale and the church members by millions**, it shall be that any that escape shall come to the works of Pastor Russell to learn the meaning of the downfall of 'Christianity.' "—*The Finished Mystery,* 1917, p. 485 (DP 84)

1925: "...**1925** shall mark the resurrection of the faithful worthies of old....**based upon the promises set forth in the divine Word**, we must reach the positive and **indisputable conclusion** that millions now living will never die."—*Millions Now Living Will Never Die,* 1920, p. 97 (DP 85)

1940's: "It would therefore appear that there is no reasonable or Scriptural injunction to bring children into the world immediately before Armageddon, **where we now are**."—*The Watchtower,* November 1, 1938, p. 324 (DP 86)

1975: "Reports are heard of brothers selling their homes and property and planning to finish out the rest of their days in this old system in the pioneer service. Certainly **this is a fine way to spend the short time remaining before the wicked world's end**."—*Kingdom Ministry,* May 1974, p. 3 (DP 87)

Most people who are familiar with the history of this organization realize that since the first *Watchtower* in 1879, it has had a history of proclaiming the end of the world on several dates: 1914, 1915, 1918, 1925, 1940's, 1975. But, does this mean that the Watch Tower Society is a false prophet? Let's examine what the Society says "False Prophets" are:

"Individuals and organizations **proclaiming messages that they attribute to a super human source but that do not originate with the true God** and are not in harmony with his revealed will."—*Reasoning from the Scriptures,* 1985, 1989, p. 132 (DP 88)

Deuteronomy 18:20-22 states:

"'However, the prophet who presumes **to speak in my name** a word that I have not commanded him to speak or who speaks in the name of other gods, **that prophet must die**. And in case you should say in your heart: "How shall we know the word that Jehovah has not spoken?" When the prophet speaks in the name of Jehovah and **the word does not occur or come true, that is the word that Jehovah did not speak**. With presumptuousness the prophet spoke it. You must not get frightened at him.'" [21]

Under the section, "Have not Jehovah's Witnesses made errors in their teachings?" on page 136 of the Society's *Reasoning from the Scriptures* book, they state:

"Jehovah's Witnesses do not claim to be inspired prophets. They have made mistakes." (DP 89)

Is it true that the Society doesn't claim to be an "inspired" prophet? Let's examine the following statements from various Watchtower publications:

"What is here meant by the word 'inspired'? It means that God, the Creator of heaven and earth, **moved these men by his spirit** or invisible empowering force, putting into their minds what they should write down as his 'word,' or message, for mankind." —*Good News,* 1976, p. 14 (DP 90)

---

[21] All Scripture quotations are from the *New World Translation* Bible of Jehovah's Witnesses.

"The Source of all true prophecy is Jehovah God. **He transmits it by means of his holy spirit or, occasionally, by spirit-directed angelic messengers.**" —*Insight on the Scriptures, vol. 2,* 1988, p. 691 (DP 91)

"Consider, too, the fact that Jehovah's organization alone, in all the earth, **is directed by God's holy spirit** or active force....That same holy spirit **and angelic direction** still affect the preaching activities of Christian ministers."—*The Watchtower,* July 1, 1973, pp. 402, 405 (DP 92-93)

"These **angels** are invisible to human eyes and are there to carry out the orders of the Lord. Not doubt they first hear the instruction which the Lord issues to his remnant and **then these invisible messengers pass such instruction on to the remnant**. The facts show that the angels of the Lord with him at his temple have been thus rendering service unto the remnant since 1919."—*Vindication III,* 1932, p. 250 (DP 94)

"There Ezekiel is definitely told that he is henceforth to serve as a prophet. **He is commissioned to speak in the divine name**....He was thus, in an outstanding way, made a witness of Jehovah. Not alone were the **inspired words** of Ezekiel prophetic, but he himself was a prophetic figure in his action....**Who is Ezekiel's present-day counterpart**, whose message and conduct correspond with that of that ancient prophet of Jehovah?...**So it is with the modern-day counterpart of Ezekiel: it is, not one person's body, but a composite body, made up of many members**....were commissioned to serve **as the mouthpiece** and active agent of Jehovah....Why, though, are all these facts of history brought to our attention? It is to show the fulfillment of prophecy. **Jehovah has found and**

commissioned his modern-day 'Ezekiel.' "
—"*The Nations Shall Know THAT I AM JEHOVAH — How?*", 1971, pp. 56, 58-59, 66 (DP 95-97)

"The scroll was doubtless delivered to Ezekiel by the hand of one of the cherubs in the vision. **This would indicate that Jehovah's witnesses today make their declaration of the good news of the Kingdom under angelic direction and support.** (Rev. 14:6,7; Matt. 25:31, 32) **And since no word or work of Jehovah can fail, for he is God Almighty, the nations will see the fulfillment of what these witnesses say as directed from heaven.** Yes, the time must come shortly that the nations will have to know that really a 'prophet' of Jehovah was among them."
—*The Watchtower,* April 1, 1972, p. 200 (DP 98)

As can be clearly seen, although the Society declares that they "do not claim to be inspired prophets," they claim to get their information **the same way** inspired prophets do (through angels and the Holy Spirit), and they claim to be on par with "inspired" prophets such as Ezekiel. Just like Ezekiel was a spokesman for God, the Society also claims to be Jehovah's "mouthpiece," and thus, they claim that they are speaking the very words of Jehovah. Note the following statements:

"The **interpretation** of prophecy, therefore, **is not from man, but is from Jehovah**; and Jehovah causes events to come to pass in fulfillment of the prophecy in due time."—*The Watchtower,* May 1, 1938. p. 143 (DP 99)

"**He merely uses the 'servant' class to publish the interpretation after the Supreme Court by Christ Jesus reveals it.**"—*The Watchtower,* July 1, 1943, p. 203 (DP 100)

"**This is not giving any credit to the magazine's publishers**, but is due **to the great Author of the Bible** with its truths and prophecies, **and who now interprets its prophecies. He it is that makes possible the material that is published in the columns of this magazine...**"—*The Watchtower,* April 15, 1943, p. 127 (DP 101)

"We see no reason for changing the figures—**nor could we change them if we would. They are, we believe, God's dates, not ours.** But bear in mind that the end of 1914 is not the date for the *beginning,* but for the *end* of the time of trouble."—*Zion's Watch Tower,* July 15, 1894, p. 226 (DP 102)

Certainly humans make mistakes and even Jesus' disciples had wrong expectations as to when the end would come. However, remember that at the time when the Watch Tower Society was making these prophecies about the end of the world, they were telling their followers that these "prophecies" and "dates" were "God's dates, not ours." They were proclaiming these prophecies in Jehovah's name.

According to the standard for testing prophets, discussed in Deuteronomy 18:18-22 and in the Society's *Reasoning* book, which category does the Watch Tower Society fall into? Are they a true or a false prophet? Do you agree with the Society's statement in the May 15, 1930 p. 156 issue of *The Watchtower* which states that once a person discovers a "false prophet" the "people should no longer trust them as safe guides"? (DP 103)

Throughout its history, each time the Watch Tower Society set a date for the end, Jehovah's Witnesses were often encouraged to sell their homes, put off education, and even put off having children, because, according to the Society, the "end" was so very near. Instead of putting your trust in an organization which has made substantial "mistakes" in the past and continues to make "mistakes," why not put your complete trust in Jesus alone, who openly invites each one of us to come to Him.

> "**Come to me**, all YOU who are toiling and loaded down, and **I will refresh YOU**. Take **my yoke** upon YOU and learn **from me**, for I am mild tempered and lowly in heart, and YOU will find refreshment for YOUR souls. For my yoke is kindly and my load is light." —Matthew 11:28-30

Jesus also warns that in the last days, false prophets will arise and claim that He came back when He did not:

> "Then if anyone says to YOU, '**Look! Here is the Christ**,' or, 'There!' do not believe it. For false Christs and **false prophets will arise** and will give great signs and wonders so as to mislead, if possible, even the chosen ones." —Matthew 24: 23-24

Jehovah's Witnesses presently believe that Jesus' presence began in 1914 and that he has been reigning "invisibly" in the heavens ever since. However, from 1879-1929, the Watch Tower Society proclaimed Christ's "invisible presence" began in 1874.[22] Therefore, we see that even according to the Society's present position, they falsely proclaimed Christ's presence for 50 years.

Under oath, at the *Douglas Walsh Trial*, Hayden Covington (former vice president of the Watch Tower Society) gave this testimony concerning the 1874 date:

> A. ...**that was the publication of a false prophesy, it was a false statement or an erroneous statement in fulfilment of a prophesy that was false or erroneous.**

---

[22] *Jehovah's Witnesses—Proclaimers of God's Kingdom,* 1993, pp. 133-134; *Prophecy,* 1929, p. 65 (DP 104-106)

Q. If a member of Jehovah's Witnesses took the view himself that the prophesy was wrong and said so he would be disfellowshipped?

A. Yes....Our purpose is to have unity.

Q. And unity based upon an enforced acceptance of a false prophecy?

A. That is conceded to be true.

—*Douglas Walsh Trial,* 1954, pp. 346-348
(DP 107-108)

Why would Jehovah appoint a false prophet to be His representative to mankind, especially since Jesus warned His followers not to follow prophets who would falsely prophesy His return? To try to smooth over their history of false prophecies, the Society states:

"Matters on which corrections of viewpoint have been needed **have been relatively minor when compared with the vital Bible truths** that they have discerned and publicized. Among these are the following:...**Since 1914 we have been living in the last days of the global wicked system of things.**"—*Reasoning from the Scriptures,* 1985, 1989, pp. 136-137 (DP 89)

As has already been pointed out, the Society has made quite a substantial doctrinal change when they changed their date for "Christ's presence" from 1874 to 1914. When we examine the record, we also discover that their current claim to have always taught the so-called "Bible truth" that "Since 1914 we have been living in the last days" has also been CHANGED. Note the following statements in earlier Watchtower publications:

"The 'Time of the End,' a period of one hundred and fifteen (115) years, from A.D. 1799 to A.D. 1914, is particularly marked in the Scriptures."
—*Thy Kingdom Come,* (1891), 1914 edition, p. 23
(DP 109)

" 'The time of the end' embraces a period from A.D. 1799, as above indicated, to the time of the complete overthrow of Satan's empire and the establishment of the kingdom of the Messiah. **The time of the Lord's second presence dates from 1874, as above stated.**"—*The Harp of God,* (1921), 1924 ed., p. 231 (DP 110)

On top of all this, the Society endeavors to cover-up their history by stating in their 1993 history book, *Jehovah's Witnesses—Proclaimers of God's Kingdom,* p. 135:

"As the years passed and they examined and reexamined the Scriptures, their faith in the prophecies remained strong, and they did not hold back from stating what they expected to occur. **With varying degrees of success, they endeavored to avoid being dogmatic about details not directly stated in the Scriptures.**" (DP 111)

Did they really, "avoid being dogmatic about details not directly stated in the Scriptures"?

"Surely there is **not the slightest room for doubt** in the mind of a truly consecrated child of God that the Lord Jesus is present and has been since 1874..." —*The Watch Tower,* January 1, 1924, p. 5 (DP 112)

"We see not reason for changing the figures—nor could we change them if we would. They are, we believe, **God's dates, not ours.**"—*Zion's Watch Tower,* July 15, 1894, p. 226 (DP 102)

"The typical Jubilee cycles pointed out A.D. 1874 as the date of our Lord's return....And this testimony was made **doubly strong** by proofs from two standpoints—**the Law and the Prophets....**"

—*Thy Kingdom Come,* (1891), 1914 ed., p. 125 (DP 113)

"In this volume we offer a chain of testimony on the subject of God's appointed times and seasons, **each link of which we consider Scripturally strong....therefore cannot be of human origin**." —*The Time is at Hand,* (1886), 1917 ed., p. 15 (DP 114)

And they avoided being "dogmatic"??

"Jehovah, the God of the true prophets, will put all false prophets to shame either by not fulfilling the false prediction of such self-assuming prophets or by having his own prophecies fulfilled in a way opposite to that predicted by the false prophets. **False prophets will try to hide their reason for feeling shame by denying who they really are**."—*Paradise Restored to Mankind—By Theocracy!,* Watch Tower Society, 1972, pp. 353-354 (DP 115-116)

Jesus said, "and YOU will know the truth, and the truth will set YOU free. ... Therefore if **the Son sets YOU free, YOU will be actually free**." —John 8:32, 36 Why not place your complete trust in Jesus alone? He will always reveal to you the truth because He is the truth:

"Jesus said to him: '**I am** the way and **the truth** and the life. No one comes to the Father **except through me**.' " —John 14:6

"**I have come as a light** into the world, in order that everyone **putting faith in me may not remain in the darkness**." —John 12:46

"YOU are searching the Scriptures, because YOU think that by means of them YOU will have everlasting life;

and these are the very ones that bear witness **about me**. And yet YOU do not want to **come to me** that YOU may have life."—John 5:39-40

"Therefore they said to him: 'Lord, always give us this bread.' Jesus said to them: 'I am the bread of life. He that **comes to me** will not get hungry at all, and he that **exercises faith in me** will never get thirsty at all. ...Everything the Father gives me **will come to me**, and the one that **comes to me I will by no means drive away**.' " —John 6:34-37

"I leave YOU peace, I give YOU **my peace. I** do not **give it to YOU** the way that the world gives it. Do not let YOUR hearts be troubled nor let them shrink for fear."—John 14:27

"**Come to me**, all YOU who are toiling and loaded down, and **I will refresh YOU**. Take **my yoke** upon YOU and learn **from me**, for I am mild tempered and lowly in heart, and YOU will find refreshment for YOUR souls. For **my yoke is kindly** and **my load is light**." —Matthew 11:28-30

"If YOU ask anything in **my name, I will do it**." —John 14:14

Jesus invites people everywhere to come to Him in prayer and to lay their burdens at His feet. You don't need an organization or a special "mediator class" between you and God.[23] "For there is one God, and **one mediator** between God and men, a man, Christ Jesus..."—1 Timothy 2:5 Jesus is the **only** Mediator. "...No one comes to the Father **except through me**."—John 14:6 Why not come to Him today? He truly wants to be your Savior.

---

[23] The Society teaches that Jesus is NOT the Mediator for "all" mankind. See *Worldwide Security Under the "Prince of Peace"*, 1986, p. 10 (DP 117)

"And this is the witness given, that God **gave us everlasting life**, and this life is in his Son. **He that has the Son has this life**; he that does not have the Son of God does not have this life. I write YOU these things that **YOU may know** that YOU have life everlasting, YOU who put YOUR faith in the name of the Son of God." —1 John 5:11-13

"...Look! **Now** is the especially acceptable time. Look! **Now is the day of salvation**.' "—2 Corinthians 6:2

DOCUMENTATION REFERENCE INDEX

1. *The Watchtower,* November 15, 1981, p. 21
2. *United in Worship of the Only True God,* 1983, pp. 166-167
3. *The Independent,* Friday 8 January 1993, p. 5
4. *Blood, Medicine And The Law of God,* 1961, pp. 54-55
5. *School And Jehovah's Witnesses,* 1983, p. 13
6. *School And Jehovah's Witnesses,* 1983, p. 14
7. *School And Jehovah's Witnesses,* 1983, p. 15
8. *School And Jehovah's Witnesses,* 1983, p. 16
9. *School And Jehovah's Witnesses,* 1983, p. 17
10. *School And Jehovah's Witnesses,* 1983, p. 18
11. *School And Jehovah's Witnesses,* 1983, p. 19
12. *School And Jehovah's Witnesses,* 1983, p. 20
13. *School And Jehovah's Witnesses,* 1983, p. 21
14. *School And Jehovah's Witnesses,* 1983, p. 23
15. *The Watchtower,* March 15, 1962, p. 178
16. *The Watchtower,* March 15, 1962, p. 179
17. *The Watchtower,* March 15, 1986, p. 12
18. *The Watchtower,* March 15, 1986, p. 19
19. *The Watchtower,* September 15, 1981, p. 25
20. *The Watchtower,* September 15, 1981, p. 29
21. *The Watchtower,* September 15, 1981, p. 30
22. *The Truth That Leads To Eternal Life,*1968, p. 13
23. *Jehovah's Witnesses—Proclaimers of God's Kingdom,* 1993, p. 45
24. *Jehovah's Witnesses—Proclaimers of God's Kingdom, ,* 1993, p. 46
25. *The Finished Mystery (Studies vol. 7),* cover
26. Advertisement for Russell's *Studies in the Scriptures*
27. *Jehovah's Witnesses—Proclaimers of God's Kingdom, ,* 1993, p. 200
28. *The Watch Tower And Herald of Christ's Presence,* October 15, 1914, cover
29. *The Watch Tower,* April 15, 1904, p. 125
30. *The Divine Plan of The Ages,* 1886, 1925ed., p. 7
31. *1975 Yearbook of Jehovah's Witnesses,* p. 88
32. *Zion's Watch Tower,* December 1, 1894, p. 384
33. *Zion's Watch Tower,* September 15, 1895, p. 216
34. *Zion's Watch Tower,* December 1881, pp. 2-3 (Reprints, p. 301)
35. *Zion's Watch Tower,* November 1881, p. 10 (Reprints, p. 298)
36. *The Atonement Between God And Man (Studies, vol. 5),* 1899, 1916ed., p. 85
37. *Zion's Watch Tower,* November 1879, p. 4 (Reprints, p. 48)
38. *The Plan of the Ages,* 1891, p. 178
39. *Jehovah's Witnesses—Proclaimers of God's Kingdom, ,* 1993, p. 201
40. *Zion's Watch Tower,* November 15, 1907, p. 351
41. *Zion's Watch Tower,* December 1, 1904, p. 364
42. *Zion's Watch Tower,* July 1, 1898, p. 204
43. *Zion's Watch Tower,* August 1, 1898, p. 231

44. *Zion's Watch Tower,* October 1, 1900, p. 296
45. *Zion's Watch Tower,* July 15, 1902, p. 216
46. *The Watch Tower,* March 15, 1913, p. 84
47. *Pennsylvania Superior Court Reports, vol. 37,* p. 351
48. *Thy Kingdom Come, (Studies, vol. 3),* 1891, 1914ed., p. 327
49. *The Finished Mystery (Studies, vol. 7)* 1917, p. 60
50. *Douglas Walsh Trial,* Scotland, 1954, p. 114
51. *The Watchtower,* May 15, 1976, p. 304
52. *Zion's Watch Tower,* February 1881, p. 3 (Reprints, p. 188)
53. *New World Translation,* 1984, Foreword, p. 5
54. *Douglas Walsh Trial,* Scotland, 1954, p. 1
55. *Douglas Walsh Trial,* Scotland, 1954, p. 7
56. *Douglas Walsh Trial,* Scotland, 1954, p. 8
57. *Douglas Walsh Trial,* Scotland, 1954, p. 9
58. *Douglas Walsh Trial,* Scotland, 1954, p. 88
59. *Douglas Walsh Trial,* Scotland, 1954, p. 91
60. *Douglas Walsh Trial,* Scotland, 1954, p. 92
61. *Douglas Walsh Trial,* Scotland, 1954, p. 102
62. *Douglas Walsh Trial,* Scotland, 1954, p. 103
63. *The Kingdom Interlinear Translation,* 1969, Title page
64. *The Kingdom Interlinear Translation,* 1985, p. 5
65. *The Kingdom Interlinear Translation,* 1985, p. 9
66. *The Kingdom Interlinear Translation,* 1985, p. 10
67. *The Kingdom Interlinear Translation,* 1985, p. 883
68. *The New Thayer's Greek English Lexicon of the New Testament,* 1974, p. 288
69. *The Kingdom Interlinear Translation,* 1985, p. 880
70. *The Kingdom Interlinear Translation,* 1985, p. 830
71. *The Kingdom Interlinear Translation,* 1985, p. 822
72. *The Kingdom Interlinear Translation,* 1985, p. 872
73. *The Kingdom Interlinear Translation,* 1985, p. 869
74. *The Kingdom Interlinear Translation,* 1985, p. 401
75. *The Kingdom Interlinear Translation,* 1985, p. 451
76. *The Kingdom Interlinear Translation,* 1985, p. 452
77. *The Kingdom Interlinear Translation,* 1985, pp. 482-483
78. *The Kingdom Interlinear Translation,* 1969, pp. 1158-1159
79. *A Grossly Misleading Translation,* Dr. Mantey, p. 1
80. *A Grossly Misleading Translation,* Dr. Mantey, p. 2
81. *The Watchtower,* April 1, 1972, p. 197
82. *The Time Is At Hand (Studies, vol. 2),* 1889, p. 101
83. *The Time Is At Hand (Studies, vol. 2),* 1889, 1917ed, p. 101
84. *The Finished Mystery,* 1917, p. 485
85. *Millions Now Living Will Never Die,* 1920, p. 97
86. *The Watchtower,* November 1, 1938, p. 324
87. *Kingdom Ministry,* May 1974, p. 3
88. *Reasoning from the Scriptures,* 1985, 1989, p. 132
89. *Reasoning from the Scriptures,* 1985, 1989, pp. 136-137
90. *Good News,* 1976, p. 14
91. *Insight On The Scriptures, vol. 2,* 1988, p. 691

92. *The Watchtower,* July 1, 1973, p. 402
93. *The Watchtower,* July 1, 1973, p. 405
94. *Vindication III,* 1932, p. 250
95. *"The Nations Shall Know That I Am Jehovah,"* 1971, p. 56
96. *"The Nations Shall Know That I Am Jehovah,"* 1971, pp. 58-59
97. *"The Nations Shall Know That I Am Jehovah,"* 1971, p. 66
98. *The Watchtower,* April 1, p. 200
99. *The Watchtower,* May 1, 1938, p. 143
100. *The Watchtower,* July 1, 1943, p. 203
101. *The Watchtower,* April 15, 1943, p. 127
102. *Zion's Watch Tower,* July 15, 1894, p. 226
103. *The Watch Tower,* May 15, 1930, p. 156
104. *Jehovah's Witnesses—Proclaimers of God's Kingdom, ,* 1993, p. 133
105. *Jehovah's Witnesses—Proclaimers of God's Kingdom, ,* 1993, p. 134
106. *Prophecy,* 1929, p. 65
107. *Douglas Walsh Trial,* Scotland, 1954, p. 346
108. *Douglas Walsh Trial,* Scotland, 1954, p. 347-348
109. *Thy Kingdom Come (Studies vol 3),* 1891, 1914ed., p. 23
110. *The Harp of God,* 1921, 1924ed., pp. 230-231
111. *Jehovah's Witnesses—Proclaimers of God's Kingdom, ,* 1993, p. 135
112. *The Watch Tower,* January 1, 1924, p. 5
113. *Thy Kingdom Come,* 1891, 1914ed. p. 125
114. *The Time is At Hand,* 1889, 1917ed., p. 15
115. *Paradise Restored To Mankind—By Theocracy!,* 1972, p. 353
116. *Paradise Restored To Mankind—By Theocracy!,* 1972, p. 354
117. *Worldwide Security Under The "Prince of Peace,"* 1986, p. 10

PHOTOCOPIED DOCUMENTATION

to "shout a great of Jericho fell

what will happen. he who "does the ne who "remains

CTIVITY

God's will for our Jesus' prophecy: kingdom will be ted earth for a wit- d then the end will o true Christians, e, in effect, a com- the good news of incoming new or- s been obeyed by hese "last days." tthew 28:19, 20.) ed their time and ners about God's this earth. As a ork, upwards of ighout the world 's new order and

obeyed the command 's kingdom in all the

NOVEMBER 15, 1981

his provision for salvation through Jesus Christ by meeting together this past April to observe the Memorial of Christ's death.

[16] As Jehovah's forward-moving organization approaches the final years of its preaching activity toward this world, there is no doubt that the scope of the work will grow. Recall what the Israelites were instructed to do just before God destroyed Jericho. First, they were instructed to march around the city once a day for six days. But then they were told: "On the seventh day you should march round the city seven times and the priests should blow the horns. And it must occur that when they sound with the horn of the ram, when you hear the sound of the horn, all the people should shout a great war cry; and the wall of the city must fall down flat."—Josh. 6:2-5.

[17] On that seventh and last day, the Israelites were to increase their activity seven times! Then they were to "shout a great war cry." Exactly as instructed, they did this. "It came about on the seventh day that they proceeded to get up early, as soon as the dawn ascended, and they went marching round the city in this manner seven times. . . . And it came about on the seventh time that the priests blew the horns, and Joshua proceeded to say to the people: 'Shout; for Jehovah has given you the city.' . . . And it came about that as soon as the people heard the sound of the horn and the people began to shout a great war cry, then the

wall began to fall down flat."—Josh. 6: 15, 16, 20.

[18] We can expect a similar expansion of our preaching activity now, at this climax of the ages. No doubt, before the "great tribulation" is finished, we will see the greatest witness to God's name and kingdom in the history of this world. And while now the witness yet includes the invitation to come to Jehovah's organization for salvation, the time no doubt will come when the message takes on a harder tone, like a "great war cry." Revelation 16:21 shows that "a great hail with every stone about the weight of a talent [nearly 100 pounds] descended out of heaven upon the men, and the men blasphemed God due to the plague of hail, because the plague of it was unusually great." Hailstones are frozen, hardened water. So this pictures how, at the end, Jehovah's judgment message sent down upon disobedient mankind will be like a barrage of hard-hitting hail. The fact that the plague of hailstones is spoken of as being "unusually great" suggests that at the very end there will be a hard proclamation of Jehovah's "day of vengeance" by Jehovah's servants.

[19] So, then, we do well to say, as Peter did, "Since all these things are thus to be dissolved, what sort of persons ought you to be in holy acts of conduct and deeds of godly devotion"! (2 Pet. 3:11) Surely, we need to "keep comforting one another and building one another up." We should "always pursue what is good toward one another." (1 Thess. 5:11, 15) "Really, then, as long as we have time favorable for it, let us work what is good toward all, but especially toward those related to us in the faith." (Gal. 6:10) To this end, do not fail to 'stay awake and keep your senses.'—1 Thess. 5:6.

16. 17. (a) What instructions were given to the nation of Israel before God destroyed Jericho? (b) How were those instructions carried out?

18. What do we anticipate as regards the scope and manner of the preaching activity before this system comes to its end?
19. In view of the immediate future, 'what kind of persons ought we to be'?

THE WATCHTOWER — NOVEMBER 15, 1981

21

I.

166   UNITED IN WORSHIP OF THE ONLY TRUE GOD, 1983

12 In sharp contrast, the clergy of Christendom are very much involved in the political affairs of the world. In some lands they actively campaign for or against candidates. Some of the clergy themselves hold political office. Others exert great pressure on politicians to favor programs that the clergy approve. Elsewhere the "conservative" clergy are close allies of the men in power while "progressive" priests and ministers may be supporting guerrilla movements working for their overthrow. However, Jehovah's Witnesses do not meddle in politics, no matter what the country in which they live. They do not interfere with what others do as to joining a political party, running for office or voting in elections. But, since Jesus said that his disciples would be "no part of the world," Jehovah's Witnesses take no part whatsoever in political activities.

13 As Jesus foretold, during this "time of the end" nations have repeatedly gone to war, and even factions within nations have taken up arms against one another. (Matt. 24:3, 6, 7) But in the face of all of this, what position have Jehovah's Witnesses taken? Their neutrality regarding such conflicts is well known in all parts of the world. Consistent with the position taken by Jesus Christ and later demonstrated by his early disciples, *The Watchtower*, in its issue of November 1, 1939, stated: "All who are on the Lord's side will be neutral as to warring nations, and will be entirely and wholly for the great Theocrat [Jehovah] and his King [Jesus Christ]." The facts show that Jehovah's Witnesses in all nations and under all cir-

---

12. (a) How does the neutrality of the Witnesses contrast with practices of the clergy? (b) What does neutrality as to politics include for Jehovah's Witnesses?
13. As to their participating in war, what do the facts show that the position of Jehovah's Witnesses has been?

"THEY ARE NO PART OF THE WORLD"   167

cumstances continue to hold to this position. They have not allowed the world's divisive politics and wars to break up their international brotherhood as worshipers of Jehovah.—Isa. 2:3, 4; compare 2 Corinthians 10:3, 4.

14 An examination of the historical facts shows that not only have Jehovah's Witnesses refused to put on military uniforms and take up arms but, during the past half century and more, they have also declined to do noncombatant service or to accept other work assignments as a substitute for military service. Why? Because they have studied God's requirements and then made a personal, conscientious decision. No one tells them what they must do. Nor do they interfere with what others choose to do. But when called on to explain their position, Jehovah's Witnesses have made it known that, as persons who have presented themselves to God in dedication, they are obligated to use their bodies in his service and who are acting contrary to God's purpose.—Rom. 6:12-14; 12:1, 2; Mic. 4:3.

15 The result has been as Jesus said: "Because you are no part of the world . . . the world hates you," (John 15:19) Many of Jehovah's Witnesses have been imprisoned because they would not violate their Christian neutrality. Some have been treated brutally, even to the point of death. Others have continued to demonstrate their neutrality during years of confinement. The book *Values and*

---

14. (a) Because of their neutral position, what else have the Witnesses refused to do? (b) How do they explain the reason for this?
15. (a) Because of maintaining separateness from the world, what have Jehovah's Witnesses experienced? (b) Even when they were imprisoned, how have Christian principles guided them?

2.

(LONDON)

Friday 8 January 1993   🦅 THE INDEPENDENT   5

Jehovah's Witness dies after refusing blood transfusion

A JEHOVAH'S Witness died yesterday after refusing a blood transfusion following a car crash.

Bob Bain, 45, a father of two, was freed from the wreckage of his car after the accident on the M40 and taken to the John Radcliffe Hospital in Oxford, where he died. A hospital spokesman said he declined a transfusion in accordance with his religious beliefs.

A passenger in the car, Mark Southall, 29, also a Jehovah's Witness, refused a transfusion and was in a critical condition last night after having a leg amputated.

A spokesman for the Jehovah's Witnesses said yesterday that the faith did not allow transfusions because "we feel that blood is a very special category of substance. The Bible repeatedly enjoins people not to take blood into their bodies and we accept that."

He said most Jehovah's Witnesses carried a card, stating their opposition to the treatment in case they became unconscious.

"We try very hard to look after ourselves, but we do not accept blood transfusions. We accept any other medical treatment, but no transfusions. There are alterna-

tives. If someone is haemorrhaging badly, the key to successful treatment is to stop the bleeding and to make up the circulating volume."

Tony Stapleton, the hospital's general manager, said: "Our policy is to respect the wishes of patients and their families in cases where they are able to make their wishes clear and we did not give him blood."

The accident happened on Wednesday night between junctions six and seven, near Thame, Oxfordshire. Paramedics and ambulance crews fought to keep Mr Bain, an engineer from Rugeley, Staffordshire, alive as firefighters struggled for two hours to free him from the wreckage. He was conscious throughout.

A post-mortem examination is due to be held today and an inquest will be held.

The question of whether or not Jehova's Witnesses can be forced to have transfusions is fraught with legal complications.

Members of the faith claim they cannot, and cite a Court of Appeal decision last year by Lord Donaldson, former Master of the Rolls. He stated that if a doctor

learnt that a patient was a Jehovah's Witness, but had no evidence of a refusal to accept blood transfusions, he or she should avoid administering blood for as long as possible.

But a British Medical Association spokeswoman said that although Jehovah's Witnesses may carry cards refusing transfusions, these are not legally binding.

She added: "Dealing with an unconscious Jehovah's Witness who cannot say for himself whether doctors can give a blood transfusion is one of the most difficult dilemmas doctors and surgeons face today."

Then it is up to the medical team to consult with friends and relations but the final clinical decision must come from the surgeons themselves.

Legal experts have suggested doctors could even be sued if they give a blood transfusion to a Jehovah's Witness who has not been able to give express permission.

In life-and-death situations involving children, doctors can fight to make a minor a ward of court. Then the court can decide whether or not to authorise a transfusion.

3

32

If such maneuvers to overrule parental rights continue to have the approval of judges and the public, it is wise for all parents to consider what it can lead to. Are they prepared to accept the thesis that, when parents disagree with a physician on any form of treatment, their child has in the eyes of the law become a "neglected" child, and can for that reason be taken by the state and subjected to the treatment in spite of parental protest? Is the right of parents to exercise their good judgment in the upbringing of their children going to be offered up in sacrifice before the ancient Spartan theory that children are the property of the State? The application of this rule in Nazi Germany meant that boys were taken from their parents to be trained for the "Hitler Youth," and young girls were used for breeding, out of wedlock, what the rulers proclaimed would be a scientifically superior race. Those considered unfit were sterilized; many were even put to death. When doctors and the courts conspire together to override family rights and force the application of certain medical procedures that are currently in vogue, it is but one step in the destruction of freedom. Once the God-given rights of Jehovah's witnesses to exercise their discretion in harmony with God's Word in the upbringing of their children have been trampled underfoot, whose rights will be next?

Jehovah's witnesses do not reject blood for their children due to any lack of parental love. They have sincere love for their children and will do anything within their means to help them, but they are not foolish enough to think that they do good for their offspring by turning their back on God. They know that if they violate God's law on blood and the child dies in the process, they have endangered that child's opportunity for everlasting life in God's new world. Their love is not moti-

---

BLOOD, MEDICINE AND THE LAW OF GOD   55

vated by overriding emotion that seeks satisfaction only at the moment, but their love is deep, seeking the everlasting welfare of their loved ones.

MAINTAINING INTEGRITY TO GOD

Realistically viewed, resorting to blood transfusions even under the most extreme circumstances is not truly lifesaving. It may result in the immediate and very temporary prolongation of life, but that at the cost of eternal life for a dedicated Christian. Then again, it may bring sudden death, and, that forever. (Matthew 10:39) How much better to abide by the law of Jehovah God, the Source of life, and abstain from blood than to incur his disapproval as a lawbreaker. At all times, and certainly when one's life forces are ebbing, the course of wisdom is to put confidence in the One in whose hands rests the power of life. God will not forsake those who lovingly obey his commands concerning the sanctity of life. He will reward their confidence in his means of salvation by extending to them the life-giving benefits of the blood of his Son—benefits that will sustain them, not for mere days or years, but forever. They know that none who trust in Jehovah God and his now-glorified Son "will by any means come to disappointment."—1 Peter 2:6.

Even if blood could be administered with absolutely no danger from a medical viewpoint—which cannot be done—would it show love for the patient for others to insist that he accept it in an endeavor to extend his present life, when disobedience to God means the forfeiture of the reward of everlasting life? No! It is a time when all interested persons, whether doctors or friends or relatives, can show their sincere concern for the patient and their fear of God by encouraging the patient to hold fast his faith, not to fear, but to trust in God, who is Almighty.

TING

areas of our
olves patriot-
lings may be
those teach-
th sensitivity
hy Jehovah's
observances

st Christians
irs. As Jesus
vorld, just as
Rather, they
government,
ene A. Colli-
g them in the
tey preferred
t they might

d closely the
i's Witnesses
6:15; 18:36)
itral position
cal affairs:

and was re-
d the pagan
iin duties of
itical office."
ry (1937), by
es 237, 238.

ians enemies
oman army.
which meant
flag does to
iir religion."
dith McCall,
67, 68.

As you may appreciate, following a similar course of neutrality today affects our young people's participation in a number of school exercises and activities. What conscientious position on these matters have Jehovah's Witnesses taken earth wide?

The Flag Salute

Even though we do not salute the flag of *any* nation, this certainly is not meant to indicate disrespect. We *do* respect the flag of whatever country we live in, and we show this respect by obedience to the country's laws. We never engage in antigovernment activity of any kind. In fact, we believe that present human governments constitute an "arrangement of God" that he has temporarily permitted to exist. So we consider ourselves under divine command to pay taxes, tribute and honor to such "superior authorities."—Romans 13:1-7.

'But why, then,' you may ask, 'do you not honor the flag by saluting it?' It is because we view the flag salute as an act of worship. Although we do not discourage others from saluting the flag, we cannot conscientiously give what we view as worship to anyone or anything except our God, Jehovah. (Matthew 4:10) Of course, many people do not consider the flag sacred or that saluting it is an act of worship. However, consider what secular authorities say about this:

"The flag, like the cross, is sacred. . . . The rules and regulations relative to human attitude toward national standards use strong, expressive words, as, 'Service to the Flag,' . . . 'Reverence for the Flag,' 'Devotion to the Flag.' "—*The Encyclopedia Americana* (1942), Volume 11, page 316.

"Nationalism's chief symbol of faith and central object of worship is the flag, and curious liturgical forms have

Jehovah's Witnesses view the flag salute as an act of worship

13

34

been devised for 'saluting' the flag, for 'dipping' the flag, for 'lowering' the flag, and for 'hoisting' the flag. Men bare their heads when the flag passes by; and in praise of the flag poets write odes and children sing hymns."—*What Americans Believe and How They Worship* (1952), by J. Paul Williams, pages 359, 360.

You may feel that the above are extreme views. However, it is interesting that in the colonial days of America the Puritans objected to the British flag because of its red cross of "Saint" George. According to *The Encyclopædia Britannica* (1910-1911), they did this, "not from any disloyalty to the mother country, but from a conscientious objection to what they deemed an idolatrous symbol."

One of the Ten Commandments forbids making an object to worship with "a form like anything that is in the heavens above or that is on the earth underneath." (Exodus 20:4, 5) As Christians, we also feel bound by the Bible's command to 'guard ourselves from idols.' —1 John 5:21.

We appreciate it when teachers are understanding regarding our beliefs and help our children to abide by them. Others have expressed an understanding of the position we have taken that the flag salute is related to worship, as the following comments show:

"Christians refused to . . . sacrifice to the [Roman] emperor's genius—roughly equivalent today to refusing to salute the flag or repeat the oath of allegiance."—*Those About to Die* (1958), by Daniel P. Mannix, page 135.

"The key assumption is that saluting a flag constitutes an act of religious devotion. . . . This view, while odd, is not entirely without biblical support. . . . If saluting is a religious act, then it is forbidden by God's law *however worthy the object of respect*. In other words, refusal to salute need imply no disrespect for flag or country."—*Render Unto Caesar, The Flag-Salute Controversy* (1962), David R. Manwaring, assistant professor of political science, Hobart and William Smith Colleges, page 32.

We would like to emphasize that we intend no disrespect for any government or its rulers by our refusal to salute the flag. It is just that we will not, in an act of worship, bow down to or salute an image repre-

"*Christians refused to . . . sacrifice to the [Roman] emperor's genius —roughly equivalent today to refusing to salute the flag*"

14

senting th
up in the
the nation:
Court of tl
previous d

"We thi
ling the fl
limitations
tellect an
Amendme:
cial contr
v. *Barnett*

So then,
our childre
emony. Bu
conducted
evidence of
young ones
not march i
support of
main neutr:

Natic

A nation:
a prayer se
(1956) says
country are
and in man:
sentiment."
fundamenta
allegiance t
basis for the
world, we d
earthly nati
When nat
a person ha
ments of th
ness youths
already stan

SCHOOL AND JEHOVAH'S WITNESSES, 1983

6.

ipping' the flag,
e flag. Men bare
in praise of the
hymns."—*What
ip* (1952), by J.

extreme views.
e colonial days
he British flag
rge. According
-1911), they did
ıother country,
at they deemed

ıids making an
thing that is in
h underneath."
) feel bound by
es from idols.'

understanding
ren to abide by
standing of the
ılute is related
show:

e [Roman] em-
to refusing to
iance."—*Those*
page 135.

lag constitutes
', while odd, is
If saluting is
l's law *howev*-
words, refusal
flag or coun-
e Controversy
essor of politi-
eges, page 32.

intend no dis-
by our refusal
rill not, in an
ı image repre-

---

senting the State, like the one Nebuchadnezzar raised up in the plain of Dura, or like the modern flags of the nations. (Daniel 3:1-30) Significantly, the Supreme Court of the United States, in a historic reversal of a previous decision, stated:

> "We think the action of the local authorities in compelling the flag salute and pledge transcends constitutional limitations on their power and invades the sphere of intellect and spirit which it is the purpose of the First Amendment to our Constitution to reserve from all official control."—*West Virginia State Board of Education* v. *Barnette* (1943).

So then, while others salute and pledge allegiance, our children stand quietly during the flag salute ceremony. But if, for some reason, the flag ceremony is conducted in such a way that simply standing gives evidence of one's participation in the ceremony, our young ones remain seated. In addition, our youths do not march in patriotic parades, which would show their support of the thing honored by the parade. We remain neutral.

National Anthems and School Songs

A national anthem often is, in effect, a hymn or a prayer set to music. *The Encyclopedia Americana* (1956) says: "Love of fatherland and pride in one's country are the keynotes of most national anthems, and in many, religious feeling is blended with patriotic sentiment." Actually, patriotic songs express the same fundamental ideas that are embodied in the pledge of allegiance to the flag. And since there is no Scriptural basis for the nationalistic pride that has so divided our world, we do not join in singing songs that extol any earthly nation.—Acts 17:26; John 17:15, 16.

When national anthems are played, usually all that a person has to do to show that he shares the sentiments of the song is to stand up. In such cases, Witness youths remain seated. However, if our youths are already standing when the national anthem is played,

As faithful Hebrew youths refused to worship an image of the State, so Jehovah's Witnesses do not salute the flag

15

SCHOOL AND JEHOVAH'S WITNESSES, 1983

7.

they would not have to take the special action of sitting down; it is not as though they had specifically stood up for the anthem. On the other hand, if a group are expected to stand *and* sing, then our young people may rise and stand out of respect. But they would show that they do not share the sentiments of the song by refraining from singing.

Do school songs come into the same category as national anthems? Yes, they are viewed the same way by those in the school as national anthems are by the nations. They are often sung with religious fervor and with cheers. Our youths do not share the sentiments of such songs.

Elective Offices and Positions

In many schools, students are voted into an office or a position, such as class president. Some schools have small-scale political campaigns, including campaign buttons and posters advertising candidates. The purpose is to familiarize young people with the machinery of politics. However, Witness youths do not mix in school politics, either by accepting an elective office or by voting others into office. So if either nominated for or elected to an office, they tactfully decline. In this way they follow the example of Jesus who withdrew when the people wanted to make him king.—John 6:15.

However, we consider an appointment by the teacher as something different. So if Witness youths are appointed to help in traffic direction or some other such activity, they are encouraged to cooperate to the extent possible.

Of course, our young ones realize that not all voting is political. Sometimes students are called on by the teacher to give their opinions. There may be no violation of Bible principles to express one's preference for certain activities or to provide one's appraisal of a talk or composition. When persons express opinions by a show of hands as to the quality of something, this is not the same as electing another politically to an office.

Witness youths do not mix in school politics

16

HOLI
CELEI

The fact t
in most holi(
be somewha
following he
matter so s(

Perhaps t(
ized, many
them have a
this that ma
nesses. We
Christian ap

"What fel
have? Or wh
Further, wh
Belial [a fa
person have
out from an
Jehovah."—

So if a ho
to other goo
trary to ou:
do not take

Birthday
ous giving t(
15:22-25; A
ing gifts an
the year. H(
mentioned i
true believe
the Roman
day celebrat
Mark 6:21-2
torical refe:
toward birt!

SCHOOL AND JEHOVAHS WITNESSES, 1983

8.

ction of sitting
cifically stood
if a group are
ng people may
y would show
of the song by

e category as
the same way
ms are by the
ous fervor and
he sentiments

's

into an office
Some schools
ncluding cam-
andidates. The
th the machin-
do not mix in
ective office or
nominated for
ecline. In this
who withdrew
g.—John 6:15.
by the teach-
ss youths are
or some other
operate to the

not all voting
led on by the
ty be no viola-
preference for
raisal of a talk
opinions by a
ing, this is not
to an office.

HOLIDAYS AND
CELEBRATIONS

The fact that Jehovah's Witnesses do not participate in most holiday observances and other celebrations can be somewhat perplexing to a teacher. We hope the following helps you to understand why we take the matter so seriously.

Perhaps to a greater extent than you may have realized, many holidays and the customs associated with them have a non-Christian religious background. It is this that makes them objectionable to Jehovah's Witnesses. We try to follow the principle stated by the Christian apostle Paul:

"What fellowship do righteousness and lawlessness have? Or what sharing does light have with darkness? Further, what harmony is there between Christ and Belial [a false god]? Or what portion does a faithful person have with an unbeliever? . . . 'Therefore get out from among them, and separate yourselves,' says Jehovah."—2 Corinthians 6:14-17.

So if a holiday or a celebration is in some way linked to other gods or goddesses, or if observing it is contrary to our understanding of Biblical principles, we do not take part.

➔ **Birthdays:** Enjoying a feast or a party and generous giving to loved ones are certainly not wrong. (Luke 15:22-25; Acts 20:35) Jehovah's Witnesses enjoy giving gifts and having good times together throughout the year. However, the only two birthday celebrations mentioned in the Bible involved people who were not true believers. They were a Pharaoh of Egypt and the Roman ruler Herod Antipas, each of whose birthday celebrations had deadly results. (Genesis 40:18-22; Mark 6:21-28) So it is not surprising to see these historical references to the attitude of early Christians toward birthday celebrations:

Early Christians did not celebrate their birthdays

17

SCHOOL AND JEHOVAH'S WITNESSES, 1983
9.

38

"The notion of a *birthday festival* was far from the ideas of the Christians of this period in general."—*The History of the Christian Religion and Church, During the Three First Centuries* (New York, 1848), by Augustus Neander (translated by Henry John Rose), page 190.

"Of all the holy people in the Scriptures, no one is recorded to have kept a feast or held a great banquet on his birthday. It is only sinners (like Pharaoh and Herod) who make great rejoicings over the day on which they were born into this world below."—*The Catholic Encyclopedia* (New York, 1911), Volume X, page 709 (quoting Origen Adamantius of the third century).

Additionally, birthday celebrations tend to give excessive importance to an individual, no doubt one reason why early Christians shunned them. (Ecclesiastes 7:1) So you will find that Jehovah's Witnesses do not share in birthday festivities (the parties, singing, gift giving, and so forth).

Christmas: As you are probably aware, December 25 was not the birthday of Jesus Christ. You may feel that this does not matter—that the event is the important thing. But the way the Christmas holiday developed shows that there is more to it than that. The following encyclopedias explain:

"The observance of Christmas is not of divine appointment, nor is it of N[ew] T[estament] origin. The day of Christ's birth cannot be ascertained from the N[ew] T[estament], or, indeed, from any other source. The fathers of the first three centuries do not speak of any special observance of the nativity."—*Cyclopedia of Biblical, Theological, and Ecclesiastical Literature* (Grand Rapids, Michigan, 1981 reprint), by John McClintock and James Strong, Volume II, page 276.

"Most of the Christmas customs now prevailing in Europe, or recorded from former times, are not genuine Christian customs, but heathen customs which have been absorbed or tolerated by the Church. . . . The Saturnalia in Rome provided the model for most of the *merry* customs of the Christmas time."—*Encyclopædia of Religion and Ethics* (Edinburgh, 1911), edited by James Hastings, Volume III, pages 608, 609.

It is commonly known that Christmas was not originally a celebration of Christ's birth. *U.S. Catholic* of

18

December 1!
separate Chr
azine explair

"The Ror
began on De
unconquerec
Somewhere
savvy officia
25 would m:
the 'sun of 1

When lea:
have some t
pedia (1982)
1600's . . . C
parts of the l
in the past r
its pagan ori
hovah's Witn
part in Chris
of gifts, or in
with Christm

Jehovah's
tal nonpartic
holidays that
is that these
Christian wo
worship ofter
following exa

Easter: A
memorate Ch
thorities say

"Easter. C
Teutonic go
Saxon as Es
was transfe:
festival desig
—*The Westr*
1944), by Jol

"Everywhe
brought by
play, but th

as far from the
ι general."—*The*
urch, During the
3), by Augustus
:), page 190.

es, no one is re-
t banquet on his
and Herod) who
vhich they were
ic *Encyclopedia*
(quoting Origen

end to give ex-
) doubt one rea-
m. (Ecclesiastes
Vitnesses do not
es, singing, gift

vare, December
hrist. You may
he event is the
ristmas holiday
o it than that.

divine appoint-
gin. The day of
he N[ew] T[es-
ce. The fathers
ık of any spe-
dia of Biblical,
(Grand Rapids,
ock and James

evailing in Eu-
e not genuine
hich have been
The Saturnalia
he *merry* cus-
lia of Religion
ımes Hastings,

s was not orig-
.S. *Catholic* of

December 1981, page 32, notes: "It is impossible to separate Christmas from its pagan origins." The magazine explains:

"The Romans' favorite festival was Saturnalia, which began on December 17 and ended with the 'birthday of the unconquered sun' (*Natalis solis invicti*) on December 25. Somewhere in the second quarter of the fourth century, savvy officials of the church of Rome decided December 25 would make a dandy day to celebrate the birthday of the 'sun of righteousness.' Christmas was born."

When learning these facts about Christmas, how have some been affected? *The World Book Encyclopedia* (1982) observes under "Christmas": "During the 1600's . . . Christmas was outlawed in England and in parts of the English colonies in America." Since people in the past refused to celebrate Christmas because of its pagan origins, it should be understandable why Jehovah's Witnesses do not celebrate it today. We take no part in Christmas parties, plays, singing, exchanging of gifts, or in any other such activity that is associated with Christmas.

Jehovah's Witnesses take the same position of total nonparticipation in other religious or semireligious holidays that occur during the school year. The reason is that these holidays, too, are connected with non-Christian worship; in fact, certain features of such worship often dominate the celebrations. Consider the following examples:

Easter: Although this holiday is supposed to commemorate Christ's resurrection, note what secular authorities say regarding it:

"Easter. Originally the spring festival in honor of the Teutonic goddess of light and spring known in Anglo-Saxon as Eastre. As early as the 8th century the name was transferred by the Anglo-Saxons to the Christian festival designed to celebrate the resurrection of Christ." —*The Westminster Dictionary of the Bible* (Philadelphia, 1944), by John D. Davis, page 145.

"Everywhere they hunt the many-colored Easter eggs, brought by the Easter rabbit. This is not mere child's play, but the vestige of a fertility rite, the eggs and

"Christmas was outlawed in England and in parts of the English colonies in America"

"This is not mere child's play, but the vestige of a fertility rite, the eggs and the rabbit both symbolizing fertility"

19

SCHOOL AND JEHOVAHS WITNESSES, 1983
11.

40

the rabbit both symbolizing fertility."—Funk & Wagnalls *Standard Dictionary of Folklore Mythology and Legend* (New York, 1949), Volume 1, page 335.

Halloween: Though celebrated as a Christian holiday, Halloween finds its origins in pre-Christian festivals that propagate false ideas about life after death. Interestingly, we read: "After the Reformation, Protestants rejected this feast along with other important ones such as Christmas and Easter. Nevertheless, Halloween folk customs of pagan origin flourished."—*Encyclopœdia Britannica* (1959), Volume 11, page 107.

All Saints' Day: "There is little doubt that the Christian church sought to eliminate or supplant the Druid festival of the dead by introducing the alternative observance of All Saints' day on Nov. 1. This feast was established to honour all saints, known or unknown, but it failed to displace the pagan celebration of Samhain."—*Encyclopœdia Britannica* (1959), Volume 11, page 107.

New Year's Day: "In ancient Rome, the first day of the year was given over to honoring Janus, the god of gates and doors and of beginnings and endings. . . . New Year's Day became a holy day in the Christian church in A.D. 487."—*The World Book Encyclopedia* (1982), Volume 14, page 237.

Valentine's Day: "Valentine's Day comes on the feast day of two different Christian martyrs named Valentine. But the customs connected with the day . . . probably come from an ancient Roman festival called *Lupercalia* which took place every February 15. The festival honored Juno, the Roman goddess of women and marriage, and Pan, the god of nature."—*The World Book Encyclopedia* (1973), Volume 20, page 204.

May Day: "May Day festivals probably stem from the rites practiced in honor of a Roman goddess, Maia, who was worshiped as the source of human and natural fertility. . . . [The] Maypole is believed by most scholars to be a survival of a phallic symbol formerly used in the spring rites for the goddess Maia."—*The New Funk & Wagnalls Encyclopedia* (1952), page 8294.

20

Mother's
of mother
worship, wit
Mother of
March thro
tannica (19

These are
monly obse
expected to
ties. Howev
reasons do
ities—wheth
plays, marc
ing parties,
the same ti
such holiday
very much
from partic
commemora

Natio

Other ho
These are
unique to a
be national
may also be
nation's war
a country c
national her

Jehovah's
participating
respect the
reside, for c
what we vie
toward all
Jesus' word
part of the
—John 17:1

SCHOOL AND JEHOVAH'S WITNESSES, 1983

12.

unk & Wagnalls
ogy and Legend

a Christian holi-
-Christian festi-
life after death.
formation, Prot-
other important
vertheless, Hal-
lourished."—*En-*
11, page 107.

doubt that the
or supplant the
icing the alter-
on Nov. 1. This
ints, known or
pagan celebra-
tannica (1959),

e, the first day
: Janus, the god
nd endings. . . .
n the Christian
k Encyclopedia

comes on the
martyrs named
vith the day . . .
i festival called
bruary 15. The
dess of women
e."—*The World*
page 204.

ibly stem from
goddess, Maia,
ian and natural
by most schol-
formerly used
iia."—*The New*
page 8294.

Mother's Day: "A festival derived from the custom of mother worship in ancient Greece. Formal mother worship, with ceremonies to Cybele, or Rhea, the Great Mother of the Gods, were performed on the Ides of March throughout Asia Minor."—*Encyclopædia Britannica* (1959), Volume 15, page 849.

These are just a sampling of holidays that are commonly observed, and in which schoolchildren often are expected to participate by sharing in certain activities. However, Jehovah's Witnesses for conscientious reasons do not take any part in these holiday activities—whether it be singing, playing music, acting in plays, marching in parades, drawing pictures, attending parties, eating and drinking, and so forth. Yet, at the same time, we do not object to others celebrating such holidays nor try to hinder them. We appreciate it very much when teachers kindly excuse our children from participation in all activities that in any way commemorate these holidays.

National Holidays

Other holidays are somewhat different in nature. These are not so universally celebrated, but may be unique to a particular country. For example, there may be national days of thanksgiving. In some places there may also be a certain day set aside to memorialize a nation's war dead, or a day to remember the birth of a country or certain prominent presidents, rulers or national heroes.

Jehovah's Witnesses also respectfully refrain from participating in such national holidays. Though we respect the authorities in whatever country we may reside, for conscientious reasons we do not give them what we view as worshipful honors. We remain neutral toward all such celebrations. This is in keeping with Jesus' words regarding his followers: "They are no part of the world, just as I am no part of the world." —John 17:16.

For conscientious reasons, Jehovah's Witnesses do not take part in holiday activities

21

SCHOOL AND JEHOVAH'S WITNESSES, 1983

13

42

LAR

t there should be
d work. Some ex-
ıl hours provide a
you may have no-
not participate in
by the schools. A
derstand our views

rsuing a program
heir worship. And
recreation in this
nts arranging and
rtainment of their
along with them,

ıay get together to
t. They also travel
larger gatherings
:onventions. These
; to visit museums,
ltural interest. At
ıeet and enjoy the
; from other parts
goal they have of

; enjoy this whole-
· of the deteriorat-
ƒ today. Jehovah's
ʌvarning: "Bad as-
s noted before, we
t to his followers:
'orinthians 15:33;
e view of Witness
·ricular activities,

Sports: Bodily training, such as we get in sports, is good for us. But placing the matter in proper perspective, the Bible says: "Be training yourself with godly devotion as your aim. For bodily training is *beneficial for a little;* but godly devotion is beneficial for all things." (1 Timothy 4:7, 8) In keeping with this advice, Jehovah's Witnesses appreciate the value of physical education courses that are conducted during school hours.

At the same time, however, Witness parents feel that schools often overemphasize sports. Therefore in training their children, they try to moderate the emphasis on athletic achievement. They hope their young ones will want to pursue careers, not as athletes, but as ministers of God. So Witness parents encourage their children to use after-school hours principally to pursue spiritual interests, rather than to excel in some sport.

Participation in organized sports, we believe, would expose Witness youths to unwholesome associations. We also feel that the competitive spirit in modern sports—'the winning isn't everything, it's the ONLY thing' ideology—has harmful effects. So if Witness youths feel the need for extra recreation, their parents encourage them to seek such recreation with fellow believers, yes, "along with those who call upon the Lord out of a clean heart."—2 Timothy 2:22.

Cheerleader and Homecoming Queen: At athletic events it is the responsibility of cheerleaders to orchestrate the crowd in frenzied cheering for a school. They also encourage the people into hero worship and lead them in standing for the school song. Jehovah's Witnesses consider it inappropriate to do this. Similarly, we feel that for a Witness youth to serve as a homecoming or beauty queen would be in violation of

23

SCHOOL AND JEHOVAH'S WITNESSES, 1983
14

178   *The* WATCHTOWER.   BROOKLYN, N. Y.

sincerity to see Jehovah's work accomplished, to his praise.

THE QUALIFICATIONS DESIRED

[11] As seen, there is a great need for dedicated ministers in the New World society, ministers of sound judgment, deep knowledge and love, men who possess the qualifications the Scriptures outline for overseers at 1 Timothy 3:1-7: "The overseer should therefore be irreprehensible, a husband of one wife, moderate in habits, sound in mind, orderly, hospitable, qualified to teach, not a drunken brawler, not a smiter, but reasonable, not belligerent, not a lover of money, a man presiding over his own household in a fine manner, having children in subjection with all seriousness; . . . not a newly converted man, for fear that he might get puffed up with pride and fall into the judgment passed upon the Devil. Moreover, he should also have a fine testimony from people on the outside."

[12] Preparing yourself for theocratic responsibilities, then, means that you must first become spiritually-minded, that you must place spiritual values above material values. You must feed your mind with things upbuilding by regular personal study and by attendance at all the congregation meetings. You must learn to work closely with the organization and learn the value of unity. You will want to gain valuable experience by working with mature ministers in the field ministry. You will set personal goals of achievement so that you will make constant improvement. Desire to deliver better sermons, work at the art of teaching, learn Scriptural arguments so that you will be able to overcome objections, learn how to explain the deep things of God. When you have reached one goal, set a new one. In that way you will make

---

11. What qualifications must overseers meet?
12. How does one show one is reaching out for greater responsibility?

advancement and not stand still.—1 Tim. 4:15, 16.

[13] Never overlook such qualities as dependability and reliability. See that you develop these qualities in yourself. Do you make appointments and not keep them? Do you turn down assignments on the service meeting program or in the Theocratic Ministry School for no good reason at all? Do you sense the need for being dependable and reliable? Do what you are assigned to do. Work at it whole-souled as to Jehovah and he will bless you. (Col. 3:23) Do not feel that you are ready to advance unless you have cultivated these essential qualities in yourself.

YOUTHS, TOO, SHOULD ASSUME RESPONSIBILITY

[14] Youthful ministers of Jehovah should not hold back from advancing toward greater responsibility. Many young persons today are choosing a variety of careers for which they are being trained. Others seem to pass through school without any particular career or goal in mind. But this should not be so with young people who have dedicated their lives to serve Jehovah God. By their dedication they have already chosen their career—the career of the ministry. Theirs is the highest career, for it is the only one that guarantees the reward of everlasting life!—John 5:24.

[15] If you have chosen the ministry as your career and your goal is fixed on accepting responsibility in the New World society, then you will want to beware of becoming overly involved in extracurricular school activities, such as sports and other activities that might involve you in potentially bad associations and stunt your Christian growth. These activities may

---

13. What two qualities are essential, and why?
14. What career have many youths chosen, and why is it the highest career?
15, 16. (a) Against what should schoolchildren be on guard, and why? (b) In what way can parents be an encouragement to children?

MARCH 15,

keep you
meetings an

[16] Parents
who want t
world will
ward goals o
sibility. To
gave this a
with godly d
ly training
godly devoti
as it holds p
which is to c
and deservi
statement."

[17] Pursuin
ly devotion i
make. There
career. It is t
to bear the
essential to
course that i
is not in vain
—1 Cor. 15:

OVERSEER

[18] When ar
overseer or
Christian cor
spiritual qua
not stop the
itself. Paul c
tention to yo
among which
you overseer
tion of God."
never lose si
bility that is
in their posit
lead in Christ
and love.

---

17. Why is the n
18. Why must ov
tion of their res

tand still.—1 Tim.

h qualities as de-
ity. See that you
1 yourself. Do you
not keep them? Do
nts on the service
ie Theocratic Min-
reason at all? Do
being dependable
ou are assigned to
ded as to Jehovah
Col. 3:23) Do not
to advance unless
ie essential quali-

LD ASSUME
.ITY

f Jehovah should
dvancing toward
ny young persons
ety of careers for
ned. Others seem
thout any partic-
d. But this should
le who have dedi-
Jehovah God. By
e already chosen
of the ministry.
eer, for it is the
s the reward of
:24.

the ministry as
d is fixed on ac-
le New World so-
to beware of be-
i extracurricular
sports and other
ve you in poten-
and stunt your
activities may

lal, and why?
i chosen, and why is

ichoolchildren be on
y can parents be an

keep you away from essential studies,
meetings and ministerial service.

¹⁶ Parents who love their children and
who want to see them alive in God's new
world will encourage and guide them toward goals of increased service and responsibility. To the young lad Timothy, Paul
gave this advice: "Be training yourself
with godly devotion as your aim. For bodily training is beneficial for a little; but
godly devotion is beneficial for all things,
as it holds promise of the life now and that
which is to come." He then adds: "Faithful
and deserving of full acceptance is that
statement."—1 Tim. 4:7-9.

¹⁷ Pursuing the responsible course of godly devotion is certainly the wise choice to
make. There is no finer or more rewarding
career. It is the course that will enable you
to bear the fruitage of the holy spirit so
essential to Christian maturity. It is a
course that is not in vain, for "your labor
is not in vain in connection with the Lord."
—1 Cor. 15:58; Gal. 5:22, 23.

OVERSEERS REACH OUT FOR GREATER
RESPONSIBILITY

¹⁸ When anyone has been appointed an
overseer or a ministerial servant in the
Christian congregation on the basis of his
spiritual qualifications, his growth should
not stop there but continue to manifest
itself. Paul counsels overseers: "Pay attention to yourselves and to all the flock,
among which the holy spirit has appointed
you overseers, to shepherd the congregation of God." (Acts 20:28) Overseers must
never lose sight of the precious responsibility that is theirs. They must, therefore,
in their position of responsibility take the
lead in Christian conduct, teaching, service
and love.

17. Why is the ministry a rewarding career?
18. Why must overseers continue to grow in appreciation of their responsibility?

¹⁹ As to the manner in which such responsibility should be discharged, the apostle Peter writes: "To the older men among
you I give this exhortation, for I too am
an older man like them and a witness of
the sufferings of the Christ, a sharer even
of the glory that is to be revealed: Shepherd the flock of God in your care, not
under compulsion, but willingly; neither
for love of dishonest gain, but eagerly; neither as lording it over those who are God's
inheritance, but becoming examples to the
flock." (1 Pet. 5:1-3) Shepherd God's flock,
the apostle says, but not under compulsion,
not begrudgingly, as if you had to, as if
you were being overly burdened, tied down
with too much responsibility. Shepherd the
flock lovingly, willingly, eagerly, joyfully.

²⁰ Remember, the sheep belong to God.
Then there is no reason for overseers to
'lord it over those who are God's inheritance,' is there? Neither should any overseer feel himself too superior to be
reached, thus making himself unap-
proachable. He must care for God's sheep.
How can he do it if he is aloof or too busy
to be bothered with their problems or so
interested in running a superefficient organization that he forgets the sheep entirely? If he desires to see his congregation warm, united, happy and fruitful,
then Peter's advice is: 'Become an example to the flock' in faith, in virtue, in
knowledge, in self-control, in endurance, in
godly devotion, in brotherly affection and
in love.—1 Pet. 5:3; 2 Pet. 1:5-8.

DISCHARGE RESPONSIBILITY EFFECTIVELY

²¹ Fulfilling the responsibility of a shepherd of God's flock is not a simple task. It
requires much patience, strength and skill.
Diligent study, an understanding of right

19, 20. (a) How should overseers discharge their responsibility, according to Peter? (b) What counsel
is given regarding aloofness and keeping the congregation warm and united in love?
21, 22. (a) Why is an overseer's task not an easy one?
(b) To what dangers and responsibilities will an overseer be alert?

16

Do you wisely destroy apostate material?

⁶ The apostle Paul expressed this concern: "I am afraid that somehow, as the serpent seduced Eve by its cunning, your minds might be corrupted away from the sincerity and the chastity that are due the Christ." (2 Corinthians 11:3) Paul found it necessary to write regarding some erroneous teachings that were circulating in his day. In his second letter to the congregation at Thessalonica, he wrote: "We request of you *not to be quickly shaken from your reason* nor to be excited either through an inspired expression or through a verbal message or through a letter as though from us, to the effect that the day of Jehovah is here. Let no one seduce you in any manner."—2 Thessalonians 2: 1-3.

6. (a) What concern did Paul express regarding some in the Corinthian congregation? (b) How was this same concern reflected in what was written to the congregation in Thessalonica?

12   THE WATCHTOWER—MARCH 15, 1986

Have No Dealings With Apostates

⁷ Now, what will you do if you are confronted with apostate teaching—subtle reasonings—claiming that what you believe as one of Jehovah's Witnesses is not the truth? For example, what will you do if you receive a letter or some literature, open it, and see right away that it is from an apostate? Will curiosity cause you to read it, just to see what he has to say? You may even reason: 'It won't affect me; I'm too strong in the truth. And, besides, if we have the truth, we have nothing to fear. The truth will stand the test.' In thinking this way, some have fed their minds upon apostate reasoning and have fallen prey to serious questioning and doubt. (Compare James 1:5-8.) So remember the warning at 1 Corinthians 10:12: "Let him that thinks he is standing beware that he does not fall."

⁸ With loving help from caring brothers, some having doubts sown by apostates have recovered after a period of spiritual turmoil and trauma. But this pain could have been avoided. At Proverbs 11:9 we are told: "By his mouth the one who is an apostate brings his fellowman to ruin, but by knowledge are the righteous rescued." Jude told fellow Christians to "continue showing mercy to some that have doubts; save them by snatching them out of the fire." (Jude 22, 23) Paul advised the overseer Timothy to instruct "with mildness those not favorably disposed; as perhaps God may give them repentance leading to an accurate knowledge of truth, and they may come back to their proper senses out from the snare of the Devil, seeing that they have been caught alive by him for the will of that one."—2 Timothy 2:25, 26.

7. (a) What questions arise if apostate literature is received by mail? (b) As regards safeguarding oneself from the influence of apostates, why is overconfidence dangerous?
8. What assistance is needed by some who have been overcome by doubts?

⁹ Tragically, ot plete darkness, e tendom's erroneo Peter wrote abou some who first then turned asid after having esca of the world by a the Lord and Sav involved again wi are overcome, th become worse fo Peter said they a turns to its von that turns back t —2 Peter 2:20-2:

¹⁰ When a fellov read this' or, 'Do may be tempted remember, in this who tells us in hi what does he say them" (Romans in company with 5:11); and "nev your homes or sa (2 John 9, 10). Th clear directions. were to read the apostate, would t inviting this ene into our home t relate his apostat

¹¹ Let us illustr Suppose your tee pornographic mat would you do? If l out of curiosity, v

9. What is the tra abandon true worsh
10. (a) What does to apostates? (b) H would amount to doi
11, 12. (a) What ill appreciate that we c tate literature? (b) Jehovah's concern fc

17

46

· it down. Abstaining
ı the body is just as
ng from fornication
lemned in the same
of the apostles and
·m.—Acts 15:19, 20,

a critical attitude
organization is too
off social contacts
! persons. (2 John
ıch critics feel that
close family tie or
friend that they are
lty to Jehovah and
uirements? Consid-
ng to accord social
ed person, even one
nay lead the erring
ıis course is not so
his further harm.
: such association
raving for what he
to regain it. Jeho-
st, and it is for our
erbs 3:5.
ın may incorrectly
res do not support
ıouse to house. But
eady dislikes this
looking for an ex-
f God and neighbor
see the urgency of
gain, endurance is
ıl spoke of his own
ly bearing witness
he taught publicly
e. (Acts 20:18-21)
should we not loy-
nple? Look at the

ıyalty not cause us to
ement that we avoid
e who are disfellow-

we have regarding
: to house?

→ *Busy and happy servants of Jehovah 'allow no place for the Devil' or for apostate ideas*

thousands who have been gathered into the "one flock" because of Jehovah's blessing upon the house-to-house work! (John 10:16) And do not forget the fine benefits we receive in training and discipline, in strengthening our faith, by going from door to door so as to reach people with the good news.—Compare Acts 5:42; 1 Timothy 4:16.

[14] Finally, we might consider what the Society has published in the past on chronology. Some opposers claim that Jehovah's Witnesses are false prophets. These opponents say that dates have been set, but nothing has happened. Again we ask, What is the motive of these critics? Are they encouraging wakefulness on the part of God's people, or are they, rather, trying to justify themselves for falling back into sleepy inactivity? (1 Thessalonians 5:4-9) More importantly, what will you do if you hear such criticism? If a person is questioning whether we are living in "the last days" of this system, or perhaps is entertaining ideas that God is so merciful that he surely will not cause the death of so many millions of people during the "great tribulation," then this individual already has prepared his heart to listen to such criticisms.—2 Timothy 3:1; Matthew 24:21.

[15] Yes, Jehovah's people have had to revise expectations from time to time. Because of our eagerness, we have hoped for the new system earlier than Jehovah's timetable has called for it. But we display our faith in God's Word and its sure promises by declaring its message to others. Moreover, the need to revise our understanding somewhat does not make us false prophets or change the fact that we *are* living in "the last days," soon to experience the "great tribulation" that will pave the way for the earthly Paradise. How foolish to take the view that expectations needing some adjustment should call into question the whole body of truth! The evidence is clear that Jehovah has used and is continuing to use his one organization, with "the faithful and discreet slave" taking the lead. Hence, we feel like Peter, who said: "Lord, whom shall we go away to? You have sayings of everlasting life."—John 6:68.

→ 14. How do you think we should react when critics accuse Jehovah's Witnesses of being false prophets?

15. Rather than being false prophets, what proves that Jehovah's Witnesses have faith in God's Word and its sure promises?

THE WATCHTOWER—MARCH 15, 1986 19

18

ation, or you em-
m that happened?
e contractually or
ntinue the business
sent, you certainly
erent attitude to-
d individual. Dis-
ters with him or
: be necessary, but
i social fellowship
past. In that way
your obedience to
e barrier for your-
press on him how
n in various ways.

**ELLOWSHIPED
D PERSON?**

od's righteousness
ing arrangement
should not speak
person, not even
have wondered
sus' advice to love
reet our brothers

dom God did not
le situation. What
nse of what Jeho-
nt of a disfellow-
we can strive to
ugh the apostle

ahead and does not
the Christ does not
mes to you and does
ver receive him into
ting to him. For he
n is a sharer in his
-11.

e that wise warn-
d knew well what
eeting others. He
mon greeting of

hat advice about speak-
on?
l speaking to expelled

that time was "Peace." As distinct from some personal "enemy" or worldly man in authority who opposed Christians, a disfellowshiped or disassociated person who is trying to promote or justify his apostate thinking or is continuing in his ungodly conduct is certainly not one to whom to wish "Peace." (1 Tim. 2:1, 2) And we all know from our experience over the years that a simple "Hello" to someone can be the first step that develops into a conversation and maybe even a friendship. Would we want to take that first step with a disfellowshiped person?

²⁴ 'But what if he seems to be repentant and needs encouragement?' someone might wonder. There is a provision for handling such situations. The overseers in the congregation serve as spiritual shepherds and protectors of the flock. (Heb. 13:17; 1 Pet. 5:2) If a disfellowshiped or disassociated person inquires, or gives evidence of wanting to come back into God's favor, the elders can speak to him. They will kindly explain what he needs to do and might give him some appropriate admonition. They can deal with him on the basis of facts about his past sin and his attitude. Others in the congregation lack such information. So if someone felt that the disfellowshiped or disassociated person 'is repentant,' might that be a judgment based on impression rather than accurate information? If the overseers were convinced that the person was repentant and was producing the fruits of repentance,* he would be reinstated into the congregation. After that occurs, the rest of the congregation can warmly welcome him at the meetings, display forgiveness, comfort him and confirm their love for him, as Paul urged the Corinthians to do with the man reinstated at Corinth.—2 Cor. 2:5-8.

* For a discussion of repentance, see The Watchtower of September 1, 1981.

THE WATCHTOWER — SEPTEMBER 15, 1981

NOT SHARING IN WICKED WORKS

²⁵ All faithful Christians need to take to heart the serious truth that God inspired John to write: "He that says a greeting to [an expelled sinner who is promoting an erroneous teaching or carrying on ungodly conduct] is a sharer in his wicked works."—2 John 11.

²⁶ Many of Christendom's commentators take exception to 2 John 11. They claim that it is 'unchristian counsel, contrary to the spirit of our Lord,' or that it encourages intolerance. Yet such sentiments emanate from religious organizations that do not apply God's command to "remove the wicked man from among yourselves," that seldom if ever expel even notorious wrongdoers from their churches. (1 Cor. 5:13) Their "tolerance" is unscriptural, unchristian.—Matt. 7:21-23; 25:24-30; John 8:44.

²⁷ But it is not wrong to be loyal to the righteous and just God of the Bible. He tells us that he will accept 'in his holy mountain' only those who walk faultlessly, practice righteousness and speak truth. (Ps. 15:1-5) If, though, a Christian were to throw in his lot with a wrongdoer who has been rejected by God and disfellowshiped, or has disassociated himself, that would be as much as saying 'I do not want a place in God's holy mountain either.' If the elders saw him heading in that direction by regularly keeping company with a disfellowshiped person, they would lovingly and patiently try to help him to regain God's view. (Matt. 18:18; Gal. 6:1) They would admonish him and, if necessary, 'reprove him with severity.' They want to help him remain 'in God's holy mountain.' But if he will not cease to fellowship with the expelled person, he thus has made himself 'a sharer (supporting or participating) in the wicked works' and must be

25, 26. What does God counsel about becoming a "sharer" with a disfellowshiped person?
27. How might a Christian become such a "sharer," and with what result?

25

19

48

ime, he has
ie. But they
prayers to
, 146) What
ı the home
family reads
Bible study?
· present to
ıch them or

wshiped, the
ıysical needs
ıd discipline.
ble study di-
n participat-
hat he would
ı the family
attention to
ı publications
is. (Prov. 1:
4) They can
, and sit with
hoping that
ıl counsel.

ive, such as a
ot live in the
subsequently
? The family
ending on the

wshiped par-
r able to care
hysically. The
Scriptural and
(1 Tim. 5:8)
· to bring the
orarily or per-

iers and ministerial
ns from Readers''
1978.

a disfellowshiped

t a disfellowshiped
ie?

:d to be
children

manently. Or it may appear advisable to arrange for care where there is medical personnel but where the parent would have to be visited. What is done may depend on factors such as the parent's true needs, his attitude and the regard the head of the household has for the spiritual welfare of the household.

[16] This could be true also with regard to a child who had left home but is now disfellowshiped or disassociated. Sometimes Christian parents have accepted back into the home for a time a disfellowshiped child who has become physically or emotionally ill. But in each case the parents can weigh the individual circumstances. Has a disfellowshiped son lived on his own, and is he now unable to do so? Or does he want to move back primarily because it would be an easier life? What about his morals and attitude? Will he bring "leaven" into the home?—Gal. 5:9.

[17] In Jesus' parable of the prodigal son, the father ran to meet and then accepted his returning son. The father, seeing the lad's pitiful condition, responded with natural parental concern. We can note, though, that the son did not bring home harlots or come with a disposition to continue his sinful life in his father's home. No, he expressed heartfelt repentance and evidently was determined to return to living a clean life.—Luke 15:11-32.

DISFELLOWSHIPED RELATIVES NOT LIVING AT HOME

[18] The second situation that we need to consider is that involving a disfellowshiped or disassociated relative who is *not* in the immediate family circle or living at one's home. Such a person is still related by blood or marriage, and so there may be

---

16, 17. (a) How might parents react to the possibility of a disfellowshiped child's moving back home? (b) What can we learn on this from the parable of the prodigal son?
18, 19. (a) How should Christians view association with disfellowshiped relatives who are outside the immediate family? (b) Why is this position appropriate? (2 Tim. 2:19)

THE WATCHTOWER — SEPTEMBER 15, 1981

The prodigal son did not return home to continue his sinful living, but was repentant. His father accepted him back

some limited need to care for necessary family matters. Nonetheless, it is not as if he were living in the same home where contact and conversation could not be avoided. We should keep clearly in mind the Bible's inspired direction: "Quit mixing in company with *anyone* called a brother that is a fornicator or a greedy person . . . , not even eating with such a man."—1 Cor. 5:11.

[19] Consequently, Christians related to such a disfellowshiped person living outside the home should strive to avoid needless association, even keeping business dealings to a minimum. The reasonableness of this course becomes apparent from reports of what has occurred where relatives have taken the mistaken view, "Though he is disfellowshiped, we are related and so can treat him the same as before.' From one area comes this:

29

"One person who was disfellowshiped was related to about one third of the congregation. All of his relations continued to associate with him."

And a highly respected Christian elder writes:

"In our area some disfellowshiped ones with large families have been met, as they enter the lobby of the Kingdom Hall, with a fanfare of backslapping and handshaking (even though the disfellowshiped one was known by them to be still living immorally). I feel a deep concern that those who have been disfellowshiped need to see that their course is hated by Jehovah and by his people and that they should feel a real need to become genuinely repentant. What will help these disfellowshiped ones to change when they are continually greeted by all in their large families who know of their practices?"

[20] There must have been congregations in the first century where many were related. But when someone was disfellowshiped, were all the relatives to carry on as normal as long as they did not discuss Scriptural matters with the disfellowshiped person? No. Otherwise the congregation would not really be applying the command: "Remove the wicked man from among yourselves."—1 Cor. 5:13.

[21] Great care needs to be exercised that a person's situation as a disfellowshiped sinner is neither overlooked nor minimized. As the sons of Korah well demonstrated, our chief loyalty must be to Jehovah and his theocratic arrangement. We can be sure that when we uphold his standards and prefer association with his organized people, rather than with wrongdoers, we will have his protection and blessing.—Ps. 84:10-12.

SOCIAL GATHERINGS AND DISFELLOWSHIPED RELATIVES

[22] Normally, relatives are often together at meals, picnics, family reunions or other social gatherings. But when someone has unrepentantly pursued sin and has had to be disfellowshiped, he may cause difficulties for his Christian relatives in regard to such gatherings. While they realize that they are still related to him, they do not want to ignore Paul's advice that faithful Christians should "quit mixing in company" with an expelled sinner.

[23] There is no point in looking for some rule as to family members being at gatherings where a disfellowshiped relative might be present. This would be something for those concerned to resolve, in keeping with Paul's counsel. (1 Cor. 5:11) And yet it should be appreciated that if a disfellowshiped person is going to be at a gathering to which nonrelative Witnesses are invited, that may well affect what others do. For example, a Christian couple might be getting married at a Kingdom Hall. If a disfellowshiped relative comes to the Kingdom Hall for the wedding, obviously he could not be in the bridal party there or "give away" the bride. What, though, if there is a wedding feast or reception? This can be a happy social occasion, as it was in Cana when Jesus attended. (John 2:1, 2) But will the disfellowshiped relative be allowed to come or even be invited? If he was going to attend, many Christians, relatives or not, might conclude that they should not be there, to eat and associate with him, in view of Paul's directions at 1 Corinthians 5:11.

[24] Thus, sometimes Christians may not feel able to have a disfellowshiped or disassociated relative present for a gathering that normally would include family members. Still, the Christians can enjoy the association of the loyal members of the congregation, having in mind Jesus' words: "Whoever does the will of God, this one is my brother and sister and mother." —Mark 3:35.

[25] The fact i
gives himself c
disfellowshiped,
proved standing
the happy co
sweet fellowship
ing much of th
Christian relativ
he has caused i

[26] Should he
arrangements f
problem. His
like to have ha
Hall, if that is i
would not be fit
from the congi
giving evidence
God's forgivene
practice sin an-
meetings, some
allow him to gi
neral home or
comments about
provide a witne
fort to the relat
fellowshiped per
ing false teachi
even such a talk
—2 John 9-11.

LESSON

[27] All of us ne
Jehovah's judgr
29:26) That is ti
for the Bible sho
that God detest:
is also true as tc
uals. Jehovah's
"unrighteous per
the "works of tl
his kingdom. (1 C
Such persons hav
will they fit in

20, 21. When it comes to disfellowshiped relatives, why do we need to be careful? (2 Tim. 2:22)
22. Why may family gatherings pose special problems as to disfellowshiped relatives?

23. What would be the situation with a disfellowshiped relative and a Christian wedding?
24. Loyal Christians can most enjoy what association? (Prov. 18:24)

25, 26. If a disfellows
be the situation as tc
27. How should we v

THE WATCHTOWER —

30

THE WATCHTOWER — SEPTEMBER 15, 1981

21

through it; whereas narrow is the gate and cramped the road leading off into life, and few are the ones finding it." (Matthew 7:13, 14) How clearly those words answer our questions! They show that many people are not worshiping God in a way that pleases him. Only a few are on the road leading to life.

3 Probably you find yourself readily agreeing with the fact that much religion is not approved by God. No doubt there are many things done in the name of religion that you do not approve. For example, if you look around in the churches and observe persons who live immoral lives but who make a pretense at being righteous, you know that something is wrong. (2 Timothy 3:4, 5) And when you read in the newspaper that some clergymen are publicly approving of sex relations between unmarried persons and that they are saying that homosexuality is all right under certain conditions, you are well aware that this is not what God says. You may remember that God destroyed the ancient cities of Sodom and Gomorrah. And why? Because they practiced such things! So you know that God is not going to approve of a religion that tells people it is all right to act like that. —Jude 7.

4 However, you have no doubt heard people say: "It doesn't matter what you believe, as long as you lead a clean moral life and deal kindly with your neighbors." But is that all there is to worshiping God in an acceptable way? These things are necessary, but God requires more. Doctrines are

3. Are there things done in the name of religion of which you do not approve?
4. (a) Besides our being moral and kind, what else must we consider about our religion, in view of Jesus' words at John 4:23? (b) Why do we need to examine the doctrines that we have been taught?

also involved. The Bible informs us that "the true worshipers will worship the Father with spirit and truth." (John 4:23) If our worship is to be acceptable to God, it must be firmly rooted in God's Word of truth. Jesus reproved those persons who claimed to serve God but who relied heavily on the traditions of men in preference to God's Word. He applied to them God's own words from Isaiah 29:13, saying: "It is in vain that they keep worshiping me, because they teach commands of men as doctrines." (Matthew 15:9) Since we do not want our worship to be in vain, it is important for each one of us to examine his religion.

5 We need to examine, not only what we personally believe, but also what is taught by any religious organization with which we may be associated. Are its teachings in full harmony with God's Word, or are they based on the traditions of men? If we are lovers of the truth, there is nothing to fear from such an examination. It should be the sincere desire of every one of us to learn what God's will is for us, and then to do it.—John 8:32.

6 The mere fact that church members may have the Bible or that it is occasionally read to them from the pulpit does not of itself prove that all the things they are taught are in the Bible. It is good to have the Bible; each and every person should. But we must also know what it says and believe it. If a religion really accepts the Bible as God's Word, it is not going to use certain parts of it and reject other parts. "All Scripture is inspired of

5. Why should we examine, not only our personal beliefs, but also the teachings of any religious organisation with which we may be associated?
6. (a) Does the fact that the Bible is occasionally used in a church prove that all the church doctrines are from the Bible? (b) Why must religion approved by God agree in all details with the Bible?

exposition was not en-
-establish my wavering
- show that the records
. What I heard sent me
study with more zeal
ver before, and I shall
Lord for that leading;
ventism helped me to
it did help me greatly
ng of errors, and thus
: the Truth."

ig renewed young Rus-
ion to search for Scrip-
sent him back to his
: eagerness than ever be-
on came to believe that
ar for those who served
ne to a clear knowledge
. So, in 1870, fired by
and a few acquaintanc-
i and nearby Allegheny
d formed a class for Bi-
rding to a later associate
: small Bible class was
his manner: "Someone
iestion. They would dis-
ould look up all related
ie point and then, when
ied on the harmony of
ey would finally state
n and make a record of
later acknowledged, the
.870 to 1875 was a time
wth in grace and knowl-
of God and his Word."
searched the Scriptures,
iings became clearer to
ruth seekers. They saw
truths pertaining to the
ie human soul and that
is a gift to be attained by

those who became joint heirs with Christ in his heavenly Kingdom. (Ezek. 18:20; Rom. 2:6, 7) They began to grasp the doctrine of the ransom sacrifice of
Jesus Christ and the opportunity that this provision
made possible for humankind. (Matt. 20:28) They
came to recognize that although Jesus first came to
the earth as a man in the flesh, at his return he would
be invisibly present as a spirit person. (John 14:19)
They further learned that the object of Jesus' return
was, not to destroy everyone, but to bless the obedient families of the earth. (Gal. 3:8) Russell wrote:
"We felt greatly grieved at the error of Second Adventists, who were expecting Christ in the flesh, and
teaching that the world and all in it except Second
Adventists would be burned up."

The Scriptural truths that became clear to this little Bible class were certainly a departure from the pagan doctrines that had filtered into Christianity during the centuries-long apostasy. But did Russell and
his spiritually-minded associates gain these truths
from the Bible unaided by others?

Influence of Others

Russell referred quite openly to the assistance in
Bible study he had received from others. Not only did he acknowledge his
indebtedness to Second Adventist Jonas Wendell but he also spoke with
affection about two other individuals who had aided him in Bible study.
Russell said of these two men: "The study of the Word of God with these
dear brethren led, step by step, into greener pastures." One, George
W. Stetson, was an earnest student of the Bible and pastor of the Advent
Christian Church in Edinboro, Pennsylvania.

The other, George Storrs, was publisher of the magazine *Bible Examiner,* in Brooklyn, New York. Storrs, who was born on December 13,
1796, was initially stimulated to examine what the Bible says about the
condition of the dead as a result of reading something published (though
at the time anonymously) by a careful student of the Bible, Henry Grew,
of Philadelphia, Pennsylvania. Storrs became a zealous advocate of what
was called conditional immortality—the teaching that the soul is mortal
and that immortality is a gift to be attained by faithful Christians. He also
reasoned that since the wicked do not have immortality, there is no eternal
torment. Storrs traveled extensively, lecturing on the subject of no immortality for the wicked. Among his published works was the *Six Sermons,*

> **George W. Stetson**
> **—"A Man of Marked Ability"**
>
> C. T. Russell gratefully acknowledged
> the assistance that was given him by
> George W. Stetson, of Edinboro,
> Pennsylvania, in studying the Scrip-
> tures. Stetson died on October 9, 1879,
> at the age of 64. The following month
> the "Watch Tower" carried an an-
> nouncement of Stetson's death that re-
> vealed 27-year-old Russell's deep re-
> spect for him. "Our brother was a man
> of marked ability," wrote Russell, "and
> surrendered bright prospects of world-
> ly and political honors to be permitted
> to preach Christ." Stetson's dying re-
> quest was that C. T. Russell preach his
> funeral sermon; Russell complied with
> the request. "About twelve hundred
> persons attended the funeral services,"
> reported Russell, "thus giving evidence
> of the high esteem in which our broth-
> er was held."—The "Watch Tower,"
> November 1879.

Photocopied Documentation

George Storrs
—"A Friend and Brother"

C. T. Russell felt a sense of indebtedness to George Storrs, who was some 56 years his senior. Russell had learned much from Storrs about the mortality of the soul. So when Storrs lay seriously ill late in 1879, Russell offered to print in the "Watch Tower" a statement of Storrs' condition. "Our brother," Russell wrote, "so long the editor of 'The Bible Examiner' is known to most of our readers; also that he has been obliged by severe illness to discontinue his paper." In Russell's estimation, Storrs had "much reason to thank God for being privileged to spend so long a life and one so consecrated to the Master." Storrs died on December 28, 1879, at the age of 83. An announcement of his death appeared in the February 1880 issue of the "Watch Tower," which said: "We mourn the loss of a friend and brother in Christ yet, 'not as those who have no hope.'"

George Storrs

which eventually attained a distribution of 200,000 copies. Without a doubt, Storrs' strong Bible-based views on the mortality of the soul as well as the atonement and restitution (restoration of what was lost due to Adamic sin; Acts 3:21) had a strong, positive influence on young Charles T. Russell.

Yet, another man who had a profound effect on Russell's life also caused his loyalty to Scriptural truth to be put to the test.

Time Prophecies and the Presence of the Lord

One morning in January 1876, 23-year-old Russell received a copy of a religious periodical called *Herald of the Morning*. From the picture on the cover, he could see that it was identified with Adventism. The editor, Nelson H. Barbour, of Rochester, New York, believed that the object of Christ's return was not to destroy the families of the earth but to bless them and that his coming would be not in the flesh but as a spirit. Why, this was in agreement with what Russell and his associates in Allegheny had believed for some time!* Curiously, though, Barbour believed from Biblical time-prophecies that Christ was already present (invisibly) and that the harvest work of gathering "the wheat" (true Christians making up the Kingdom class) was already due.—Matt., chap. 13.

Russell had shied away from Biblical time prophecies. Now, however, he wondered: "Could it be that the *time prophecies* which I had so long despised, because of their misuse by Adventists, were really meant to indicate when the Lord would be *invisibly present* to set up his Kingdom?" With his insatiable thirst for Scriptural truth, Russell had to learn more. So he arranged to meet with Barbour in Philadelphia. This meeting confirmed their agreement on a number of Bible teachings and provided an opportunity for them to exchange views. "When we first met," Russell later stated, "he had much to learn from me on the fulness of *restitution* based upon the sufficiency of the ransom given for all, as I had much to

---

* Neither Barbour nor Russell was the first to explain the Lord's return as an invisible presence. Much earlier, Sir Isaac Newton (1642-1727) had written that Christ would return and reign "invisible to mortals." In 1856, Joseph Seiss, a Lutheran minister in Philadelphia, Pennsylvania, had written about a two-stage second advent—an invisible *pa·rou·si′a*, or presence, followed by a visible manifestation. Then, in 1864, Benjamin Wilson had published his *Emphatic Diaglott* with the interlinear reading "presence," not "coming," for *pa·rou·si′a*, and B. W. Keith, an associate of Barbour, had drawn it to the attention of Barbour and his associates.

---

learn fro
sell that (

"Resolve
C. T.
Christ's i
others. H
the harve
er had be
the Truth
vote him

To co
the pamp
lished in 1
Worlds, a
subjects o
had been t
to *combin*
view that

As Ru
thing mor
watered. T
bour deci
pended be
contribute
editors.

All we

Russell B
In the
article by I
Russell, wl
was, in fac
very next
Atonemen
The contro
months. F
Mr. Barbo

C. T. F
enough; th
must be pr

* A clearer
"Growing in /

25

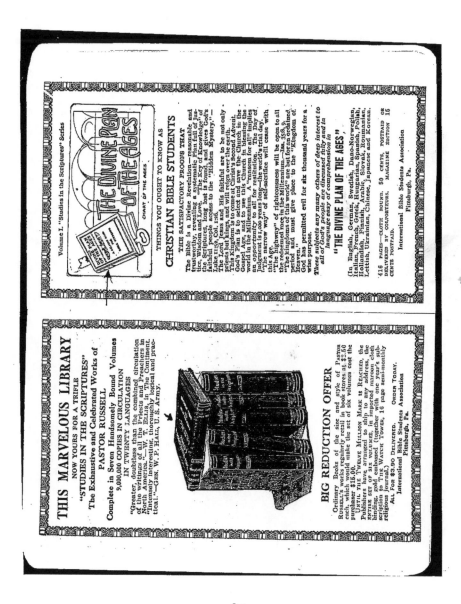

26

1993

Helping Their Fellowman

Reverence toward the gods was at the heart of the social and cultural life of the Roman Empire. Since Christians abstained from sharing in anything tainted by the pagan gods, the people viewed Christianity as an affront to their way of life; and according to the historian Tacitus, Christians were said to be haters of mankind. Conveying a similar feeling, Minucius Felix, in his writings, quotes a Roman as saying to a Christian acquaintance: "You do not attend the shows; you take no part in the processions . . . abhor the sacred games." The populace of the ancient Roman world little understood the Christians.

Similarly today, Jehovah's Witnesses are not understood by many in the world. People may admire the high moral standards of the Witnesses but feel that the Witnesses should share with the world around them in its

activities and get involv
ever, those who get to l
is a Biblical reason for e

Far from shutting t
Witnesses devote their l
Christ set the example.
with the problems of li
the guidelines for life th
with their neighbors Bi
look on life. At the cor
passing away," that soor
tem to an end, and that
of the world and put the

Practices That Have Been Abandoned

This Christmas celebration at Brooklyn Bethel in 1926 was their last. The Bible Students gradually came to appreciate that neither the origin of this holiday nor the practices associated with it honored God

For years, Bible Students wore a cross and crown as a badge of identification, and this symbol was on the front cover of the "Watch Tower" from 1891 to 1931. But in 1928 it was emphasized that not a decorative symbol but one's activity as a witness showed he was a Christian. In 1936 it was pointed out that the evidence indicates that Christ died on a stake, not a two-beamed cross

In their "Daily Manna" l
of birthdays. But after th
and when they realized ti
giving undue honor to cr
Christians never celebrat
dents quit this practice to

27

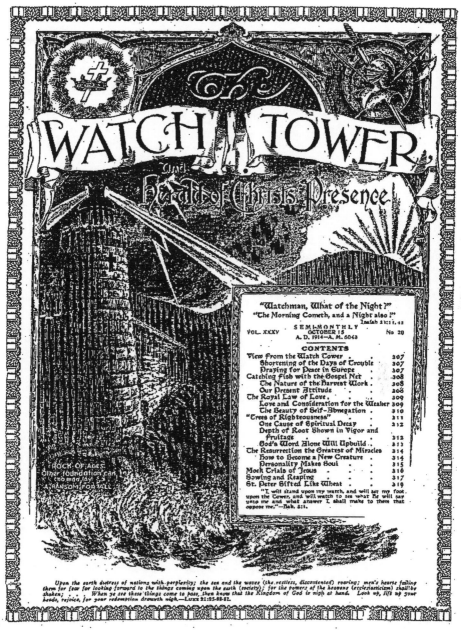

WATCH TOWER,

Herald of Christ's Presence

ROCK OF AGES
Other foundation can
no man lay
A RANSOM FOR ALL

"Watchman, What of the Night?"
"The Morning Cometh, and a Night also!"

Isaiah 21:11, 12

VOL. XXXV   SEMI-MONTHLY   No 20
OCTOBER 15
A. D. 1914—A. M. 6043

CONTENTS

"I will stand upon my watch, and will set my foot
upon the Tower, and will watch to see what He will say
unto me, and what answer I shall make to them that
oppose me."—Hab. 2:1.

Upon the earth distress of nations with perplexity; the sea and the waves (the restless, discontented) roaring; men's hearts failing
them for fear for looking forward to the things coming upon the earth (society); for the powers of the heavens (ecclesiasticism) shall be
shaken; . . . When ye see these things come to pass, then know that the Kingdom of God is nigh at hand. Look up, lift up your
heads, rejoice, for your redemption draweth nigh.—Luke 21:25-28-31.

28   10/15/14

1904 apr 15

(126-127)　　　　　ZION'S WATCH TOWER　　　　ALLEGHENY, PA.

an interpretation we are met with several difficulties, however. (1). To suppose such a class in the church would be to recognize what is elsewhere denied—to recognize a clerical or authoritative class as distinct and separate from the remainder of the church, because this steward is to dispense the meat in due season to the household, to the fellow-servants. The church of Christ, we hold, is not composed of clergy and laity; but, "ye are all one in Christ Jesus," and "one is your Master, even Christ." There would be no violation of principle, however, in supposing that the Lord at the time indicated would specially use one member of his church as the channel or instrument through which he would send the appropriate messages, spiritual nourishment appropriate at that time; because at various times in the past the Lord has used individuals in such a manner. For instance, Peter used the "keys" of the kingdom of heaven at Pentecost, and again at the home of Cornelius, and in both places he was used as a special servant in connection with the dispensing of special truths. This did not constitute Peter a lord over the other apostles or over the church, but merely a servant.

(2) However much we might endeavor to apply this figure to the Lord's people collectively, the fact would still remain that the various items stated would not fit to a company of individuals. For instance, in the 42nd verse, in the common version it is rendered, that faithful steward; the revised version, the faithful steward; as though a particular one were meant and the term not used indefinitely for a number. Turning to the Greek text we find that the emphasis is there also and in double-form—the faithful, the wise steward. If it were a case in which we could apply this text to Christ, there would be no difficulty, or if it were a case in which it could be applied to the whole body of Christ, there could be no difficulty, in harmonizing the one with the many members of the one body of Christ; but since the servant mentioned is to dispense food to the other members of the body, his fellow-servants, the term seems to be limited to some particular individual. However, just as we said of Peter, that he was not by reason of special use made a lord over the brethren, so we say of whoever is meant in this passage, that in no sense of the word would this constitute him a lord, or dictator or master, or imply his inspiration. All that we could say would be that it would be one who would be privileged to be a servant, and not many, seem anxious to fill such a position in the true sense of the word. This servant, if found faithful, would be intrusted more and more with the distribution of every feature of present truth as represented in the parable, by his being given the

dispensing of the food in due season to the household. Unfaithfulness on the part of this appointed one would mean his degradation from this service, and presumably the service would go on at the hands of another, his successor.

The expression, "Verily I say unto you, He shall make him ruler over all his goods," should not be understood to apply to future glories and honors, but merely to a more general charge or stewardship as respects the dispensing of the Lord's "goods," or truths due to be protected or disbursed during the remainder of this "harvest" time. In other words, the steward through whom the Lord will dispense present truth in this "harvest," will, if found vigilant, humble, faithful, be continued in the stewardship and be used of the Lord more and more in the service of the household—down to the close of the "harvest."

"NOT AS LORDS OVER GOD'S HERITAGE"

That this servant must not act or be regarded as a lord is clearly indicated in the 45th verse, which shows that such a misuse of his appointment would work his downfall. At no time has the church ever had need to be on guard against its servants who really endeavored to serve it and to hand forth from the Lord's treasure house the meat in due season. The church's dangers have always arisen from those who sought to lord it over God's heritage, and to dispense their own wisdom or the wisdom of other men instead of the Word of the Lord.

Verses 47, 48, seem to imply that the servant's responsibility to the Lord will be in proportion to his knowledge of the Lord's will; and that the Lord will deal with him on the principle that having had much knowledge and opportunity, the requirements at his hands will be proportionately large. While this exhortation in general seems to apply to one particular servant through whom the other servants are to be supplied (see Matt. 24:45-51), we can see that the same principles in a general sense would apply to each servant in turn, as he would receive either food or stewardship. His responsibility would, be in proportion to what he received or had opportunity to receive, and to the manner in which he used the blessing. We of today, living under such great favor from the Lord, enjoying the light of present truth as we do, have every reason to give thanks and more and more to appreciate the things new and old from the Master's storehouse of truth that he is now dispensing to us, and which each in turn is privileged to dispense to others and has responsibility for in proportion to his knowledge. The Lord help us each to be faithful, and to remember that our Lord was a servant as well as a Son, and that our highest privilege as sons is to be faithful servants, stewards of the manifold grace of God.

INTERESTING QUESTIONS ANSWERED

CONCERNING BAPTISM OF JEWS

Question.—Would a Jew coming into Christ today symbolize consecration just as do Gentiles, or would his baptism signify repentance for remission of sins, as per Acts 2:38?

Answer.—The special favor of God toward natural Israel as a nation ended at the time of Christ's rejection when their house was "left desolate." A personal favor continued, with the true Israelites for a further 3½ years to the end of their covenanted 70 weeks of years. It is possible that some sort of special favor continued with this class until the full end of the Jewish "harvest," A. D. 69, but certainly no longer.

The Apostle Paul refers to this change, saying that "the middle wall of partition" between Jew and Gentile had been broken down. It follows, therefore, that Jews could not now come into relationship with Christ on any other terms than could Gentiles. As natural branches they are "broken off," and would require re-engrafting just the same as would the wild-olive branches.—Rom. 11:19-24.

Question.—Was there any difference between the immersion of John and that mentioned by Peter (Acts 2:38)?

Answer.—Yes; John's preaching of repentance was merely an exhortation to renounce sin and prepare for a coming Messiah. The exhortation of Peter was to repent of sin, because the Messiah had come, and the sin to be repented of included the national sin of rejecting Messiah and crucifying him; hence, of the latter it is said that it is a baptism in the name of Jesus.

Question.—In Eph. 4:5 we read that there is "one Lord, one faith, one baptism." How does this agree with the thought that the Jews were immersed for the remission of sins, whereas the Gentiles were immersed into Christ?

Answer.—The one baptism is not the symbolic one, but the actual one, viz., the burial into Christ. This, in the case of those who are Gentiles, signifies a full consecration and full burial into the will of Christ; but this same baptism to the Jew would mean a transfer from Moses to Christ, from being

dead in Moses to being dead in Christ. The sin of violation of the Jewish Law Covenant being repented of and forgiven, the Jew who was under that covenant is thenceforth counted as being under the New Covenant, and to him the outward form or symbol of baptism would mean a repentance from the works of the Law and his failure under the Law Covenant, and his acceptance in Christ, the new Mediator of the New Covenant. To us who are by nature Gentiles there can be no such repentance from the dead works of the Law; for we were never under that Law, and there can be no such transfer from Moses to Christ, because we never were in Moses.

Question.—Does Rom. 10:12 have any bearing on this question? "There is no difference between the Jew and the Greek; for the same Lord over all is rich unto all that call upon him."

Answer.—It has a bearing, but not as contradicting the foregoing. There is no difference between the Jew and the Greek when both have come into Christ—thenceforth they are on the same plane, on the same footing; but there was a difference in the way the Jew and the Greek properly attested their coming to Christ at the opening of this Gospel age.

Question.—Was the re-immersion mentioned in Acts 19:3-5 made necessary because the persons were Gentiles, and had symbolized their baptism in a manner appropriate only to the Jews?

Answer.—We think it was, for the latter reason.

HOW DOES THE ANTITYPICAL SCAPEGOAT CLASS BEAR THE SINS OF THE PEOPLE?

Question.—What is represented in the typical confession of sin by the high priest over the "scapegoat" in the Tabernacle sacrifices, as recorded in Lev. 16:20-22?

Answer.—We understand that this goat represents a consecrated class which fails to perform sacrifice; and that its being sent into the wilderness at the hand of the "fit" man represents that all the consecrated who have not sacrificed

* See June 15, 1919, issue for critical examination of Covenants.

29　[3356]

Biography

the age," during, which the Lord has been conducting his great harvest work; that, in harmony with the Lord's own statement, this harvest work is separating true Christians, designated as "wheat," from merely professing Christians, designated as "tares," and gathering the true saints into the kingdom of the Lord. It is here interesting to note that Jesus said: "Who then is a faithful and wise servant, whom his Lord hath made ruler over his household, to give them meat in due season? Blessed is that servant, whom his Lord, when he cometh, shall find so doing. Verily I say unto you, that he shall make him ruler over all his goods." Thousands of the readers of Pastor Russell's writings believe that he filled the office of "that faithful and wise servant," and that his great work was giving to the household of faith, meat in due season. His modesty and humility precluded him from openly claiming this title, but he admitted as much in private conversation. For a more detailed account of his work, reference is made to THE WATCH TOWER of June 1st, 1916.

In 1910 Pastor Russell visited Palestine and Russia. He there delivered to thousands of orthodox Jews lectures on the regathering of the Jews to Palestine. In 1911 he was one of a committee of seven who made a journey around the world and especially examined into the conditions of missionary work in Japan, China, Korea, and India. On the same occasion he again visited the Jews in Palestine and Galatia, explaining to them that the prophecies teach that the Jews at an early date will again be established in Palestine. On his return to America he was given a great ovation at the New York City Hippodrome by thousands of Jews, his discourse on that occasion being published by Hebrew papers both in America and in Europe.

During the forty-two years of Pastor Russell's Christian work he never directly or indirectly solicited money.

Biography

ferent languages. At the same time he was pastor of more than 1,200 congregations of Bible Students, in different parts of the world. These he visited and taught as often as possible.

Pastor Russell organized and conducted a Lecture Bureau which constantly employed seventy Bible lecturers, who traveled and delivered lectures on the Scriptures. He organized and managed an auxiliary lecture bureau of seven hundred men who gave a portion of their time to lecturing on Bible teachings. Each year he wrote practically all of the copy for the BIBLE STUDENTS MONTHLY, the annual distribution of which amounted to approximately fifty million copies.

His weekly sermons were handled by a newspaper syndicate. More than 2,000 newspapers, with a combined circulation of fifteen million readers, at one time published his discourses. All told, more than 4,000 newspapers published these sermons.

The Continent, a publication whose "editor" often opposed Pastor Russell, once published the following significant statement concerning him:

"His writings are said to have greater newspaper circulation every week than those of any other living man; a greater, doubtless, than the combined circulation of the writings of all the priests and preachers in North America; greater even than the work of Arthur, Brisbane, Norman Hapgood, George Horace Lorimer, Dr. Frank Crane, Frederick Haskins, and a dozen other of the best known editors and syndicate writers put together." ...

... HARVEST WORK

Pastor Russell adhered closely to the teachings of the Scriptures. He believed and taught that we are living in the time of the second presence of our Lord, and that this presence dates from 1874; that, since that time, we have been living in the "time of the end," the "end of

THE DIVINE PLAN OF THE AGES, 1886, 1925 edition

30

88

hardships can be borne. Peter told fellow believers: "Beloved ones, do not be puzzled at the burning among you, which is happening to you for a trial, as though a strange thing were befalling you; but, on the contrary, go on rejoicing forasmuch as you are sharers in the sufferings of the Christ."—1 Pet. 4:12, 13.

Jehovah and his "messenger of the covenant," Jesus Christ, came to inspect the spiritual temple in 1918 C.E. Judgment then began with the "house of God" and a period of refining and cleansing commenced. (Mal. 3:1-3; 1 Pet. 4:17) Something else also occurred. Men manifesting the marks of an 'evil slave" came forward and figuratively began 'beating' their fellow slaves. Jesus Christ had foretold how such ones would be dealt with. At the same time he showed that a "faithful and discreet slave" class would be in evidence, dispensing spiritual food.—Matt. 24:45-51.

The identity of the "faithful and discreet slave," or "faithful and wise servant" (*King James Version*), was a matter of quite some concern back in those years. Much earlier, in 1881, C. T. Russell wrote: "We believe that every member of this body of Christ is engaged in the blessed work, either directly or indirectly, of giving meat in due season to the household of faith. 'Who then is that *faithful* and *wise servant* whom his Lord hath made ruler over his household, to give them meat in due season? It is not that little flock of consecration vows—the body of Christ—and is not the whole body individually and collectively, giving the meat in due season to the household of faith—the great company of believers?'"

So it was understood that the "servant" God used to dispense spiritual food was a class. With the passing of time, however, the idea adopted by many was that C. T. Russell himself was the "faithful and wise servant." They felt that all the truth God saw fit to reveal to his people had been presented through Brother Russell, that nothing more could be brought forth. Annie Poggensee writes: "This caused a great sifting out of those who chose to stay back with Russell's works." In February 1927, this erroneous thought that Russell himself was the "faithful and wise servant" was cleared up.

Shortly after Brother Rutherford became president of the Watch Tower Society, a real conspiracy developed. The seed of rebellion was planted and then the trouble spread, as explained below.

C. T. Russell had seen the need to send someone from headquarters to Britain to strengthen the Bible Students there after the outbreak of World War I.

89

He intended to send Paul S. L. Johnson, a Jew who forsook Judaism and became a Lutheran minister before coming as a knowledge of God's truth. Johnson had served as one of the Society's traveling speakers and was well known for his ability. Out of respect for Russell's wish, the executive committee that served for a short time before Rutherford's election as president sent Johnson to England, giving him certain papers that would facilitate entry into that country. He was to learn all he could about the work in England and then make a full report to the Society, but he was to make no personnel changes at the British headquarters. However, his reception in England during November 1916 seemed to warp his judgment and finally his reason, "until," as A. H. Macmillan stated, "he came to the ridiculous conclusion that he was the 'steward' of Jesus' parable of the penny. He later thought he was the 'messenger' throughout England. In discourses to Bible Students throughout England, Johnson characterized himself as Russell's successor, contending that the mantle of Pastor Russell had fallen upon him just as Elijah's cloak ("official garment") fell upon Elisha.—2 Ki. 2:11-14.

Evidently, Johnson's aspirations had developed even earlier, for brother Kessler recalls: "In 1915 I left Bethel and before going for the vacation I visited a couple of old friends I had known for years, P. S. L. Johnson by name. Satan was already showing his ugly underhanded methods to gain control, no matter how. Johnson said, 'I'd like to talk with you. Let's sit in the living room, which we did. He commenced by saying: 'Sister, we know that it is possible for Brother Russell to pass on most anytime, but the friends need not be fearful when that happens. I can step into his place and take right over without any stopping of the work.'"

While in England, Johnson endeavored to take complete control of the British field of activity, even trying, without authority, to dismiss certain members of the London headquarters staff. So much confusion resulted that the branch overseer complained to Brother Rutherford. In turn, Rutherford appointed a commission of several brothers in London who were not members of the headquarters staff. They met, heard and weighed the facts and recommended that Johnson be recalled. Rutherford told Johnson to return. Instead of doing so, Johnson sent letters and cablegrams charging the committee with bias, and also trying to justify his course. Seeking to make his position indispensable in Britain, he improperly used the documents furnished him by the Society and impounded its funds in the

31

Photocopied Documentation

a people for the reception of the gospel (whether they had profited by it or not), that they were expected to recognize both the harvest message and the appointed and attested messengers; and their opportunity for either receiving or rejecting them, was the first applied test of their worthiness of the special favors then about to be offered to them. It was on this account that the harvesters were instructed to go to that people in a manner to impress them with a sense of their obligations as a covenant people to receive and gladly to entertain the messengers of the Lord to them. Throughout the whole nation the fame of the Messiah and the divine attestations of his power and authority had spread (Matt. 4:23-25; Mark 1:28, 32-34, 45; 6:31-34; 8:26, 27; Luke 4:14, 15, 36, 37; Matt. 9:26, 31; 14:1, 2), and these now sent forth in his name represented him, so that in receiving them they were receiving him, and in rejecting them they were rejecting him. Hence the blessing promised on their reception, and denunciations that followed their rejection. (Verses 11-15) When they departed out of the city or house that rejected them, they were to shake off the very dust of their feet for a testimony against them, because that in so doing they were violating their most solemn covenant with God and bringing upon themselves the just condemnation of such a course. That condemnation, however, was not to eternal death, but to deprivation of the privileges and blessings of the new dispensation then about to be offered to them, but of which they proved themselves unworthy. Nor was the condemnation, either then or at the full end of their age, an individual one; for, although the nation as a whole was cast off from divine favor and blinded, and destined to remain so until the gospel favor had passed over to the Gentiles, yet during this time, if any individual of the nation repented and severed his ties with the nation and family (which the persecuting spirit of the nation has always compelled) he might, through such tribulation, enter into the embryo kingdom—the Gospel church.

In this harvest the circumstances attending the work are in many respects quite different. Though here also the Lord has a consecrated people—nominal spiritual Israel—they are not a local nation within a circumscribed boundary, but they are scattered here and there as wheat in the midst of tares. The reapers here must therefore search them out singly, while there they were grouped in cities and families and a nation.

Again, the circumstances here are the reverse of those there in that the testimony to the truth is given in the midst of a very babel of voices, all claiming to teach the truth; and so great is the confusion that only the consecrated and faithful souls, whose practiced ears know the Master's voice from all others, are able to discern it. They have an affinity for the truth: the holy Spirit within them recognizes the same spirit in the message, as well as in the messengers, and it satisfies their longings as nothing else can do.

Thus the harvest message becomes a test of faithfulness to God's covenant people here, and as a sickle it accomplishes the reaping. These different circumstances and conditions of this harvest make necessary the very reverse of the former method of the dependence of the messengers upon the hospitality of the people. Now, in order to make manifest that no mercenary motives, or motives of indolence, or love of ease, or popularity, or of desire to impose on others prompt the reapers of this harvest, the Lord in his providence has so arranged the work here that all such motives are manifestly eliminated from the harvest work; and it is seen to be a self-sacrificing labor of love, prompted by that devotion and zeal which the truth alone inspires. And this truth commands the truth to the attention of the Lord's people where the messenger comes in contact with them, though often it reaches them through the printed page alone, where the luster of the truth is its own commendation.

This difference in the two harvests was aptly illustrated by the Lord when he likened the Jewish nation to wheat and chaff, and his work there to a fan for blowing the chaff away—thus indicating the compactness of that people; while here his professed people are likened to wheat and tares, thus indicating their scattered and confused condition and the necessity of careful searching and gathering out.

It would therefore be entirely out of order for the reapers in this harvest to denounce or shake off the dust of their feet for a testimony against any city now, for no city or community as such is now in covenant relations with God as was Israel; and so different are the customs and circumstances of this time that a man might brush the dust and denounce the people for a week and not be noticed, or, if noticed, merely considered as of unsound mind, as intent are the masses of the people on pursuing their own course and grasping after gain.

The consequence now to those who recognize and yet reject the truth will be very similar to those which followed Israel's

rejection, (their complete overthrow in the midst of great tribulation), excepting that the increased light and privilege of this time will merit and receive the greater punishment—"a time of trouble *such as never was* since there was a nation." (Dan. 12:1) Surely, then, it will be more tolerable for the land of Sodom and Gomorrah (Matt. 10:15) in the day of judgment (the Millennial age) than for the condemned house of Israel, either fleshly or spiritual, which are judged unworthy of the grace of God, because they cast it from them. The judgment upon condemned fleshly Israel was a terrible overthrow in the midst of harrowing scenes of war and desolation and famine, leaving them utterly desolate and scattering them as fugitives among all nations; while that which is shortly to come upon nominal spiritual Israel is described as a time of unparalleled trouble, such as never has been and never again shall be.

Another point of contrast which this lesson suggests is that between the Lord's methods for the harvest work of the Jewish age and and the subsequent methods of the inspired apostles, equally under the Lord's direction and supervision, which not only winnowed the grain of that harvest, but also sought to systematically store it. The wheat of that dispensation was to form the nucleus of the Christian church—the embryo kingdom of heaven—which as a compact and sympathetic body subject to Christ, imbued with his spirit, and representing his truth, was to stand before the world as a living testimony to his truth and to the power of his grace for nearly two thousand years. It was necessary, therefore, as believers multiplied in the days of the apostles, to adopt some simple method of recognition which would serve to unify them and to make them helpful one to another as members of one body.

But as that work of organizing the church of the new Gospel dispensation was no part of the harvest work of the old Jewish dispensation, so the present harvest work or reaping of the Gospel dispensation is also separate and distinct from the work of the new Millennial dispensation now drawing on. But there is this difference between our days and those of the apostles: the wheat of the Gospel age is not to form the nucleus of another church for the Millennial age; and those gathered out from among the tares are not beginning, but are finishing their course on earth, and the time of their sojourn in the flesh is very short and cannot go beyond the twenty years of harvest yet remaining. Their organization for the work of the new dispensation will be beyond the vail, when they are changed to the glorious likeness of the Lord.

In view of these facts and also of the nature of the harvest work, and the additional fact that each one so gathered is expected to enter into the harvest work as a reaper, and will do so to the extent of his ability and opportunity, it is plain that the forming of a visible organization of such gathered out ones would be out of harmony with the spirit of the divine plan; and if done would seem to indicate on the part of the church a desire to conform to the now popular idea of organization or confederacy. (See Isa. 8:12) The work now is not organization, but division, just as it was in the Jewish harvest proper (Matt. 10:34-36). And this harvest, as illustrated by the natural, is the busiest time of all the age, because the time is short and the "winter" is fast approaching. What is to be done must be done quickly, and there is abundant room in the great field for every member of the body of Christ to reap.

While, therefore, we do not esteem a visible organization of the gathered ones to be a part of the Lord's plan in the harvest work, as though we expected as an organization to abide here for another age, we do esteem it to be his will that those that love the Lord should speak often one to another of their common hopes and joys, of trials and perplexities, communing together concerning the precious things of his Word, and so help one another, and not forget the assembling of themselves together as the manner of some is; and so much the more as they see the day approaching.—Heb. 10:25.

Let us, then, give ourselves diligently to the great harvest work, observing and carefully following the providential lines for the guidance of the work as indicated by the Lord of the harvest—the same Lord, and just as truly present and active in this harvest as in the Jewish harvest, though invisible to mortal sight. What dignity and grandeur and blessed inspiration does the realization of this truth give our humble services! Truly it is not a glory which the world can discern, but faithfulness to the end of our course will bring an exceeding and eternal weight of glory which will appear to all God's intelligent creatures of every name and order; for in the ages to come he will show forth the exceeding riches of his grace in his loving kindness toward us who are in Christ Jesus (Eph. 2:7); and, praise the Lord! our exaltation and glory will be for a grand and benevolent service—even the privilege of scattering universal blessings.

[1743]

32

(215-216) ZION'S WATCH TOWER ALLEGHENY, PA.

prayer and receive that strength and sympathy and consolation and help we so much need. Let us live in the presence of the Father and the Son who have promised to abide with us. It will sweeten our days and comfort our nights and ease our burdens and lighten our cares and brighten our hopes, and, in a word, it will lift us up above the world into a higher and purer atmosphere. Such is the will of heaven concerning us: let us appreciate and avail ourselves of the privilege.

By all the encouragements of precept and example, the Lord assures us that the fervent prayer of a righteous man (a justified and consecrated child of God) availeth much. (Jas. 5:16) We are urged also to come in faith. Jesus said, "If ye have faith and doubt not, . . . all things whatsoever ye shall ask in prayer, believing, ye shall receive." (Matt. 21:22) As he was addressing his consecrated disciples, it must of course be understood that all their petitions would be subjected to divine wisdom, and therefore the answers to their prayers, though always sure, might not always be in the way expected, but they would always be considered and answered in some way for their highest good.

What a blessed privilege, dear fellow-disciples of the Lord, is ours, to be instant in prayer, to pray always—to lift up our hearts and minds to God at any time and in any place and to realize thus daily and hourly that the Father and our dear Lord Jesus continually abide with us. And then, when the active duties of the day have been performed under his eye and supervision, or at any time when the soul realizes its necessity, how precious is the privilege of entering into our closets and there alone with God unburdening our hearts at the throne of grace.

While secret prayer is the blessed privilege of every child of God, and one without which his spiritual life cannot be sustained, it is also the privilege of Christians to unite their petitions at the throne of grace. This united prayer is specially commended by the Lord. (Matt. 18:19) "Again I say unto you, that if two of you shall agree on earth as touching anything that they shall ask, it shall be done for them of my Father; for where two or three are gathered together in my name, there am I in the midst of them."

With such promises as these, together with an experience of their fulfilment, who can doubt the love and favor of our God and of our Lord and Saviour, Jesus Christ? Therefore let us be encouraged to pray always and not to faint when the answers seem to tarry long, for time is often required to work out the deep designs of an allwise and loving Providence. Remember the words of the angel to Daniel. Daniel said, "While I was speaking and praying and confessing my sin and the sin of my people Israel, and presenting my supplication before the Lord my God, for the holy mountain of my God; yea, while I was speaking in prayer, the answer came by the hand of an angel who said, "O Daniel, I am now come forth to give thee skill and understanding. At the beginning of thy supplications the commandment came forth, and I am come to show thee; for thou art greatly beloved."—Dan. 9: 20-23.

On another occasion, when Daniel had mourned three weeks, fasting and praying, because of his inability to understand, the angel of the Lord came and said, "Fear not, Daniel, for from the first day that thou didst set thine heart to understand, and to chasten thyself before thy God, thy words were heard, and I am come for thy words."—Dan. 10:2, 3, 10-12.

Even so shall it ever be with all the beloved of the Lord: at the beginning of our supplications God begins to set in operation the influences and to shape the circumstances which are designed to work out the intended blessing for us—if we faint not, but continue instant in prayer, thereby evincing our continued earnestness of desire, and if we confess our sins, and set our hearts to understand, and chasten ourselves before him. How many prayers are not heard; or are hindered because the one who asks does not first purify himself of evil in his own heart? "Ye ask, and receive not, because ye ask amiss, that ye may consume it upon your lusts;" i. e., you ask selfishly and without regard to the will of God. (Jas. 4:3) But to the chastened and sanctified comes the promise—"Before they call [reading, the desire of the heart; even before it finds expression in words] I will answer [will begin so to shape events as to bring the answer soon or later]; and while they are yet speaking I will hear." (Isa. 65:23, 24) While this is in connection with a prophecy relating to the Lord's people in the Millennial age, it nevertheless is true of all his faithful ones of this age. Praise the Lord for all his loving kindness to even the least of his lowly children.

CONCERNING PROFITABLE MEETINGS.

We have received a number of requests from friends of the truth for advice as to the most profitable methods of conducting meetings. One brother writes:

"A few brethren who have been reading DAWN express their willingness to meet somewhere to study in consecutive order, and I ask suggestions for a plan suited to beginners. Pray for us, that we may commence this study in the right way, and be the recipients of many blessings.

"Yours in the faith, J. W. McLANE."

Another brother recently removed to a new neighborhood says:

"I find in this locality a fine field for labor. Several here to whom I have given tracts already manifest interest. I have conversed freely with them on Bible subjects, and have their promise to attend meetings at my house. So if you can aid me by suggestions I will be thankful.

"I am, dear brother, yours in the service of the Master, JOSHUA L. GREEN."

Another Brother writes:—

"We have a number of persons here who wish to assemble themselves together for worship. We would be pleased to have some instructions from you as to how to go about it.

"I hope you can give us some way which will be satisfactory. Some of us have left the churches and are now free from all precepts of men. To speak for myself, I left the Presbyterian church.

"Yours in Christ, C. C. FLEMING."

We are glad to note the increasing desire for the study of God's plan of the ages; and also to see that the importance of method and order are recognized in this. We give our advice as follows:—

(1) You would best first re-read some things already written which bear upon this subject—in our issues of May 1, '93, page 131; Sept. '93, page 259; Oct. 15, '93, page 307; Mar. 1, '94, page 73; April 1, '95, page 78; May 1, '95, page 109.

(2) Beware of "organization." It is wholly unnecessary. The Bible rules will be the only rules you will need. Do not seek to bind others' consciences, and do not permit others to bind yours. Believe and obey so far as you can understand God's Word today, and so continue growing in grace and knowledge and love day by day.

(3) The Bible instructs you whom to fellowship as "brethren,"—only believers who are seeking to walk, not after the flesh, but after the spirit. Not believers, of any and every thing, but believers of the Gospel record—that mankind is fallen into sin and its penalty, death, and that only in Christ is there salvation, "through faith in his blood" "shed for the remission of sins," as "a ransom [a corresponding price] for all." Any who merely believe in Christ as a noble and good person, a grand example of righteous living, etc., may be agreeable as neighbors or business acquaintances, but they are not "believers," and hence are not "brethren," any more than are Jews, Mohammedans, Infidels, publicans and sinners—for practically these also acknowledge him.

(4) You come together, then, as God's children, bought back from sin and death with the great price, and resolved henceforth to live not unto yourselves, but unto him who died for you. (2 Cor. 5:15) Your meetings should have certain objects in view, viz.:—

(a) Worship, praise and prayer.

(b) Mutual helpfulness in waging victorious warfare against the world, the flesh and the devil within and without.

(c) And to these ends you meet also for the study of God's Word, which he provided for our instruction and help in the narrow way which leads to those blessings prepared by him for those who love him and who demonstrate their love by their efforts to serve, honor and obey him.

(5) Thus seen, a knowledge of doctrines is not our ultimate object in meeting, but the building up of characters, which, as attempted copies of the character of God's dear Son, will be "accepted in the Beloved." But God declares that knowledge of the doctrines which he has revealed in his Word will be of great value to us in our endeavors to grow in his grace.

Hence, after worship, praise and prayer, Bible study should be recognized in its two parts,—(a) The study of God's plan,—what he tells us he is doing for us and for the world; what he has done; and what he will yet do; that we may be enabled as sons to enter into the very spirit of the great work of God and be intelligent co-workers with him. (b) The study of our duties and privileges in God's service, toward each other and toward those that are without, to the end that

[1866] 33 September 15, 1895

NOTTINGHAM, ENGLAND,
November, 8th, 1881.

MY DEAR SIR—Permit me though a stranger to assure you, that I can never feel sufficiently thankful that out of the thousands of copies of your book, "*Food for Thinking Christians*," distributed in this town—a copy fell into my hands: apparently it was the merest accident; but really I regard it as a direct providence. It has thrown light upon subjects which have perplexed me for years; and has made me feel more than ever, what a glorious book the Bible is, how worthy of our profoundest study. At the same time, I came from the study of your book with the conviction that a very large proportion of the Theology of our Churches and Schools, is the merest scraps of human notions, and that our huge *systems of Theology* upon the study of, which, some of us have spent so many laborious years—only to be the worse confused and perplexed—are infinitely more the work of mistaken men, than the inspiration of the allwise God.

However I may differ from the book in a few minor details, I found the main argument to be resistless, commending itself to both my head and my heart. Again let me thank you on my own behalf, for the good I have received.

I find at the close of it, you make an offer to send copies to any who have reason to believe they can make a good use of them. In my church and congregation, there is a number of intelligent persons who are interested in the second coming, and who would be only too glad to read your book, I could distribute 60 or 70 copies with advantage, you say, "ask and ye shall receive"—I have faith in your generosity. Believe me to remain yours, Most faithfully

LOUISVILLE, KENTUCKY,
November 22, 1881.

GENTLEMEN—Having read with the most profound interest your publication entitled; "Food for Thinking Christians," and being fairly dazzled by the wonderful light it reveals on the great "subject," I find myself thirsting for more knowledge from this seemingly inspired pen.

Therefore, in accordance with the invitation extended by you on the cover of this little work I ask that you send me a few copies of "The Tabernacle and its Teachings," if in print.

With reference to the first named book, permit me to say, that I have never yet read or heard anything equal to that little volume in its influence upon my heart and life; and to my mind, it answers most grandly and conclusively the great question, "Is life worth living." Such views as it sets forth, are bound to find response in the minds and hearts of all unbiased thinking christians for they bear the stamp of something greater than mere human conception. I only wish we could hear it from the pulpits; but I think this must shortly follow. It is good seed and in its "*due time*" will come forth.

Believe me, I am

Very Truly Yours

"A LITTLE WHILE."

A little while, our fightings shall be over;
A little while, our tears be wiped away;
A little while, the presence of Jehovah
Shall turn our darkness into Heaven's bright day.

A little while, the fears that oft surround us
Shall to the memories of the past belong;
A little while, the love that sought and found us
Shall change our weeping into Heaven's glad song.

A little while! His presence goes before us,
A fire by night, a shadowy cloud by day;
His banner, love-inscribed, is floating o'er us;
His arm almighty is our strength and stay.

A little while! 'Tis ever drawing nearer—
The brighter dawning of that glorious day;
Blest Saviour, make our spirits' vision clearer,
And guide, oh, guide us in the shining way.

A little while! Oh, blessed expectation!
For strength to run with patience, Lord we cry;
Our hearts up-leap in fond anticipation,
Our union with the Bridegroom draweth nigh.

—Selected.

"YE ARE GODS."

"I have said, Ye are Gods; and all of you are children of the Most High. But ye shall die like men, and fall like one of the princes," [literally heads]. Psa. 82:6.

Our high calling is so great, so much above the comprehension of men, that they feel that we are guilty of blasphemy when we speak of being "*new creatures*"—not any longer human, but "partakers of the *divine nature.*" When we claim on the scriptural warrant, that we are begotten of a divine nature and that Jehovah is thus our father, it is claiming that we are divine beings—hence all such are Gods. Thus we have a family of God, Jehovah being our father, and all his sons, being brethren and joint-heirs; Jesus being the chief, or first-born.

Nor should we wonder that so few discern this grand relationship, into the full membership of which, we so soon hope to come. The apostle tells us that the *natural* man receiveth not the things of the Spirit of God . . . *neither can he know them* because they are spiritually discerned." (1 Cor. 2:14). Just so it was, when our great Head and Lord was among men: He, having consecrated the human at 30 years of age was baptized of the spirit, and became a part-taker of the divine nature. When Jesus said he was *a son of God* the Jews were about to stone him, reasoning thus, that if a son of God he was making himself to be also a God, or of God family. (Just what we claim. "Beloved, now are we the sons of God"—The God and Father of our Lord Jesus "hath begotten us.") (1 John 3:2 and 1 Pet. 1:3).

Jesus does not deny that when he said he was a son, it implied that he was of the divine nature, but he quotes to them the above passage from the Psalms as being good authority and it seems as though it satisfied them, for they did not stone him. Jesus said, "Is it not written in your law, I said, Ye are Gods"? Then he proceeds to show that the "Gods" there mentioned, are the ones who receive obediently his words and example, and concludes his argument by asking whether if God calls such ones as receive his (Jesus,) teachings, Gods, whether they think that he the teacher, whom the Father had specially set apart as the head of *those Gods* could be properly said to blaspheme, when he claimed the *same relationship as a son of God.* (John 10:35).

These ones of God, like him from whom they heard the word of truth by which they are begotten, are yet in disguise; the world knoweth us not for the same reason that it knew him not. Our Father puts no outward badge or mark of our high relationship, but leaves each to walk by faith and not by sight all through the earthly pilgrimage—*down into death.* His favor and love and the Glory and Honor which belong to our station, we can now see by the eye of faith, but soon it will be realized in fact. Now we appear like men, and all die naturally like men, but in the resurrection we will rise in our true character as Gods.

"It doth not yet appear,
How great we must be made;
But when we see him as he is,
We shall be like our Head."

How forcibly this is expressed by the prophet and how sure it is too, Jesus says—It cannot be broken; "I have said ye are Gods, all of you sons of the Most High. But, ye *shall die like men*, and fall like one of the princes," [lit. *heads*—Adam and Jesus are the two heads.]

Then the whole family—head and body are addressed as one, as they will be under Christ their head, saying—"Arise O God, judge [rule, bless] the earth: for thou shalt inherit all nations." The Mighty God, and everlasting Father of the nations, is Christ whose members in particular we are. He it is that shall inherit all things and He it is that promised his body that they too should have power over the nations, and of whom Paul says "Know ye not that the saints shall judge the world?"

How forcible this scripture in connection with the thought that *all* must die like men—like the (last) one of the heads. [See article "Who Can Hear It."—*November Number, 1881,* Z. W. T.]

(10)   ZION'S WATCH TOWER   Pittsburgh, Pa.

propriate to Our Lord Jesus Christ. And we might add that so perfectly, is his Bride—body—church, associated with him, both in filling up the measure of the sufferings—being joined in sacrifice, and also in the Glory that shall follow, that the same titles are applicable to the Church as his body—for "He that hath freely given us Christ, shall he not with him also freely give us all things?" "Therefore all things are yours, and ye are Christ's and Christ is God's."

After the sacrifice—soon follows the power which will, under him as our head, constitute the whole body of Christ, the "Mighty God" (el—powerful one) to rule and bless the nations —and the body with the head, shall share in the work of restoring the life lost in Adam, and therefore be members of that company which as a whole will be the Everlasting Father to the restored race.

PRACTICAL PREACHING

It is objected that practical preaching is the right kind of preaching, and that prophecy is not practical. Is this true? It is not true. The preaching of the Ten Commandments, the social virtues, and the neighborly and moral duties may be called practical preaching by some, but it is not so in the Christian sense of the word. The most successful preaching is the preaching of the cross in which Paul gloried, and the crown for which he waited. The two advents are the poles around which the orb of duty rolls—the strong foundation on which the morality of the new man reposes. Faith lays hold of the cross, the fountain of divine mercy, and out of love to Him that first loved us, brings forth in the heart and life of the believer the fruits of righteousness. Hope looks forward to the crown and the kingdom, and the promised inheritance, to nerve us for the trials and duties of life, and make us victorious over all our spiritual enemies. This is practical religion. Doctrine is the root and basis and motive of practice; and in the whole range of theology there is not a more practical doctrine than the second advent —no, not one. I challenge you to show me a duty of which it is not in one way or another made the motive.

Read, and consider the following texts of Scripture. It is the motive for patient waiting, 1 Thess. 1:10; for divine hope, Titus 2:13; for moderation in all things, Phil. 4:5;

for prayer to be counted worthy to stand before the Son of man, Luke 21:36; for long-suffering patience, James 5:8; for heavenly-mindedness, Luke 21:34; for perseverance in spite of persecution, 1 Pet. 1:7; of godliness and holy conversation, 2 Pet. 3:11, 12; it is the motive for earnest preaching, 2 Tim. 4:1-3; for fighting the good fight of faith, 2 Tim. 4:7, 8; for reverence and godly fear, Heb. 7:26-28; for sobriety and watching unto prayer, 1 Pet. 4:7. This is practical preaching; but if you preach these duties without the Advent, which is their chief motive and strength, you are asking the people for bricks without giving them the straw—the steam is taken from the engine and the train stops.—Messiah's Herald.

If the belief of the coming of the Lord has so much power to mould and influence the child of God, what indescribable power and influence should and does the belief that he has come—is now present! a spiritual being—the "harvest" now progressing under his supervision as the chief reaper, and the gathering of the ripe wheat now being in progress and soon to be finished and the righteous then made to shine forth as the Sun in the kingdom of their Father—what effect as a separator and sanctifying power should this truth have we enquire! What preaching can be so powerful?

FROM BRO. J. B. ADAMSON

DEAR BRO:—Your letter received. I shall try to go on in strong faith in all circumstances, believing the "many and exceeding precious promises" "so Christ shall be magnified in my body" by life or by death. Am working more each day, for delivering personally, calls for more preaching to twos and threes, and is very precious to them and me. I avoid those "wise" men who know it all, whose creed is all and in all for them, and go to those really truth hungry, among whom I find Christ's most precious people and also many infidels. Some days do not get far and then have appointments for the evening. Truly the views we hold are true Gold to a large and increasing class. Most timely was the tract project, from every point of view. As the poor teaching and want of teaching among the clergy increases, many look out to gather rays of light. I am asked to come Sunday at one o'clock to make the third meeting with an intelligent couple, members of the M. E. church who let me talk by the half hour and hour, seeming to drink in the doctrine and rejoice in it. Last night I spent an hour with them before prayer-meeting when I was asked

to go along and testify, there of these precious things. I had to remind them I dare not do so fully, and of the opposition and even abuse I met almost everywhere. I may give you some incidents in detail again that will rejoice your heart. Found the Free Methodist's very fair. The treatment better than I got anywhere else. Gave the pamphlet to sixteen preachers and one hundred of the most intelligent of the church membership, attending the conference from all over the state, beside in a large number of cases, also adding a word that will make the book more living for the personality attaching to it. That is the reason I talk to so many that I give the books to; so I get their attention to the book more fully. Am generally asked for explanations of our views, and though neither powerful nor eloquent of speech, I get attention to the book by complying. Thank God for the wider field thus opening. May the will of God be done in poor me, and His name get honor and blessing forever.

Yours in Christ,   J. B. A.

YOUR LETTER

We have been so much engaged by the tract work during the past three months that the issuance of the last two numbers of the W. T. has, of necessity, been considerably delayed. Our apology must be found in article under the head of "In the Vineyard."

To many who may have written important letters or ones requiring some answer, the same apology must be offered. The distribution of the pamphlets and papers has brought from their readers hundreds of letters, asking questions or requesting back numbers of the paper, etc. We answered quite a good many of these, but they come so fast, and our time has been so limited, that nearly a thousand letters and postal cards

have now accumulated—unopened and unread, and probably your letter is among them.

The Lord has provided more office help (for it is difficult to get suitable assistance,) and we hope to get caught up soon.

Let us here remark that we do not send receipts for regular subscriptions—the amount is too small. You know when and what you send, and we keep a careful record of all receipts. If subscriptions are lost in the mail we will be responsible for it, and be the losers. If your paper fails to come to hand any month, inform us by card if you have paid in advance, or if as one unable to pay, you have requested to be put on the "Lord's poor list."

NO BACK NUMBERS

The demand recently has exhausted our supply of back numbers of the WATCH TOWER except a few of the July number.

For the benefit of our many new readers, we will republish a few articles which appeared in our columns about a year or two ago. Among others in next number will be an article on "The Beast and Image of Rev. 13."

ROME AND JERUSALEM.—The Roman Church maintains a steady attention to the Holy Land. At Jaffa they have erected a new hospital, they have established a branch nunnery at Ramleh, and a nunnery and schools at Bethlehem. It would appear that the Franciscans have a new establishment at Emmaus, in addition to, the large hospice at Jerusalem. On the Mount of Olives a grand sanctuary and an extensive nunnery have been erected and endowed by the Princess de la Tour d'Auvergne, who, with great devotion, spent several years on the spot, in order personally to superintend the work.

[298]

35   November 1881

84   The Atonement Mediator.

Lord Jesus, we find their testimony very explicit, harmonious and satisfactory. We will first state, in synoptical form, what we find to be the Scriptural teaching, the proofs of which we will give further along.

(1) Our Redeemer existed as a spirit being before he was made flesh and dwelt amongst men.

(2) At that time, as well as subsequently, he was properly known as "a god"—a mighty one. As chief of the angels and next to the Father, he was known as the Archangel (highest angel or messenger), whose name Michael, signifies, "Who as God," or God's representative.

(3) As he was the highest of all Jehovah's creation, so also he was the first, the direct creation of God, the "Only Begotten," and then he, as Jehovah's representative, and in the exercise of Jehovah's power, and in his name, created all things,—angels, principalities and powers, as well as the earthly creation.

(4) When he was made flesh, to be our Redeemer, it was not of compulsion, but a voluntary matter, the result of his complete harmony with the Father, and his joyful acquiescence in carrying out every feature of the divine will,—which he had learned to respect and love, as the very essence of Justice, Wisdom and Love.

(5) This humiliation to man's condition was not intended to be perpetual. It accomplished its purpose when our Lord had given himself, a human being, as our ransom, or "corresponding price." Hence, his resurrection was not in the flesh, but, as the Apostle declares, "He was put to death in the flesh but quickened in spirit."—1 Pet. 3:18.

(6) His resurrection not only restored to him a spirit nature, but in addition conferred upon him a still higher honor, and, as the Father's reward for his faithfulness, made him partaker of the *divine nature*—the very highest of the spirit natures,* possessed of immortality.

* Vol. I., Chap. x.

The Only Begotten One.   85

(7) It is this great One, who has been thus highly exalted and honored by Jehovah, whom we delight to honor and to worship and to serve, as one with the Heavenly Father, in word, in work, in purpose and in spirit.

SCRIPTURE TESTIMONY RESPECTING THE SON OF GOD.

Let us now consider the Scriptural evidences substantiating these positions. We begin with the first chapter of John's Gospel. Here our Lord, in his prehuman existence, is referred to as "The Word" (Greek, *Logos*). "In the beginning was the *Logos*." Dr. Alexander Clarke says, concerning this word *Logos*: "This term should be left untranslated for the same reason that the names *Jesus* and *Christ* are left untranslated. As every appellative of the Savior of the world was descriptive of some excellencies in his person, nature, or work, so the epithet, *Logos*, which signifies a word, a word spoken, speech, eloquence, doctrine, reason, or the faculty of reason, is very properly applied to him." The Evangelist, in his epistle, uses the same title in respect to our Lord again, denominating him "the Word of life," or the "*Logos* of life."—1 John 1:1.

The title, "Word of God"—"*Logos* of God"—is a very fitting one by which to describe the important work or office of our Master, prior to his coming into the world. The *Logos* was the heavenly Father's direct *expression* of creation, while all subsequent expressions of divine wisdom, power and goodness were made through the *Logos*. It is said that in olden times certain kings made addresses to their subjects by proxy, the king sitting behind a screen, while his "word" or spokesman stood before the screen, and addressed the people aloud on subjects whispered to him by the king, who was not seen; and such a speaker was termed "The King's *Logos*." Whether or not the legend be true, it well illustrates the use of this word "*Logos*" in connection with the prehuman existence of our Lord and Master and his very grand office as the Father's representative, which the Scriptures, in this con-

THE ATONEMENT BETWEEN GOD AN MAN (Studies In The Scriptures, Vol. 5) 1899, 1916ed.

THE NAME OF JESUS

"What's in a name?" is often asked, implying insignificance, and it may make but little difference to a man whether he be called Peter, James, John, Moses, Aaron or even Joshua (Jesus) in times when these and other names are used without any reference to their signification. But in Bible study we are impressed with the idea that names are full of meaning. They were given with reference to time, place or circumstance, past, present or future. Some names were as *monuments* to remind of some special dealings of the Lord, and others were *prophetic*. The qualities, work or destiny of an individual was often expressed by his name. When the direction of a life was changed it was sometimes indicated by a change of name. Adam, indicates man's origin—"of the earth, earthy." Cain, is "acquired," and the woman was mistaken in the value of the man she had gotten of the Lord. Abel, is "feeder," a shepherd, and fitly represents the great Shepherd of the sheep, who gave his life for them. Abraham means "father, of a great multitude," or "of many nations." His name was changed from Abram to Abraham when God made him the promise. (Gen. 17: 5,) And in reference to the same great plan Sarai was changed to Sarah, i. e., Princess. (Ver. 15) These are prophetic in their character and point to the grand success of the gospel in bringing the nations to God, the Father of all, through the agency of the "seed" of promise —Christ and the church—the antitypes of Isaac and Rebekah. David, means beloved, a type of Christ, the true King of Israel. David as a prophet personifies Christ, and God makes promises to him as if he were Christ.

The excellent language of David—"Thou wilt not leave *my* soul in the grave, neither wilt thou suffer thine holy one to see corruption,"—was fulfilled in the triumphant resurrection of Christ from the dead. The name given is made to refer to position or official relationship, so that the *position* is *meant* when the word "name" is used. Even in this sense "a good name is rather to be chosen than great riches." The success of the Lord's work is to Him "for a *name*"—an honor. (Isa. lv:13.) To the obedient the Lord promises "an everlasting *name.*" (lvi:5) "but the *name* of the wicked shall rot." (Prov. x:7.) To receive a prophet in the *name* of a prophet certainly refers to his official character. "Thou shalt call his name Jesus because He shall save His people from their sins." Jesus, means Saviour, and we are carried forward from the mere *word* to the exalted official position, on account of which he can "save to the uttermost all who come unto God by him." His *position* is contrasted with that of men and angels, as he is Lord of both, having "all power in heaven and earth." Hence it is said, "Let *all* the angels of God worship him"; [that must include Michael, the chief angel, hence Michael is not the Son of God] and the reason is, because he has "by *inheritance* obtained a more excellent *Name* than they." Michael or Gabriel are perhaps grander names than Jesus, though Jesus is grand in its very simplicity, but the *official* character of the Son of God as Saviour and King is the inheritance from his Father, which is far superior to theirs, for it pleased the Father that in him all *fullness* should dwell. He has given him a *name* which is above every name, that at the *name* of Jesus *every knee should bow* both in heaven and earth. And there is "none other name under heaven given among men whereby we must be saved."

With this view before our minds that the name refers to his official position, the importance of taking from among the Gentiles a "people for his *name*" will be appreciated. As the wife takes the name of her husband, so the church takes the name of her Head. The two made one is the fact of importance. Not one in name merely, but in *fact*, as represented by the name—one in spirit, position, aim and work. The difference between the terms Jesus and Christian may illustrate a point. The first relates to the *letter*, as Jesus is a proper name; the second relates more nearly to the *spirit*, as *Christ* means *anointed* and refers to his official position. We are not here pleading for a *name*, but what appears to be an important *idea*. There is doubtless as much danger

in using the name *Christian* as the name of a *sect*, as in using other names. The one body knows *no* divisions. All who have the spirit of Christ are *one* whether they fully realize it or not; one in spirit now and when glorified—married— one in every *possible* sense, even as the Father and Son are one. Jno. xvii:22, 23.

To be baptised into the name of Jesus (or Father, Son and holy Spirit,) as in him all fullness of the Godhead dwells, means far more than a baptismal *formula.* It is by the apostle expressed as being baptised by one spirit into one body. (1 Cor. xii:13.) There are letter and spirit in the subject of baptism as in almost every other part of God's plan. We should not ignore or belittle either. The letter represents the spirit, as a symbol or "*likeness* of his death," and "resurrection." (Rom. vi:5.) Those who can appreciate the spirit need not and are not most likely to ignore the letter, but it seems important that we should guard against mere formalism. In *spirit*, to be baptised involves a death to sin, a rising into a new life of obedience, and a consequent formation of a character;—having "your fruit unto *holiness* and the end everlasting life." (Rom. vi:22.) "As many of you as have been baptised into *Christ* have *put on* Christ." (Gal. iii:27.) "Into one body!" "Ye are *members* of Christ," as in the figure used, bone of his bone and flesh of his flesh. (Eph. v:30.) Do not confound the figure with the reality, do not imagine we will lose our individuality. The body of Christ is a body corporate, each individual acting in harmony with each other and under the direction of Christ for the manifestation of God's love in the salvation of men.

The human body is used to *represent* the church, but in this as in all other figures the reality is but dimly foreshadowed. As Jesus is the *anointed*, so are we, and for the same purpose. He is both king and priest, so we are to be kings and priests—kings to rule and priests to bless. To be baptised into his name is to become sharers in his spirit, his character, his official position and his work. The power given to him will be manifested through his saints. He is our Saviour, but the body corporate will save the *world*. He will continue to be our Head, but the church will be the head of the world. Adam was the head of his wife, but *they* were the united head of the race. The natural is the shadow of the spiritual. Our *position* will be higher than the highest angel. We, like them, will *die no more*; but as we for a *little while* have been lower than the *angels*, and in an important sense under their influence, they in this world being ministering spirits to the *heirs* of salvation, so in the world to come, the church being then exalted to the throne of him who is Lord of both angels and men, the "saints will judge (rule) angels," and "judge (rule) the world" too. In that day when every knee shall bow to the highest manifested authority—before the Messiah's throne—the Queen as well as the King will be there. Is it a false ambition, to look for such royal honor? The voice of our coming husband sounds sweetly upon our ears as we struggle on amid the trials of this life. The overcomer will sit with me in my *throne*. Will he allure us on by such a hope to *deceive* us? Are the crown, throne and kingdom promised but unmeaning words? Are our hopes in vain? Will they vanish in fulfillment? Away with the doubt; it is Satan's snare; our Lover is true and faithful, and He has "all power." Call it an unworthy ambition and selfish withal, do you? Then God never would have given the inducement. If this hope of ours is selfish, then our Saviour is selfish. For the *joy* set before him he *endureth*; but it is a *benevolent* selfishness. His power is exercised to *bless.* The greater serves the less.

How else could we enter into the *joy* of our Lord than by reaching a position from which we can pour blessing on the needy? He hath given him a *name* above every name. Oh that we may realize our privilege of sharing it!

> Baptised into the Saviour's death,
> With him we rise again;
> His spirit moves our every breath,
> With him we'll live and reign.   J. H. P.

THE DAY OF JUDGMENT

One great reason for the perverted views respecting the Messianic age, is the failure to understand the Bible meaning of the word *judgment.* It has several significations. Sometimes it means simply an examination or investigation of certain facts, testimony or arguments, in order to ascertain truth, or to reach a just decision. We also use the term to express that quality of mind which enables one to correctly grasp the true conclusion; as we speak of a person having *good judgment.* It often means the determination arrived at in the

mind; also the results flowing from the trial and decision in the distribution of the rewards or punishments.

We have been taught to associate the word, when found in the Scriptures, with the last mentioned meaning, i. e. the *executive* judgment, which signification it certainly has; nevertheless, it also and frequently refers to the trial itself while in progress. Notice the first occurrence of the word in the New Testament, (Matt. vii:1, 2,) would clearly bear this rendering: "Test not, that ye be not tested. For with what

(4)

[48]
37

to be a ransom for mankind he had to be a man, of the same nature as the sinner whose substitute in death he was to become, it was necessary that his nature be changed. And Paul tells us that he took not the nature of angels, one step lower than his own, but that he came down two steps and took the nature of men—he became a man; he was "made flesh,"—Heb. 2:16; Phil. 2:7, 8; John 1:14.

Notice that this teaches not only that angelic nature is not the only order of spirit being, but that *it is a lower nature than that of our Lord before he became a man; and he was not then so high as he is now*, for "God hath highly exalted him," because of his obedience in becoming man's willing ransom. (Phil. 2:8, 9.) He is now of the highest order of spirit being, a partaker of the divine (Jehovah's) nature.

But not only do we thus find proof that the divine, angelic and human natures are separate and distinct, but this proves that to be a perfect man is not to be an angel, any more than the perfection of angelic nature implies that angels are divine and equal with Jehovah; for Jesus took *not the nature of angels*, but a different nature—the *nature of men*; not the imperfect human nature as we now possess it, but the *perfect* human nature. He became *a man*; not a depraved and nearly dead being such as men are now, but a man in the full vigor of perfection.

Again, Jesus must have been a perfect man else he could not have kept a perfect law, which is the full measure of a *perfect man's ability*. And he must have been a perfect man else he could not have given a ransom (a corresponding price—1 Tim. 2:6) for the forfeited life of the perfect man Adam; "For since by *man* came death, by *man* came also the resurrection of the dead." (1 Cor. 15:21.) Had he been in the least degree imperfect, it would have proved that he was under condemnation, and therefore he

could not have been an acceptable sacrifice; neither could he have kept perfectly the law of God. A perfect man was tried, and failed, and was condemned; and only a perfect man could pay the *corresponding price* as the Redeemer.

Now we have the question fairly before us in another form, viz.: If Jesus in the flesh was a perfect man, as the Scriptures thus show, does it not prove that a perfect man is a human, fleshly being—not an angel, but a little lower than the angels? The logical conclusion is unmistakable; and in addition we have the inspired statement of the Psalmist (Psa. 8:5-8) and Paul's reference to it in Heb. 2:7, 9.

Neither was Jesus a combination of the two natures, human and spiritual. The blending of two natures produces neither the one nor the other, but an imperfect, hybrid thing, which is obnoxious to the divine arrangement. When Jesus was in the flesh he was a perfect human being; previous to that time he was a perfect spiritual being; and since his resurrection he is a perfect spiritual being of the highest or divine order. It was not until the time of his consecration even unto death, as typified in his baptism—at thirty years of age (manhood, according to the Law, and therefore the right time to consecrate himself as *a man*)—that he received the earnest of his inheritance of the divine nature. (Matt. 3:16, 17.) The human nature had to be *consecrated to death* before he could receive even the *pledge* of the divine nature. And not until that consecration was actually carried out and he had actually sacrificed the human nature, even unto death, did our Lord Jesus become a full partaker of the divine nature. After becoming a man he became obedient unto death; *wherefore*, God hath highly exalted him to the divine nature. (Phil. 2:8, 9.) If this Scripture is true, it follows that he was not exalted to the divine nature until the human nature was actually sacrificed—dead.

67

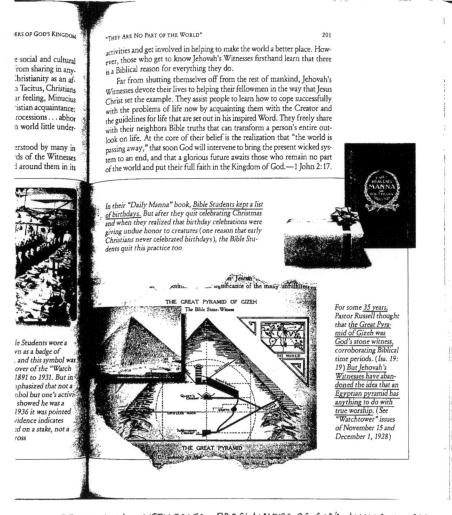

e social and cultural
rom sharing in any-
Christianity as an af-
a Tacitus, Christians
ar feeling, Minucius
ristian acquaintance:
rocessions . . . abhor
n world little under-

erstood by many in
ds of the Witnesses
i around them in its

activities and get involved in helping to make the world a better place. However, those who get to know Jehovah's Witnesses firsthand learn that there
is a Biblical reason for everything they do.

Far from shutting themselves off from the rest of mankind, Jehovah's
Witnesses devote their lives to helping their fellowmen in the way that Jesus
Christ set the example. They assist people to learn how to cope successfully
with the problems of life now by acquainting them with the Creator and
the guidelines for life that are set out in his inspired Word. They freely share
with their neighbors Bible truths that can transform a person's entire outlook on life. At the core of their belief is the realization that "the world is
passing away," that soon God will intervene to bring the present wicked system to an end, and that a glorious future awaits those who remain no part
of the world and put their full faith in the Kingdom of God.—1 John 2:17.

*In their "Daily Manna" book, Bible Students kept a list
of birthdays. But after they quit celebrating Christmas
and when they realized that birthday celebrations were
giving undue honor to creatures (one reason that early
Christians never celebrated birthdays), the Bible Students quit this practice too*

significance of the many unfulfilled

THE GREAT PYRAMID OF GIZEH
The Bible Stone-Witness

le Students wore a
vn as a badge of
. and this symbol was
over of the "Watch
1891 to 1931. But in
iphasized that not a
nbol but one's activi-
showed he was a
1936 it was pointed
vidence indicates
ed on a stake, not a
ross

THE GREAT PYRAMID

*For some 35 years,
Pastor Russell thought
that the Great Pyra-
mid of Gizeh was
God's stone witness,
corroborating Biblical
time periods. (Isa. 19:
19) But Jehovah's
Witnesses have aban-
doned the idea that an
Egyptian pyramid has
anything to do with
true worship. (See
"Watchtower" issues
of November 15 and
December 1, 1928)*

JEHOVAH'S WITNESSES - PROCLAIMERS OF GOD'S KINGDOM, 1993
39

in this instance (Nehemiah's commission) he made a considerable alteration, substituting another date of his own, so as to adapt the reign of Artaxerxes to his own theory.

"The date which stands in our Bibles for the 20th year of Artaxerxes is B. C. 446. This makes the commencement of his reign B. C. 465; but the date fixed by the best and most nearly contemporary historian will put the matter in a different light. Thucydides mentions that the accession of Artaxerxes had taken place before the flight of Themistocles. This authorizes us to adopt Ussher's date and to place the commencement of the reign 473 or 474 B. C. This would give the date of 454 or 455 B. C. as his twentieth year and the date of the commission."

It appears that Archbishop Ussher was the first to establish the date of Nehemiah's commission as 454 B. C. as a result of lecturing on the 70 weeks of Daniel in Trinity College, Dublin, in 1613. Other critics who support the date given in DAWN II. are Vitringer, Kruger and Hengstenberg, as well as Tregelles, above quoted. With much love, I remain,

Yours in the Lord,   J. P. BURNS,—England.

"SCRIPTURE STUDIES" AS CHRISTMAS GIFTS

DEAR FRIENDS:—

It might interest you to know that we are already offering the books for "Christmas gifts." We find that many secure their Christmas presents several months ahead, and that this month is the one in which many are very pleased to secure "such a beautiful, appropriate, and above all such a reasonable [in price] gift!" Often we can get orders for several sets in one home, in view of the fact that the books make such splendid gifts. Today we got more than one order on this account. We mention this because we think it might help wonderfully during the next six weeks in securing orders from people who would perhaps not buy for their own use. We say, "Many are taking them for gifts, and it is of course a compliment to a friend's intelligence to give him a book, and especially this kind, and you get the three for only 98c!"

With much Christian love and appreciating more and more the great privilege of laboring in the harvest field, we are,   Yours in Him,

J. AND L. HUTCHINSON,—Colporteurs.

CHARITY BEGINS AT HOME

Dear Brother Russell:—

Being my Pastor in a very special sense to me, and knowing of your deep interest in all who understand, even to a limited degree, the Harvest Message, I am taking the liberty to write you on a subject that has been on my mind for a long time.

I am sorry, very sorry to say it, but many times I have found, on close acquaintance with the brethren in the truth, men who professed full consecration, that they neglected their families so very badly relative to the truth. Seemingly anxious to spread the truth amongst their friends and neighbors, yet they made no provision for their wives, so that they could attend the meetings, and would even talk before their families in such a way as to leave the impression that maybe the truth was not for their wives and children.

I confess this is beyond my comprehension—how a man with brains enough to comprehend the truth, and after reading the six volumes of MILLENNIAL DAWN and the Towns, could or would do or say such!

A man can leave all the cares of the home and the care of the children to a perhaps not too strong wife, and spend all of his spare time while at home reading; and Sunday morning, instead of helping his wife and encouraging her, just get up and eat, dress and leave, and let her know he expects a hot dinner when he returns from the class, and it is no wonder she cannot go. It certainly doesn't look fair to me. Just nominal church people do better than that.

From the depths of my heart I pity the man who has the truth and objects to his children attending the nominal church Sunday school and makes no effort to teach his children and never has family prayer unless some of the colporteurs or elders call on him. These things are so. I wish I could believe otherwise.

Several cases have come to my personal knowledge where the wife was really hungering for fellowship with the class and believed all the truth she could understand, and whose husband, while himself attending the class every Sunday, was the real cause that hindered her. I feel confident a special pointed article from your pen would do good to many.

Yours in the service of the King, ———— Tenn.

VOL. XXVIII   ALLEGHENY, PA., DECEMBER 1, 1907   No. 23

VIEWS FROM THE WATCH TOWER

GETTING READY FOR FEDERATION

Unquestionably the splitting of Christendom into numerous denominations since the Reformation has been productive of a spirit of moderation in sharp contrast with the period in which many were racked, maimed, burned at the stake, etc., as "heretics." When we have pointed out that the proposed Federation of Religions would again put great power into the hands of a united majority and possibly revive the persecutions of the past, we have been laughed at. We are told that the world has so changed that persecution for religious belief would be unthinkable.

Within a month we have heard of two professed "ministers of the Gospel" whose remarks imply that nothing is lacking but the favorable opportunity for them to light the fires of persecution. Besides the most refined modes of persecution, by slander and ostracism, there may yet be opportunities for as barbarous martyrdoms for the truth's sake as were practised in our Lord's day.

REV. DR. PATTERSON'S CHRISTIAN LOVE

"There was an exciting episode at the Monday meeting of the Philadelphia ministers, and the Rev. Dr. R. M. Patterson, pastor emeritus, was the centre of it. His assignment was a discourse on John Calvin. He gave the ministers a surprise by advocating capital punishment for other felonies than murder—and for flagrant heresy. According to one reporter, he said: 'Those who spread blasphemous and immoral doctrines should also be put to death.' According to another reporter, he added that burning at the stake was too good for them."

The editor of the Philadelphia Inquirer, in answer to a query as to the very words of the reverend gentleman, replied (Oct. 18):—

"We are sorry that you should ask us to print the very words used by Rev. Dr. R. M. Patterson in his recent outburst. They were reported as follows: 'If I had my way about it I would have an executioner called in to deal with all heretics and blasphemers. Burning at the stake would be too good for those who revile religion and take the Lord's name in vain.'

The growth of heresy is such today that nothing but measures such as this can stop it.'"

Not all Presbyterians, however, feel so bitterly toward the non-elect heretics; for we read further:—

"The Rev. Dr. Henry C. McCook replied to the Rev. Dr. Patterson. 'My blood boils,' he said, 'at what I have just heard, and it astonishes me to think that a Presbyterian minister should utter such sentiments.'"

THE SPIRIT IS WILLING

Evidently, some of the "doctors of the law" in our day are as willing to do violence as were those who stoned Stephen. Their spirit is willing but their flesh is weak—because public sentiment would not stand for it. But we expect to see public sentiment grow in the same direction under the stimulus of the Federation of the Churches.

Recently the Editor preached at Morgantown, W. Va., to a large audience, which gave close attention for more than two hours. Shortly after a man who was present met one of the ministers of that city who asked him if he had heard the discourse. He replied, "Yes! and I enjoyed it very much. Did you attend?" "No," replied the minister, "I would sooner have joined in stoning him out of town!"

It is presumable that only lack of courage held back this Reverend Doctor of the Law of Love from enjoying himself at our expense. Poor blind leaders of the blind! We are so glad for them that God has a glorious plan in which they may yet share—when "all the blind eyes shall be opened and all the deaf ears shall be unstopped." Verily it is written, "They that hated you, that cast you out [rejected you] said, Let the Lord be glorified! [We do it for the good of churchianity!] But he [Christ] shall appear to your joy and they shall be ashamed."—Isaiah 66:5.

METHODIST RE-UNION IN ENGLAND

By means of re-union a new church was created in Great Britain on September 17. This event, says Dr. Robertson Nicoll in The British Weekly (London), "was a historic day of the twentieth century and marked an epoch in the Christian church." Three Methodist denominations, known as the Meth-

69

(363-365)   *ZION'S WATCH TOWER*   ALLEGHENY, PA.

The Taylor Cylinder, found in Nineveh in 1830, and now in the British Museum, describes Sennacherib's conquest of Judah in the time of Hezekiah. The stone records of Assyrian history, called the 'Eponym Canon,' discovered in 1862, in Nineveh, by Sir Henry Rawlinson, help us to gain a more exact knowledge of the dates of this period.

Our Golden Text, which constitutes the caption of this article, contains a valuable thought for any occasion, but one especially suited to this review. Looking at the history of God's earthly people, Israel after the flesh, we can readily see that all of their difficulties and failures to attain to the blessings that were before them, were closely associated with neglect of the truth set forth in our Golden Text. They did not sufficiently sanctify the Lord God in their hearts and let him be the only fear and only dread—fear to displease him, dread to come under his reproof. On the contrary, they were prone to forget the Lord and all the blessings and mercies they had received from him and the obligations they were under to him.

They forgot, too, that a part of the covenant entered into between the Lord and them was that if as a people they would honor him and serve him he would bless and honor them, but if as a people they rejected or neglected him, they were to have special disciplines and corrections. Their neglect of his favor, their seeking without the Lord to establish themselves and to have the assistance and co-operation, and to adopt the manners, customs, etc., of foreign nations, all these were a part of their failure to properly worship the Lord and serve him alone. How great was their mistake! And yet we are to remember that a remnant did not make this mistake, though they were few. This remnant already received a blessing in the present life and are to have a still greater share in the favors of God in the coming age.

Similarly nominal spiritual Israel has neglected the counsel of this Golden Text, and, instead of having the Lord first, has been disposed to forget the Lord and to affiliate with the world, to seek worldly favor and co-operation. Fear to displease the world has largely controlled churchianity; desire to have the world's favor and approval has apparently been more important before the mind of churchianity than the approval of the Lord and a fear of the loss of his favor.

As a result we see today worldly customs in the professed church of Christ, and note that these worldly customs have drawn into the nominal church, as they were intended to do, large numbers of the world, unjustified, unsanctified, "tares," and that these now quite overwhelm the few who are loyal to the Lord and the spirit of his Truth. Nevertheless there is today, and has been all throughout the Gospel age, a "little flock," a "remnant," which did indeed trust the Lord, and which did indeed sanctify the Lord God in their hearts and make him alone their fear and him alone their dread—fear to displease him, dread to lose the light of his kindness, his favor. We trust, dear friends, that the majority of those who read these words are of the latter class. If so all things are working together for good to such, because they love the Lord and have been called according to his purpose, and are seeking to make their calling and election sure by so running as to obtain the prize.

"THE PRINCE OF PEACE."

ISAIAH 9:1-7.—DECEMBER 25.

GOLDEN TEXT:—"*His name shall be called Wonderful, Counsellor, Mighty God, Everlasting Father, Prince of Peace.*"—R. V.

Even though Christmas day is not the real anniversary of our Lord's birth, but more properly the annunciation day or the date of his human begetting (Luke 1:28), nevertheless, since the celebration of our Lord's birth is not a matter of divine appointment or injunction, but merely a tribute of respect to him, it is not necessary for us to quibble particularly about the day. We may as well join with the civilized world in celebrating the grand event on the day which the majority celebrate —"Christmas day." The lesson for the occasion is a most happy choice, fitting well to the series of lessons it follows.

The first verse seems much better translated in the Revised Version, thus: "But there will be no gloom in her that was in anguish. In former time he brought into contempt the land of Zebulun and the land of Naphtali, but in the latter time hath he made it glorious, by way of the sea, beyond Jordan, Galilee of the nations." The Prophet penned these words, probably shortly after the ten-tribe kingdom known as Ephraim had gone into captivity to Assyria. Zebulun and Naphtali were the names of the principal districts of Ephraim; and Isaiah, prophetically looking from those desolated lands of his time, under the guidance of the holy Spirit, points out that in the latter time a great blessing is coming to those very lands.

It was centuries after Isaiah's prophecy that our dear Redeemer appeared among men and spent most of his time, did most of his mighty works, and performed most of his mighty miracles in these lands of Zebulun and Naphtali, called Galilee, which in the time of Isaiah had been denuded of its Jewish population and had been settled by Gentile emigrants, "Galilee of the Gentiles." Subsequently these Gentiles gathered more particularly in the vicinity of the city of Samaria, and became known as Samaritans, and, noting the hopes of the Israelites, were inclined to claim a certain share in the blessings belonging to the people into whose lands they had been introduced. The Jews, however, disowned them as being still Gentiles, and would have no dealings with the Samaritans, as the Apostle pointed out.

Our Lord himself instructed the apostles to go not in the way of the Gentiles nor into any city or the Samaritans to announce him, declaring that he was not sent to any but the lost sheep of the house of Israel. He again declared to one of these Samaritans, "Ye worship ye know not what: we [the Jews] know what we worship: for salvation is of the Jews." (John 4:22) Outside of the Samaritan districts all of Galilee became repopulated with Jews, though they represented generally the less noble class, so that it was rather as a mark of disrespect that our Lord and the apostles were called Galileans, Nazareth of Galilee being our Lord's home in his youth—a dis-esteemed city, as in the expression, "Can any good thing come out of Nazareth?" Our Lord indeed was born in Bethlehem, a more honorable city. Under divine providence he was taken to Nazareth, to the intent that a certain amount of odium might attach to him and to his cause. Thus often the Lord permits some unsavory influence to attach to the Truth, to the intent that none may receive his message except from the love of the Truth —that none should be influenced to receive it from any earthly consideration.

THE LIGHT SHINED IN THE DARK VALLEY.

The second verse of the lesson fitted well to Galilee: "The people that walked in darkness have seen a great light." As our Lord declared, "The light shined in darkness, and the darkness comprehended it not." He was the light of the world and was in the world and the world knew him not. But there is a higher and deeper and broader sense in which these words are to be understood—they apply to all peoples who have been favored with the opening of the eyes of their understanding during this Gospel age.

The people of Galilee in the day of our Lord's personal ministry, and other parts of the earth since with a similar humble class of people, have more or less had amongst them representatives of the true light, and in every case the light has shined in darkness and the darkness comprehended it not, as our Lord declared to be the case. Only a few appreciate this shining now because, as the Apostle declared, "The god of this world hath blinded the minds of them that believe not"—the eyes of their understanding are so darkened by false doctrines, misunderstanding and superstition that they cannot see these glorious things which can now be seen only by the eye of faith, the eyes of their understanding being opened.

That the prophecy was not confined to the people of Galilee is evident from the last clause of the second verse, "They that dwell in the land of the shadow of death, upon them hath the light shined." The land of the shadow of death is the whole world, for the shadow of death has been on the whole world ever since the first transgression in Eden, ever since the curse or sentence of death was pronounced against our race. As the Prophet David describes it, the Lord's true people are blessed even while in the present valley and under the shadow of death; he says, "Though I walk through the valley of the shadow of death, I will fear no evil for thou art with me." It is to this class who walk with the Lord, who trust him, that the true light now shines—not as the glorious Sun of Righteousness, as it will shine by and by when the Millennial kingdom is established, but merely as the little lamp, "Thy Word is a lamp to my feet, a lantern to my footsteps."

This lamp shines not for the world but for those who are the Lord's special people, to whom the light of his revelation, the lamp of enlightenment is granted. All these thus walking in this valley, under the guidance and care of the great Captain of our Salvation, have indeed seen a great light in him, have seen a light which the world sees not. But, thank God, the world's time to see the great light is shortly coming, drawing nigh. As soon as the present work of selecting the church,

41 [3468]   December 1, 1904

70

highway of holiness then opened up to them "shall be *destroyed* from among the people"—"the second death."—Compare Isa. 35:8; 62:10; Acts 3:23; Dawn I., Chap. 11.

WAS THE TEMPLE CLEANSED TWICE?

Question. From the various accounts would it not appear that the Temple was cleansed twice? I see that Dawn and Watch Tower always refer to the matter as tho there had been but one cleansing.—See Mark 11:15; John 2:13-17; Matt. 21:12, 13.

Answer. Many take the view suggested—that there were two cleansings; but we do not share it. It will be noticed that Matthew, Mark and John each mention the matter only once; and each mention once our Lord's riding upon the ass in fulfillment of Zechariah's prophecy (9:9-12); but only one of them *connects* these two events—Matthew. Moreover, since all agree that the riding on the ass was in fulfillment of Zechariah's prophecy, and that *there* our Lord assumed for the first time his title as *King*, it is but reasonable to suppose that the use of force in cleansing the temple followed and did not precede that assertion of regal authority. For the same reasons we accept that *same* day as the one in which our Lord wept over Jerusalem and said "Your house is left unto you desolate!" Note the Prophet's expression—"Even *today* do I declare I will render [the second half of thy] double unto thee;"—the day of the riding on the ass as King.

The disconnection so noticeable in the gospels may be accounted for (1) By remembering that the Apostles were "unlearned men," not regularly educated historians, men who recorded the wonderful words and works of their wonderful Teacher, but apparently saw little necessity for order or sequence. (2) By assuming that in this matter our Lord designed the confusion of the record, that only the faith-full and zealous might, under the leading of the holy Spirit be led to "rightly divide the Word of truth" and to get from it "meat in due season."

CHRISTIAN DUTY IF DRAFTED

Question. There are possibilities of a still greater war and of a draft which might include some of us who understand our Lord's commands to forbid our engagement in carnal warfare. What then, would be our duty?

Answer. "We know that all things shall work together for good to those who love God—to the called ones according to his purpose." If, therefore, we were drafted, and if the government refused to accept our conscientious scruples against warfare (as they have heretofore done with "Friends," called Quakers), we should request to be assigned to the hospital service or to the Commissary department or to some other non-combatant place of usefulness; and such requests would no doubt be granted. If not, and we ever got into battle, we might help to terrify the enemy, but need not shoot anybody. Meantime what an opportunity we might thus have for preaching "Jesus and the resurrection;"—for being "living epistles known and read by all" the camp;—examples of good soldiers of the Lord Jesus Christ, drilled and thoroughly equipped with the armor of God, loyal and courageous in the Christian warfare, against the world, the flesh, and the devil.

"JEHOVAH, HE IS THE GOD"

JULY 17.—1 Kings 18:30-40.

"And when all the people saw it they fell on their faces, and they said: Jehovah, he is the God."—1 Kings 18:39.

The three and a half years of drouth no doubt had an humbling effect upon King Ahab, as well as upon the people of Israel. No doubt they began to wonder where the matter would end; and to recognize it as more than an accident—as a judgment. The question would be whether it was a judgment from Baal or a judgment from Jehovah; for the people, as a result of their extended acquaintance with idolatry had a comparatively weak faith respecting the unseen Jehovah, who permitted no image or likeness of himself to be made or to be worshiped. The Lord's time had come for awakening Israel, and starting a reformation movement amongst them, and Elijah, who had been sought by the King throughout the surrounding nations, was instructed to present himself before Ahab, with a promise that rain should follow; and was permitted to be the Lord's agent in drawing the attention of the people to the true God, who alone has power over the elements.

Altho Ahab realized that the famine was a judgment of the Lord, nevertheless, after the custom of the natural man, he ignored personal responsibility, and affected to charge the evils to Elijah, saying to him, "Art thou he that troublest Israel?" It is always so with the faithful mouthpieces of the Lord. Since they cannot prophesy smooth things, but must present the truth in reproof of unrighteousness, therefore the world and the nominal Israelite hate them. They do not seem to realize that the difficulty lies in themselves, and their sins, and their separation from the Lord. But Elijah, humble yet unabashed, did not hesitate to tell the king the truth of the matter, assuring him that the trouble in Israel came from his own wrong course.

The drouth had so humbled Ahab that he did not resent the Prophet's arraignment of his sin: perhaps also he hoped that through the prophet's favor the embargo of the drouth and famine might be lifted. At all events he very promptly complied with Elijah's request that the people of Israel be assembled at Mount Carmel, together with the priests of Baal. Accordingly there was a great concourse to the flat, table-top of Mount Carmel, where Elijah awaited them, the king also coming with them; but Queen Jezebel sullenly remained at the palace in the capital city of Samaria.

Elijah, full of zeal for the Lord, and full of indignation against the idolatry, and probably counseled respecting his course by the Lord, had a plan prepared by which to demonstrate to Israel which was the true God and which the false one. In the presence of the people he made a proposition to the priests of Baal for a contest to prove the question. This proposition was so reasonable, and the interest and expectation of Israel so great, that the priests of Baal dare not refuse. They, four hundred and fifty in number, were to build an altar and to make a sacrifice thereon to their god, Baal, while Elijah would build an altar and offer a sacrifice thereon to Jehovah, and whichever god would answer by fire would thus be attested as the true God. If Baal were powerful enough to answer the prayers of his priests and to accept the offering of the altar, then the people might understand that it was because Baal was offended with them that they had experienced the drouth and the famine. But if Jehovah had the power, and would answer with fire, it would be proof to the people that the drouth and the famine were from him, and signs of his indignation because they had forsaken him and worshiped Baal.

The proposition could not be rejected: the priests of Baal prepared their altar and their sacrifice, and had the advantage of the noon-day heat of a tropical sun, sufficient almost of itself to ignite the fat of the sacrifice. They desired and prayed that the test might be granted; they cut themselves with stones until the blood gushed out, claiming that it must be because some of them, as priests of Baal, had trespassed against him, that their prayers were not heard. They kept this up for hours, until near sunset—Elijah meantime, in the hearing of the people, pouring upon them the sharpest sarcasm—the sarcasm of truth, not of falsehood. He suggested that they pray louder, as peradventure their god might be a little deaf; he urged them to keep it up, peradventure Baal might be on a journey, or attending to other business, or asleep. Thus he was giving to Israel in general the most telling lesson possible, considering their lethargy on religious subjects. He was preparing them for the final demonstration which he was about to give, that Jehovah is the true God, the only God who had power to answer both by fire and by water.

Mark how thorough the Prophet's faith in God, and how thoroughly he demonstrated that there could be no room for deception in connection with his offering. Twelve stone crocks of water were poured upon the sacrifice and the wood, and filled the trench around about it; the sun was losing its power, and the offering was thoroughly drenched, and all things were thus ready for a thorough test of Jehovah's power to send down fire.

Elijah stated the matter to the people: "How long halt ye between two opinions? If Jehovah be God, follow him; but if Baal be God, then follow him." The test was to show which was the true God, and which was the false god, and incidentally which the true and which the false prophets. Then Elijah prayed a beautiful and proper prayer. He did not say, "O Lord, cause Israel all to know how great, I Elijah, am, as a prophet of the Lord," but "Hear me, O Lord, hear me, that this people may know that thou art Jehovah God, and that thou hast turned their heart back again [—recalling them again by their experiences and these signs to be thy people]."

The answer by fire was prompt, and the effect upon the people great. They promptly acknowledged Jehovah, and slew the priests of Baal. Then, while Ahab and the people

Documented Facts Watchtower Society Doesn't Want You to Know

do some good things in harmony with the divine law, and that to that extent their conduct meets with the divine approval. But the Apostle clearly shows that neither the Jews nor the heathen do all things in harmony with the divine law, nor can they, because of inherited imperfections. Hence, neither the Jews nor the heathen would be justified under the Law. God, however, has provided through Christ a justification, under the terms of the New Covenant, which excuses and forgives whatever is not wilful sin, on the part of both Jews and heathen, who receive Christ, and through his merit. Thus it is that God will justify the heathen through faith—not all the heathen, but all the heathen who will exercise the faith when the knowledge of Christ shall reach them, in God's *due time.*

Question. I was surprised to note your advice to any who might be drafted into the army. Would not your advice seem like *compromising* to avoid trouble?

Answer. It is proper to avoid trouble in a proper manner. It is proper to compromise when no *principle* is involved, as in the case mentioned. Notice that there is no command in the Scriptures against military service. Obedience to a draft would remind us of our Lord's words, "If any man compel thee to go a mile, go with him twain." The government may compel marching or drilling, but cannot compel you to kill the foe. You need not be a good marksman.

Question. You suggested in a recent WATCH TOWER that, if drafted and in the army, we need not shoot to kill. Would such a course be right? Would it not be fraudulent?

Answer. No; it would be quite right to shoot, not to kill. You forget, perhaps, our provisos, which were that we explain our conscientious scruples against war, and seek to be excused; if not excused, that we seek non-combatant positions, as nurses, etc.; but if *compelled* to go a mile or many miles as a soldier, we still need not kill anybody.

Question. Will we know each other in the kingdom?

Answer. When the Apostle says (1 Cor. 13:12), "Now we see through a glass darkly [*i. e.*, as through an obscured glass], but then face to face; now I know in part, but then shall I know, even as I also am known," he undoubtedly included in the future knowledge the recognition of friends, even as he realized himself already known of God. If we are to be partakers of "the divine nature" and inheritors of all things, we must expect to be acquainted with the beings who form a considerable part of our heritage for a thousand years as well as with our associates in that inheritance.

Question. Were not the Psalms inspired specially for song service; and is it not therefore improper to use other hymns?

Answer. David's thought in writing the Psalms may have been merely their use in song; but the Lord's object was to give *prophecy* to assist his people of a later period. See what Peter says on this subject. (1 Pet. 1:10-12) Other prophecies of the Old Testament are written in poetical form, particularly Isaiah and Job. Our Lord quoted from both, as did also his apostles, and showed that in some of the Psalms David typified the Lord.

While some of the Psalms seem to us very suitable for singing, others we regard as less appropriate than hymns of praise of modern date. When the apostles said that we should sing "psalms and hymns and spiritual songs" (Eph. 5:19), he recognized a distinction between the three kinds of songs and commended all. We believe it is safe to follow his instructions, remembering the instruction, "Be not wise above what is written." However, on this subject we believe each one should follow his own conscience. Doubtless the Lord accepts the offering of song, whatever its form, so long as it comes from the heart,—just as with prose prayers; for hymns and psalms should be regarded as union or concert prayers.

ELISHA DOING RESTITUTION WORK

AUG. 14.—2 KINGS 4:25-37.

"Cast thy burden upon the Lord, and he shall sustain thee."—Psa. 55:22.

Elisha did receive a double portion of Elijah's spirit, or power. Not only did Jordan part before him, in obedience to his faith and at the stroke of the mantle, but other important works followed. Coming to a school of the prophets, they found that in preparing the dinner of vegetables something had gotten into the stew which they recognized to be poisonous, and the dinner was spoiled; but Elisha miraculously antidoted the poison, and made the dinner wholesome. Again, the people of Jericho complained that the fountain of water which supplied them was brackish, and he healed the waters so that the fountain became known as the fountain of Elisha, and the place is so known today.

These may be considered as typical of the restitution works which the Elisha class will introduce to the world. What do people who are religiously disposed, and who seek to understand the Word of the Lord, need, as the first feature of restitution blessings? Will it not be that something shall be put into their mess of pottage, that will destroy its poisonous errors, and make it health-giving, nutritious? Surely the peoples of civilized lands have God's Word in their hands, and its contents are good and nourishing and health-giving; but some of the theological cooks have unintentionally added doctrines of the evil one so that it is made to the people a poisonous dinner, injurious, as represented in the various creeds of Christendom. And what does the world in general need more than that the springs of the water of life (which have become corrupted and brackish, through false theories and misinterpretations of the divine Word and plan) should be corrected, healed, made sweet and pure and refreshing? And such restitution work will be accomplished, we understand, by the successors of the Gospel church in a much larger measure than the church itself is able to accomplish it now, the church's work being specifically the making of herself ready,—Rev. 19:7.

Further, we have the record of how the poor widow and her sons were helped by the prophet Elisha, to whom she appealed in her distress. A debt was upon her, and, according to the terms of the law, her sons would be bound to serve the creditor until the indebtedness had been discharged, or until the Jubilee year should be ushered in; and as she was a widow she needed her sons' assistance at home. The prophet saw her distress, sympathized with her, and assisted: the assistance being rendered in a manner which helped to develop her faith in the Lord. The only merchantable thing she had in her house was a pot of oil; and the prophet

directed her to send among her neighbors and borrow all the empty vessels that she could obtain, and to pour all full of oil, which then she could sell, and from the proceeds pay the debt and have something left; and so she did, according to directions. Does not this act of relieving the poor illustrate restitution powers and work also? Are we not told that in that time the Lord will "lift up the poor and the needy, and him that hath no helper?" There is in this a lesson of the Lord's sympathy with us in our earthly difficulties; a lesson of his willingness to assist us to pay our honest debts; and a lesson of the propriety of paying honest debts. And there is another lesson respecting how God is pleased to bless the use of the things which we have, rather than to send us other things, or to miraculously put the money into our pockets. There is also a lesson for faith, because it was in proportion to her faith that the woman gathered a large or small number of vessels, and therefore got a larger or a smaller evidence of divine bounty and mercy. Let us, when dealing with the Lord, remember that all the gold and silver are his, and the "cattle on a thousand hills," and let our works be in harmony with our faith.

We come now to the particular feature of this lesson, the Shunammite woman and her son: and this also contains a suggestion of the great restitution blessing of awakening the dead. This Shunammite has the record of the Scriptures that she was "a great woman." Apparently she and her husband were comfortably situated in life; perhaps indeed the greatness referred in part to wealth, but evidently she was a more than ordinary woman in other respects, as is indicated by the narrative. She may have been superior to her husband in intelligence, as the narrative seems to indicate. She had the kind of greatness, too, which recognizes goodness, and reverences the Lord, and those who are his. Seeing the prophet pass her place occasionally, probably on his way to the schools of the prophets, she hospitably urged him to take dinner with her, and so, apparently, every time he passed that way he stopped to partake of her hospitality. And the more this great woman saw of the Lord's prophet the more she realized that it was a favor to have him under the roof, so she said to her husband, "Behold now, I perceive that this is an holy man of God, which passeth by us continually. Let us make a little chamber, I pray thee, on the wall, and let us set for him there a bed, and a table, and a stool and a candlestick: and it shall be when he cometh to us that he shall turn in thither." Altho apparently the

[2345]

43

ciplines, corrections in righteousness, which will prevail toward all men during the Millennium.

CAN RESTITUTION CHANGE THE ETHIOPIAN'S SKIN?

The following, from the *New York World*, is the third we have seen reported. These suggest and illustrate the process of restitution soon due. The item reads:

"From Black to White He Slowly Turned"

"PARKERSBURG, W. Va., Sept. 8.—It has fallen to the lot of the Rev. William H. Draper, pastor of the Logan Memorial church, of Washington Conference, A. M. E. church, of this town, to give a living affirmative answer to the famous Biblical question, "Can the Ethiopian change his skin or the leopard his spots?" Though once as black as charcoal, the Rev. Mr. Draper is now white. His people say that his color was changed in answer to prayer. Many years ago Draper was employed by a fair-skinned man, and he was often heard to remark that if he could only be white like his employer, he would be happy. While in the white man's service Draper "experienced" religion.

"From that day forward he prayed constantly and fer-

vently that he might become white. Thirty years ago his prayer began to be answered. He first experienced a prickling sensation on his face, and upon close investigation found a number of small white spots scarcely larger than the point of a pin. He became alarmed, thinking he had some peculiar disease but he did not suffer, and aside from the prickling sensation felt nothing unusual. Gradually the white spots became larger and extended themselves, until now, after the change has been in progress for over thirty years, Draper has not a single dark spot on his body.

"Many years ago, before this strange metamorphosis took place, Mr. Draper was in charge of the same church he has now. He was popular with his flock and his departure was a source of great regret. When he recently returned to Parkersburg there was great rejoicing among the churchmen because their favorite pastor was coming back. When, however, Draper appeared in the pulpit the first Sunday, not one of the congregation recognized him. In fact, it was all he could do to convince them that he, a white man, was the same old black preacher they had years before."

DIVINE CARE FOR THE LOST

LUKE 15:1-10.—OCT. 21.

"There is joy in the presence of the angels of God over one sinner that repenteth."

Lost, as used in connection with mankind, has quite a different meaning in the Bible from that commonly given it in modern theology. The latter uses the term "lost" in connection with reprobates, for whom there is no hope; it implies, according to "orthodoxy," hopeless, endless, eternal torment. But from the Scriptural standpoint the word "lost" is used in an almost opposite sense, as will be noted in the lesson before us.

Our Lord, holy in word and in conduct, naturally would draw to himself especially the holiness people of his day, and these were the Pharisees, amongst whom, however, were many whose holiness was of a hypocritical character—delighting in outward show rather than in purity and holiness of heart. Recent lessons showed us our Lord the guest and companion of prominent Pharisees, and how he improved the opportunity to preach the gospel to them as well as to others. But the Pharisees, accustomed to thinking of themselves as the holier class of the Jews, had gradually separated themselves from the lower elements of that people, so that in our Lord's time the two classes mingled very little; the Pharisees refusing to acknowledge the others as brethren and fellow-heirs of the divine promises. Consequently, when they perceived that the lower classes of the Jews were interested in Jesus' teachings, and that Jesus did not hold himself aloof from them, but mingled with and taught them just the same as others, they wondered, and this inclined them to repudiate Jesus, whom they would have been glad to have had as one of their number if he had been willing to be known as a Pharisee and to conform to their customs. It was to correct the wrong ideas of these Pharisees that Jesus gave five parables, which we are about to consider—two of them in this lesson.

The parable of the true shepherd who, loving his sheep and caring for them, left the ninety and nine well cared for by under-shepherds in the wilds (not in a desert) and went after the one lost sheep until he found it, gives us an illustration of the divine care. Possibly our Lord meant no further lesson than this to be taken from his words; but if we shall suppose that the parable was intended to be applied in its varied particulars, and to illustrate features of the divine plan of salvation, we would be obliged to suppose that the one sheep that was lost represented Adam and the human family, and that the ninety and nine never lost, but remaining under the shepherd's care, were the angels and other spirit beings, who never wandered into sin and away from God; and who always have been under his supervision and care. In this view the shepherd going after the straying sheep would represent our Lord Jesus, leaving the glory which he had with the Father before the world was, and coming into human conditions in the interest of mankind.

To take any other detailed view of the parable than this would seem inconsistent; as, for instance, to suppose that the lost sheep represented the degraded element of humanity, and ninety-nine sheep a holiness class, would be inconsistent in two ways: (1) "There is none righteous, no, not one," is the Scriptural declaration; and again, as the prophet has declared, "we all like sheep have gone astray." (Rom. 3:10; Isa. 53:6) (2) Even if it should be claimed that the ninety-nine represented some who are relatively whole, tho not actually so, the illustration would be inapt; because it will not be questioned

that only a small minority—one in ten thousand, or one in a hundred thousand of earth's sixteen hundred millions, is even in a condition of reckoned and relative harmony with Jehovah, the Great Shepherd.

Viewing the one sheep as representing the whole of humanity, fallen in Adam and straying far from paths of righteousness, and viewing Jesus as the Good Shepherd, the representative of the Father, the Great Shepherd (Psa. 23:1), we see that the work of going after the lost sheep began at our Lord's first advent. We see the cost to our Saviour incidental to his start for the recovery of the sheep, but we do not yet see the sheep recovered; for in no sense of the word is mankind brought back into harmony with God. We do, however, see that during this Gospel age God is selecting from humanity an elect church, to be the body of Christ—members of the Good Shepherd, under Jesus as the Head; and we see that it is costing every member of the body something to prepare to join in this work of seeking the lost sheep—humanity in general—during the Millennial age.

Already the sheep is found, in the sense of being located; indeed, in that sense of the word it was not lost. But as it was lost, in the sense of having wandered from God into sin and degradation, in the same sense of the word it must be recovered or brought back, by processes of *restitution* (Acts 3:19-21) out of degradation, out of the mire of sin, and the horrible pit of iniquity and death. It will require the entire Millennial age to bring back the sheep in the full, perfect sense of the parable; but meanwhile our Lord assures us that every step in this great plan for human salvation is viewed with interest by the heavenly host, the sheep who strayed not from the Father's fold; and the figure changing a little in our Lord's explanation, and no longer represented by one sheep, but by many (even as the human family, tho originally one, is now many), he declares that there is joy in the presence of the angels of God over one sinner that repenteth—that returns to the fold, to harmony with God.

Those now returning to harmony with God are accepted in the Beloved, and justified freely from all things by the grace that was in him, and are, in the language of the Apostle, "returning to the Shepherd and Caretaker of their souls" (1 Pet. 2:25); and called to be co-laborers with the Good Shepherd, as members of his "body."

In the case of Father Adam, the one original straying sheep, as in the case of many of his posterity, the lost condition is not the desirable one—far rather would he and many others have gone back again to the fold from which he strayed; but in the degradation and mire of sin, they became so degraded and helpless that it was impossible for them to *return* in their own strength by the way in which they went. They needed a Savior—one able to save them unto the uttermost—able to recover them fully from all condemnation of sin, and to bring them back completely into the fold of God; and just such an one the heavenly Father has provided in our Lord Jesus: "He is able to save unto the uttermost all who come unto the Father through him."

True, there will be a class, as the Scriptures clearly show, who, after having received at the Lord's hands all the blessings and opportunities which his love has provided for their recovery, will still persist in wilfulness—self-will, and thus

JULY 15, 1902.   *ZION'S WATCH TOWER*   (215-216)

nations are mentioned as of one blood; and this again borne out by his statement that those who accept Christ, whether Jew or Gentile, barbarian or Scythian, bond or free, are "all one in Christ Jesus."—Gal. 3:28; Col. 3:11.

The Ethiopian eunuch to whom Philip was sent with the messages of salvation was unquestionably a black man—"Can the Ethiopian change his skin?" (Jer. 13:23; Acts 8:27) We find no suggestion on Philip's part that this Ethiopian was not a man, but a beast; but quite to the contrary, he was ready to preach the Gospel to him and to accept him as a brother in Christ upon his confession of faith.

The Queen of Sheba who visited Solomon in the height of his glory is presumed to have been a negress; the present Emperor of Abyssinia claims to be a descendant of Solomon by this Queen—he is a black man, and an able warrior and general, as the Italian army, attempting to invade his country a few years ago, learned to its cost—its serious defeat. Solomon is presumed, by some, to have referred to the Queen of Sheba in his Songs or Canticles 1:5, 6.

HOW SHALL WE ACCOUNT FOR RACIAL DIFFERENCES?

(3) Question.—If the foregoing is not the solution of the racial distinctions amongst men, what would you suggest as a reasonable explanation?

Answer.—From the Scriptural standpoint we must and do recognize all of the human family as one race, of which father Adam was the original head; a later head being Noah. Accepting as we do the Bible narrative of the flood (and it is confirmed by similar, though less explicit, narratives amongst all ancient peoples) we need not go back of Noah and his family in seeking a cause for the differences. Taking Mt. Ararat as the central joint from which postdiluvian humanity spread itself over the earth, we may reasonably suppose that his three sons and their posterity went in different directions, the one northward, the other southward, and the third eastward. There is a general consensus of opinion that it was Ham who went southward, and whose posterity afterward peopled Africa; that it was Shem who remained near the Mediterranean and became the millions of Armenia, Persia, Assyria, Egypt and India; and that Japheth went northward and eastward, and that his posterity is represented in the Turks, Russians, Chinese, etc.

In attempting to account for the wide differences between whites and blacks, and the lesser differences between these and the yellow, brown, and red, we are treading upon uncertain ground,—as all ground must be in which our imperfect knowledge and imperfect reasoning powers have not inspired direction from the Lord's Word. Hence it should be understood at the outstart that all that we or others can do is to guess on this subject—respecting the differences in shape of head, color of skin, shape of eyes, peculiarities of hair, the nose, lips, etc. Undoubtedly, the climate and the soil have much to do with these differences, just as they have much to do with changes in vegetation. For instance, the apple which reaches to a great degree of perfection in a cold climate, if transferred, even gradually, to a warm one will do poorly, and if it does not die out entirely will at least undergo a transformation, in harmony with the change of soil and climate. The same is noticeable in the quince, the plum and the grape, the orange, etc. Is there more difference between the different races of human species than between the different kinds of grapes—some sweet, some sour; some larger, some smaller; some round, some oblong, some pear-shaped; some white, some green, some reddish, some purple; some with solid meat, some half full of juice, some with seeds and some without? Yet it is not questioned that all grapes are of one family.

Again, consider the dog species. Some are sleek and some are rough; some are very woolly and some are without hair; some white, some brown, some tan; some large, some small, etc. Does any one dispute that all dogs are of one species? Appropriately, we find that locality and climate and the kind of food subsisted upon had much to do with these differences. True, we see dogs in various countries of different breeds now, yet we recognize each breed as having had originally a distinctive home: as for instance, the St. Bernard of the Alps, the Spitz of the Arctic regions, the Scotch terrier, the Collie and the Newfoundland—each had its own place, and was developed under peculiar conditions, which for the time being it separate from others. We are to remember that for long centuries neither dogs nor their masters roamed the world over as at present, but were content with their own home, country, which, with its peculiar conditions and customs, gradually fixed certain characteristics of thought, manner, language and outer appearance. As a consequence, an experienced eye will know a Scotchman fresh from his native heath as quickly as he would recognize his dog. And the same with other peoples.

When we find that Europe, which was settled much more recently by its present inhabitants, has in so short a time divided itself into so many different nations, and when we remember that Europeans have stirred, and commingled with each other far more than the peoples of other parts of the earth, it helps us to see how gradually, through many centuries, other peoples have undergone still greater changes.

In considering this matter we are not to forget the strong pre-natal influence of the mother's mind upon her offspring,—co-operating with the influences of climate and soil. To illustrate: Suppose a missionary and his wife removed to China; not only would the influence of the climate and soil be manifested upon themselves, but the same would be still more manifested in their children. Whoever will give careful attention to this matter will notice that each succeeding child born in that foreign country will have increasingly more resemblance to the Chinese—the hair, the skin, the shape of the eyes, and in general all features will bear closer resemblance with each succeeding child. We can readily suppose that if so much change occurs in a few years, ten or twenty centuries under similar conditions would turn any white people into regular Chinese, even supposing there were no intermarrying. The mother, while carrying her unborn child, has continually before her the Chinese type of countenance—eyes, hair, color, etc., and the continual impress of these upon her mind could not fail, according to the law of our being, to influence her offspring in the manner noted.

Indeed a traveler, a scientist, has lately reported to the civilized world that he found in China a district where there were ruins of a very ancient Hebrew temple, and tablets in Hebrew. The people of the district informed him that they had a tradition that their fathers once spoke and understood the language of the tablets (Hebrew), had emigrated thither many centuries before, adopting the Chinese customs and language and, gradually, their appearance also.

The effect would be similar in India. Undoubtedly the stronger contrast between the white and the black would require a longer time to be brought about; but we should expect that neither of these extremes fairly represented the original, if we may judge of Adam; Noah and Abraham by the only nation whose ancestors can be traced unblemished back to these heads of the race,—the Jews. We may suppose that they were neither as white as some of us, nor as black as the negro, but of a swarthy, tawny color. If this be true, the extreme whiteness of some peoples is not to be considered the original standard, but a deflection on the one side, as the negro and others are deflections on the other side. We are not to forget, either, that Africa is inhabited by various tribes or nations of negroes—some more and some less degraded than the average. Those brought to America as slaves were of various tribes;—from among whom no doubt the Lord is making choice of some for the prospective "royal priesthood."

While it is true that the white race exhibits some qualities of superiority over any other, we are to remember that there are wide differences in the same Caucasian (Sémitic and Aryan) family; and also we should remember that some of the qualities which have given this branch of the human family its preeminence in the world are not such as can be pointed to us in all respects admirable. Indeed we can not but wonder whether if the Gospel had been sent into Asia instead of into Europe it would have found amongst the people of India a soil much more naturally adapted to the development of the peaceable fruits of righteousness. However, that the Gospel was divinely directed into Europe is most manifest (Acts 16: 6, 9), and sooner or later we shall see the full meaning of this divine providence. Perhaps the Lord intends to show that as typical Israel was a stiff-necked generation, so also spiritual Israel will be taken from amongst similar classes; and all the more show forth the power of the truth, by taking the elect church chiefly from amongst the most quarrelsome, aggressive, selfish and dominating of humanity, and transforming these through the power of the truth into exemplifications of patience, humility, love and peace. The secret of the greater intelligence and aptitude of the Caucasian undoubtedly in great measure is to be attributed to the commingling of blood amongst its various branches; and this was evidently forced in large measure by circumstances under divine control. It remains to be proven that the similar commingling of the various tribes of Chinese for several centuries would not equally brighten their intellects; and the same with the peoples of India and Africa.

NOAH'S CHARACTER AND HIS "CURSE" UPON HAM

(4) Question.—Those who hold that the negro is a beast deny that he is the offspring of Noah's sons, and claim that the curse of Noah was not upon Ham, but upon one of Ham's sons, Canaan. They belittle Noah's curse, by saying that it

74

through Christ Jesus. After he has accepted our Lord as his Redeemer, and has offered himself in consecration, our Lord, as his Advocate, must cover his imperfections with the Robe of His own Righteousness, and present him to the Father. Then he will be accepted and given the privilege of prayer.

POSSESSORS OF PARTICULAR QUALITIES OF MIND NATURALLY DRAWN TO GOD

The question then arises, If the world cannot approach God in prayer, what is the method by which He draws men? The Scriptures say that no man can come unto Christ except the Father draw him. (John 6:44.) The answer is that the drawing cannot be done through the Holy Spirit; for the world has not yet received that Spirit. The drawing power which the Almighty exercises over humanity is in different degrees. Some have a strong desire to worship God, others have a weak desire, and others have no desire at all. This difference is due to the shape of the brain. Mankind are born with differences in this respect.—Psa. 51:5.

Various imperfections were stamped upon us before our birth. As the Scriptures say, "There is none righteous, no, not one"; "for all have sinned, and come short of the glory of God." (Rom. 3:10, 23.) All come short of that standard which God would be pleased to recognize. But amongst mankind there are some who have not lost their reverence, whatever else they may have lost in the unbalance of mind resulting from the fall. Or perhaps they have the quality of conscientiousness or appreciation of justice well developed. These qualities draw or incline their possessors toward God; and they feel as if they cannot be happy without Him. This is the drawing influence.

This drawing influence may be illustrated by the effect of a magnet. If a quantity of steel filings were scattered throughout a box of sawdust, and a magnet were held close to the surface, the steel filings would immediately respond to the attraction of the magnet. On the other hand, the sawdust would not be affected; nor would the steel filings respond to any other influence than that of a magnet, exercised either directly or indirectly.

Man was created in the image of God. The fall has greatly marred that image, but no one is totally depraved. All have unbalanced brains, some in one direction, others in another. When the Truth comes in contact with those whose organs of veneration or conscientiousness are less impaired, they are drawn to investigate it, with the hope of being drawn close to God. Those whose organs of veneration and conscientiousness are more impaired, do not have this experience, and are not drawn unto God, if haply they may find Him.

Those who are without this drawing influence are not to be blamed; for they were born under those unfavorable conditions. Those who are reverential are, however, favored in that whoever would come to God must exercise faith in Christ; for without this faith there can be no blessing. At first this blessing and privilege are not clearly discerned by the seeker after righteousness. He merely longs to know God, and as he seeks, he finds; and as he knocks, it is opened unto him.—Matt. 7:7, 8.

Any one, therefore, who seeks God will find Him; for the Scriptures promise, "Draw nigh to God, and He will draw nigh to you." (James 4:8.) Those who thus find the way to God have something for which to be thankful in the possession of the quality of mind which led them to appreciate God. Persons of a particular character will follow on in the way and will, if faithful, attain to the reward. Those who have it not will not be drawn of the Lord until they shall have been made over in the next Age.

We are not, therefore, to suppose that everybody is being drawn during the present Age.

After a person has been drawn, guided and instructed, then his *will* comes into action. It is for him to decide what course he will pursue. When he sees that no man comes to the Father except through Christ, and that the conditions are self-sacrifice, then he has the matter squarely before his mind. There are Scriptures which warn him that the path is difficult, but there are other Scriptures which tell him of the glory, honor and immortality at the end of the way. It is for the person to decide what he will do. But he does not come fully into the family of God until he has decided, and has taken the step of thorough consecration unto death; only then can he be begotten of the Holy Spirit and enter the School of Christ.

PRAYER A PRIVILEGE OF THE HOUSEHOLD OF FAITH

During the Jewish Dispensation, the Jews had the privilege of approaching God in prayer; but during the Gospel Age they have not had this privilege. As long as the Atonement Day sacrifices were offered annually, they had the privilege of prayer under the Law Covenant; but as soon as the typical sin-offerings ceased, all those privileges which that Covenant secured for them terminated; therefore the Jews have no access to God. They are still under the Law Covenant; but they have lost this special feature of it, because the typical priesthood ceased to be recognized as soon as the Antitypical Priest appeared.

The Church of Christ alone, therefore, at this time has the special privilege of coming to God in prayer; for the great Antitypical High Priest has made a satisfactory Sin-Offering of Himself. Whosoever will, through faith in Him and under the covenant relationship of sacrifice, may draw near to God in prayer, nothing doubting.

But while only the consecrated class, the under priesthood, the New Creation, are thus encouraged to approach the Throne of Grace with confidence and courage, very evidently all who in any proper sense belong to the "household of faith" may to some extent enjoy the privileges of prayer, the privileges of thanksgiving and intercession, and may rejoice in the peace of God, in a realization of the forgiveness of sins through faith in the Atonement.

During the Millennial Age, every good trait which any one possesses will be an advantage to him, and every evil trait will be a disadvantage. But no advantage will be so great that it will enable any to rise without the aid of Messiah. The less degraded will not have so far to retrace their steps; but where much grace is needed, much will be supplied. The power of the great Mediator will be adapted to all conditions; for the Scriptures give us the assurance that Christ's Kingdom will be instituted for that very purpose. Since there is none righteous, no, not one, therefore all must have the great Messiah to assist them back into full harmony with God.

PRAYER AN OPPORTUNITY AND A NECESSITY

While prayer is a privilege and not a command, yet our condition makes it a necessity. Because of the fall of man from his original perfection, our flesh has imperfections, frailties; and yet we, as New Creatures, have responsibility for these weaknesses. The only way to discharge these responsibilities is to go to the Throne of Grace and there obtain help in time of need. Whoever, therefore, goes frequently to the Throne of Grace in prayer thus indicates that he recognizes the necessity of using the opportunity which God has provided, his interest and his privilege.

Prayer is necessary to the well-being of any who would properly enjoy the blessings and privileges of his organism. We have the organ of veneration, Brain...

RUSSELL *v.* RUSSELL, Appellant.   351

348, (1908).]   Opinion of the Court.

In an analysis of the testimony it is quite difficult to understand the view of the respondent in regard to his duty as a husband to his wife. From his standpoint, he doubtless felt that
his rights as a husband were radically different from the standards imposed upon him by the law and recognized by all the
courts of this country. He stated to his wife, "I can show you
a thousand women that would be glad to be in your place and
that would know my wishes and do them." His estimation of
his own importance is gathered from his statement to a friend:
"I have been approached twice by parties who contemplate
the organization of a large bank in Pittsburg, with a capital of
three million dollars, and have been solicited to permit my
name to be used in connection with the organization as its
prospective president," and to another friend, "After reading
'The Plan of the Ages' people say, Brother Russel is great! I
will go to Allegheny and be near this great man! When they
get to Allegheny they find Brother Russel makes no claim to
greatness, and merely claims that it is God's word that is wonderful. He reasons the matter to them as though it were a
question in mathematics; and when they hear the answer, they
say, 'how simple,'" and many like expressions of self-esteem
pervade his testimony. Letters to friends furnish some idea
of his own estimation of his character. He repeatedly states
that he is not self-conceited, but meek and not boastful, and
writes that two phrenologists had examined his head and as-
sured him that he was deficient in self-esteem. From his whole
testimony, it would seem that he was right in reaching the conclusion stated by him in a letter to his wife, to wit: "I conclude
that I am adapted to no one, and that no one is adapted to me,
except the Lord. I am thankful that He and I understood each
other and have confidence in each other. The last month has
fastened the conviction upon me much against my will. I am
convinced that our difficulty is a growing one generally—that
it is a great mistake for strong-minded men and women to
marry."

From this view point his conduct is at least consistent, and
he would naturally feel warranted in feeling that any doubt as
to the correctness of his views or conclusions, would be due to

of Egypt, and a pillar [pyramid] *at the border* thereof, to the Lord. And it shall be for a sign and for a witness unto the Lord of hosts in the land of Egypt." Another fact worthy of notice is that the Great Pyramid is located in the geographical center of the land surface of the world—including North and South America, unknown for centuries after the location and construction of the Great Pyramid.

ITS SCIENTIFIC LESSONS.

The Great Pyramid speaks to us, not by hieroglyphics, nor by sketches, but only by its location, its construction and its measurements. The only original marks or figures found were in the "Construction Chambers" over the "King's Chamber;" there are none whatever in the passages and rooms of the Pyramid proper. The scientific lessons of the Great Pyramid we omit for economy of space, because not one in a hundred ordinary readers would understand the scientific terms, so as to appreciate the demonstrations, and especially because they would be no part of the gospel which it is our misson to present. Suffice it, therefore, that we merely *suggest* the manner in which it teaches the scientist. For instance: The measure of the base of the four sides, at the level of the "sockets," added, is found to be as many pyramid cubits as there are days in four years, to the fraction—including the leap-year fraction. The measures diagonally across the base from northeast to southwest, and from northwest to southeast, added, give as many inches as there are years in the precessional cycle. This cycle astronomers had already concluded to be 25,827 years, and the Great Pyramid corroborates their conclusion. The distance to the sun it is claimed is indicated, by the height and angle of the Great Pyramid, to be 91,840,270 miles, which almost exactly corresponds with the latest figures reached by astronomers. Astronomers until recently had calculated

this distance to be from ninety to ninety-six millions of miles, their latest calculation and conclusion being ninety-two millions. The Great Pyramid has also its own way of indicating the most correct standard of all weights and measures, based upon the size and weight of the earth, which it is also claimed to indicate.

Commenting upon the scientific testimony and the location of this majestic "Witness," Rev. Joseph Seiss, D. D. suggests:

"There is a yet grander thought embodied in this wonderful structure. Of its five points there is one of special pre-eminence, in which all its sides and exterior lines terminate. It is the summit corner, which lifts its solemn index finger to the sun at midday, and by its distance from the base tells the mean distance to that sun from the earth. And if we go back to the date which the Pyramid gives itself, and look for what that finger pointed to at midnight, we find a far sublimer indication. Science has at last discovered that the sun is not a dead center, with planets wheeling about it, and itself stationary. It is now ascertained that the sun also is in motion, carrying with it its splendid retinue of comets, planets, its satellites and theirs, around some other and vastly mightier center. Astronomers are not yet fully agreed as to what or where that center is. Some, however, believe that they have found the direction of it to be the Pleiades, and particularly Alcyone, the central one of the renowned Pleiadic stars. To the distinguished German astronomer, Prof. J. H. Maedler, belongs the honor of having made this discovery. Alcyone, then, as far as science has been able to perceive, would seem to be ' the midnight throne ' in which the whole system of gravitation has its central seat, and from which the Almighty governs his universe. And here is the wonderful corresponding fact, that at the date of the Great Pyramid's building, at midnight of the autumnal equinox, and hence the true beginning of the year* as still preserved in the traditions of many nations, the Pleiades were distributed

*The beginning of the Jewish year, introduced by the Day Atonement, as shown in SCRIPTURE STUDIES, VOL. II.

Joachim heretics." His application of the correct principle, "a year for a day," made in the very depths of the Dark Ages, is one of the most pathetic incidents in the history of mankind; but his study of time-prophecy brought him peace and joy of heart. He was an opponent of the prevailing "doctrine of the Trinity." William Miller, in the year 1829, was privileged to see (approximately) the correct date for the setting up of the abomination of desolation (539 A. D.), and for the beginning of the Time of the End (1799 A. D.) Morton Edgar, author of *Pyramid Passages*, has found foreshadow in the Great Pyramid of Egypt abundant evidence of the accuracy of the Bible chronology of Pastor Russell and the supplements thereto supplied by Dr. John Edgar, deceased. These findings are set forth in his work, *Pyramid Passages*, Vol. II, of which we recommend sections numbered in the following table. For convenience we give the citations to Pastor Russell's works in which the same items are discussed. The Pyramid is still there, and the measurements can be made by anybody. Pastor Russell's chronology was written before he ever saw the Pyramid.

Date Foreshown	Event	Pastor Russell's Works	Sections of Pyramid Passages
Fall 4127 B. C.	Fall of Adam.	Z 04-343	26-30-58
Fall 3127 B. C.	End of Adam's 1000-year day.	Z 04-343	25-28
Fall 2473 B. C.	Flood.	B 42	23-30
Fall 2021 B. C.	Birth of Isaac.	R 231	16-17
Spring 1918 B.C.	Death of Jacob.	R 218-232	
Spring 1615 B.C.	Exodus and giving of the Law.	R 42	11
Spring 1575 B. C.	Entrance into Canaan.	R 42	43-46
Fall 1425 B. C.	Last Jubilee.	B 185	50
Fall 607 B. C.	Desolation of the Land.	B 51	19-46-48
465 B. C.	Nehemiah's Commission.	B 67	51-52-53
2 B. C.	Birth of Christ.	B 54	10-43-43-58
29 A. D.	Baptism of Christ.	B 54	10-11-14-33-
33 A. D.	Death of Christ,	B 61	45
36 A. D.	Conversion of Cornelius.		
Spring 1378 A.D.	Wycliffe.	B 71	37
Spring 1521 A.D.	Diet of Worms.	Z 05-195	38
Fall 1846 A.D.	Evangelical Alliance.	Z 05-180	14-52
Fall 1874 A.D.	Second Advent of...	C 96-119	
Spring 1878 A.D.	Favor to Jews and sleeping Saints.	B 173-247	16-32-50
1914 A. D.	End of Times of the Gentiles.	C 233	17-28
Fall 2875 A.D.	Restitution completed.	R 73-344	19-48
Fall 2914 A.D.	Dominion restored to mankind.	Z 04-344	37
		Z 04-343	58

The chronology as it appears in the STUDIES IN THE SCRIPTURES is accurate. The year 1914 brought the end of the Times of the Gentiles, but not the end of the Harvest work. Have the teachings of the Parallels lost their value? Not at all. The point not previously noticed is that the Jewish polity was not to be destroyed in Jerusalem only, but throughout all Judea. Nor does *Judea* mean all of Palestine. The actual depopulation of the whole of Palestine did not occur until the year 135 A. D. (corresponding to our year 1980), on the ninth day of the month of Ab, the anniversary of the burning of the Temple under Titus. On that day came to an end the insurrection of Bar-Cocheba, the false Messiah, who wrought his own destruction and that of 580,000 of his followers, when he attempted to regain control of Judea and Jerusalem. The struggle was of five years' duration having begun in 130 A. D. "It was the effort, under the leadership of Bar-Cocheba, to regain their independence, that brought about actually in the depopulation of Palestine, and resulted in the depopulation of Palestine. The whole of Judea was turned into a desert; about 985 towns and villages were laid in ashes; fifty of their fortresses were razed to the ground; even the name of their capital was changed to Ælia Capitolina, and they were forbidden to approach it on pain of death; and thousands of those who had escaped death were reduced to slavery, and such as could not be thus disposed of were transported into Egypt."—McC.

When the Lord gave His wonderful prophecy in which the destinies of nominal Fleshly Israel, nominal Spiritual Israel, and the Israel of God, are set forth, in answer to three definite questions: *"When shall these things be? and what shall be the sign of Thy Parousia, and of the end of the Age?"* (Matt. 24:3.) The Lord did not ignore their question. He answered it with a reply that sweeps the history of twenty centuries. He showed that the *end* of Fleshly Israel foreshadowed the *end* of that the end of Fleshly Israel foreshadowed the *end* of the Spiritual Israel. Fleshly Israel had three ends; the destruction of Jerusalem in A. D. 70, the complete subjugation of Judea in A. D. 73, and the actual depopulation of the whole of Palestine in A. D. 135. Which did He mean? Not the end in A. D. 70, foreshadowing 1915; for the Harvest of the Gospel Age is still in progress. Not the end in A. D. 135, foreshadowing 1980; for the *Harvest is the end.* He must have meant the end in *Judea*, even as He said, "Then let them which be in *Judea* flee into the mountains." (Matt. 24:16.) See also Matt. 2:22; 3:5;

THE FINISHED MYSTERY, 1917

49

114

F.W.Franz
(Cross)

A   Q. So that what is published as the truth today by the
Society may have to be admitted to be wrong in a few years?
A. We have to wait and see. Q. And in the meantime the
body of Jehovah's Witnesses have been following error? A.
They have been following misconstructions on the Scriptures.

B   Q. Error? A. Well. error.   Q. Did not Judge Rutherford
take the view that the Beast is Satan's organisation on
earth manifested particularly in the seventh head thereof,
to wit the seventh world power. which is Great Britain?
A. Might I see that statement. Q. I have not the book.

C   but it is in "Light" volume 1.   You have read Light? A.
Yes. Q. Is that statement not in it? A. I would have
to see the statement as it is. in print not as you say it.
Q.   Did he not associate the Beast with Great Britain?
A.   Which Beast?   Q.   You are an authority on these

D   matters?   A. There are a number of Beasts mentioned.
You must specify which one you mean so that I can understand.   Q.   Perhaps we could get together if you tell
me-is-it-not the case that one of the Beasts was regarded
as Great Britain by Judge Rutherford?   A. No you are

E   not right about that. Q. Well you put me right and tell
me what was the association in Judge Rutherford's
publication between Great Britain and a Beast in
Scripture? A. In the 13th Chapter of Revelation
there is a two-horned Beast that comes up out of the

F   earth?

DOUGLAS WALSH TRIAL, Scotland, 1954
50

79

ceeded to say: 'Let light come to be.'" It later mentions the "greater luminary for dominating the day," that is, the sun, earth's principal source of light, and also of energy, without which life on earth would be impossible. The crowning act of earthly creation came when "Jehovah God proceeded to form the man out of dust from the ground and to blow into his nostrils the breath of life, and the man came to be a living soul," "in God's image." Adam, and then Eve, were created perfect, with all the senses and faculties, physical and mental, for the full use and enjoyment of both life and light.—Isa. 45:18; Gen. 1:1, 3, 16, 27; 2:7.

[14] From this it is evident that, not only is Jehovah God the Source and Author of life and light, the Creator and Life-Giver, but by virtue of such he is rightly the Supreme Authority, the Supreme Ruler in government. (Ps. 103:19; Dan. 4:17, 35; Rev. 4:11) Accepting this, we naturally want to know how there could possibly be an authority in opposition to Jehovah. What is the "authority of Satan" that Jesus mentioned? How did it come about? And how can we come out from under its domination?

[15] As the inspired account shows, Satan attempted to use his *influence* in a subtle way, and in this he was successful. How so? By insinuation and falsehood. He put forth error, under cover of a lie, as a substitute for truth. In other words, he put darkness for light.

14. On what basis is Jehovah seen to be the Supreme Authority, this giving rise to what question?
15. (a) How did Satan subtly seek to undermine God's authority? (b) How was God's word involved in this? (c) What prompted Adam and Eve in their course of action?

304

Interestingly, it was regarding life, saying that Eve would not die but would continue to live in the flesh on earth if she did as he suggested. He promised her increased enlightenment when he said, through the serpent: "In the very day of your eating from it [the forbidden fruit] your eyes are bound to be opened." Then, implying she would become free to exercise authority independent of God, he added: "You are bound to be like God, knowing [for yourselves] good and bad." (Gen. 3:1-5) Satan thus claimed that God's word and command given to Adam were not to be relied on as a true light to guide and keep him and his wife in the right roadway leading to life. First Eve and then Adam decided to disobey God's simple and direct command, and to strike out on the roadway of selfish independence, a roadway leading away from life and light in God's favor into darkness and death.—Ps. 119:105; see also 2 Corinthians 11:14.

[16] We pause here to consider one of Satan's chief tactics and how it operates. By subtle means, by deception, he tempts us to view things from a selfish viewpoint, as he did with Eve. If at heart we are, or become, governed by selfishness, then we readily fall into Satan's snare and are easily blinded and deceived. We seek to justify ourselves, and put out of our mind the fear of God. See how clearly and forcefully this is expressed in Psalm 36:1-3: "The utterance of transgression to the wicked one is in the midst of his heart; there is no dread

Adam and Eve's course of selfish independence led them away from light and life into darkness and death

16. (a) Why is it helpful to consider Satan's line of approach? (b) How do the Scriptures give enlightenment respecting this?

THE WATCHTOWER — MAY 15, 1976

of God in eyes. For he smoothly to own eyes to error so as t words of hi hurtfulness a he has cease sight for doin judgment of expressed by Isaiah: "Wo are saying bad and bad who are pu for light and ness . . . ! wise in the and discreet of their ow should certa we "become hence blinde ceptive pow Heb. 3:13.

[17] From t Eden, manki ly under S Though Sat yet man hi large extent not leave hi world of ma yet "his invi from the wo they are pe even his et that they ar with Psalm that "altho they did no they thank headed in t intelligent b 1:19-23) T

17. To what e becoming incre

THE WATCHTO

(3)   Z I O N ' S   W A T C H   T O W E R   Feb 1881, p.3

PITTSBURGH, PA.

structed concerning the evil day; there is the intimation that it will be a time of special trial, and admonitions to held fast, &c., are given as in this 38th verse. During the last six or seven years, the Lord has been leading us, his people, in a very remarkable manner. As we look backward we can see that our pathway has been as "a shining light . . . . shining more and more." It has been *progressive*, bringing us strength with "meat in due season." It has caused us to grow both in *grace and knowledge* and this growth, taken in connection with the fact that we are not obliged to look back and now call *darkness* what was then called by some of the brethren, "a great flood of light," is the very strongest grounds for confidence that the same Lord who then supplied us *light* from the word, is still providing of the same kind. We say then, "Cast not away your confidence" in our *Leader*, "the great Shepherd of the sheep."

If we were following *a man* undoubtedly it would be different with us; undoubtedly one human idea would contradict another and that which was light one or two or six years ago would be regarded as darkness now; But with God there is no variableness, neither shadow of turning, and so it is with *truth*; any knowledge or light coming from God must be like its author. A new view of *truth never can contradict a former truth.* "New light" never extinguishes older "light," but adds to it. If you were lighting up a building, containing seven gas jets you would not extinguish one every time you lighted another, but would add one light to another and they would be in harmony and thus give increase of light; So is it with the light of truth; the true increase is by adding to, not by substituting one for another.

Therefore, in mentioning grounds of our confidence; that we are in the shining path under the leading of the Spirit, we mention first that the tendency of present truth is to produce the proper fruit of the spirit, of which love is the chief. The tendency of our growth in knowledge is to growth in grace. "He that hath this hope in him *purifieth himself* even as he (Jesus) is pure." Our pathway has been one of increase of light in harmony with former light. Thus we have been led to increased confidence in our leader. Let us take

A GLANCE BACKWARD

at the steps of progress, and let all notice that the progress is not only forward but *upward*; i. e., the tendency is from the natural to the spiritual. We will look, not at any one person's experience, but at what serves to show the advance of the knowledge of truth for ten years past. Looking back to 1871, we see that many of our company were what are known as Second Adventists, and the light they held briefly stated, was that there would be a second advent of Jesus—that he would come to bless and immortalize the saints, to judge the world and to burn up the world and all the wicked. This, they claimed would occur in 1873, because the 6,000 years from the creation of Adam were complete then.

Well, 1873 came, the end of 6,000 years, and yet no *burning* of the world, &c. But prophecies were found which pointed positively to 1874 as the time when Jesus was due to be present, and the resurrection of Daniel was also due as proved by the ending of jubilee cycles and the 1335 days of Dan. xii. The autumn of 1874, anxiously expected, finally came, but the earth rolled on as ever. "All things continued as they were from the beginning of creation." All their hearts were sad. They said, "Surely we have been in error—but where? Surely it is clearly taught; that Jesus will come again; perhaps our calculation of time is at fault." Carefully they examined the chronology but it seemed faultless and positively declared that the 6,000 years ended in 1873. Then the prophetic arguments were carefully re-examined. Was an error found? No, they stood the test of all investigation and the jubilee argument and "1335 days" of Daniel could not possibly be prolonged beyond the fall of '74 or the spring of 1875 and these periods were both past.

Dark indeed seemed the outlook; all were discouraged. It had seemed as though the Lord had been leading in the past, and yet now all these things which had been thought light seemed to be proved darkness.

Just at this time Bro. Keith, (one of our contributors) was used of the Lord to throw another beam of *light* on the subject which brought order out of confusion, and caused all of the former "light" to shine with tenfold brightness. Brother K. had been reading carefully Matt. xxiv chapter, using the translation of the New Testament; when he came to the 37th and 39th verses he was much surprised to find it read as follows, viz.: "For as the days of Noah thus will be the *presence* of the son of man. For as in those days, those before the deluge they were eating and drinking, marrying and pledging in marriage till the day that Noah entered the

Ark, and *understood not* till the Deluge came and swept them all away; thus will be the *presence* of the Son of Man."

His surprise was at finding that the Greek word *parousia* which signifies *presence*, had in our common version been improperly rendered *coming*, but the new rendering showed that it was not the act of coming that resembled the days of Noah, but that *in Noah's days* the masses of the people "*knew not*" so it would be in the time of Jesus' *presence* at the second advent. Humanity will go on eating, drinking, marrying, etc., as usual and "know not" that he is *present*. The next step was, to see whether the account of the same discourse as recorded by Luke, would harmonize with this new idea of a *presence* unseen, except by the eye of faith, until the "little flock" typified by Noah had gone from among men into the condition of safety (from the coming storm) represented by the Ark—"one taken and another left."

Luke's account was in perfect accord with Matthew's, though in different words—"As it was *in the days* of Noah so shall it be also *in the days* of the Son of Man." (Luke xvii:26.)

This was communicated to others of the disappointed ones, and with the remembrance that the time arguments above referred to had been found faultless and unalterable and proved that Jesus was due here in the fall of 1874, came the thought—Can it be possible that Jesus does not come in a fleshly body at his second advent? Can it be possible that his *presence* began at the time indicated in those prophecies, and yet we went on eating and drinking, etc., and "*knew not*" of his presence?

A careful examination of the Word was begun by all deeply interested, to see whether it, as a whole, would be in harmony with this new thought. It was found to be in perfect harmony and opened up and made clear many scriptures hitherto dark: For instance the differences between *natural, earthly bodies* and *spiritual, heavenly* bodies; how that the things which are seen are temporal, natural, but the things that are not seen are eternal, spiritual; that spiritual beings could not be seen by mortals, (without a miracle) and that the object and scope of the Gospel age was, the taking out of the world of mankind a "little flock" to be associated with Jesus in the work of the future—destroying evil and blessing all the families of the earth; that God's plan was not, to destroy all mankind after the gathering of the Gospel church but to "*restore all things*" and destroy only the evil which now rules in the world; that the *fire* supposed to be literal, was "really symbolic and signified a great time of trouble which would be the close of the Gospel age and dawn of the Millennial in which all evil principles of governments and society would be manifested and destroyed, as a necessary preparation for the coming blessing.

So says the Prophet: "Wait ye upon me, saith the Lord, until *the day* that I rise up to the prey, for my determination is to gather the nations, that I may assemble the kingdoms and pour upon them mine indignation even *all* my fierce anger for all the earth, *shall be devoured with the fire of my jealousy*; For then will I turn to the people a pure language and they shall all call upon the name of the Lord to serve him with one consent." (Zeph. iii:8-9.)

As to the manner of Christ's coming other scriptures were found to be in perfect accord with the accounts of Matt. and Luke, of its being an *unseen presence*: For instance, the angel's message—Acts i. 11.

"THIS SAME JESUS SHALL SO COME IN LIKE MANNER : as ye have seen him go into heaven." This had generally been supposed to teach that Jesus would come *in the flesh*, and be seen of men, as he was there seen of the disciples. But when carefully examined the text does not say that any one will *see* him, but that he will so come as he went away not with "flaming fire" and rolling thunder and great outward demonstration, but silently, *unknown* to the world. And if he "*so comes* in like manner," how much in harmony with Matthew's and Luke's record—they will eat and drink and know not of his presence.

But the angels' language seemed peculiar—this *same* Jesus as though there had been *another* Jesus: Examination revealed the fact, that Jesus since his resurrection is a totally different being from the Jesus who died; that a great change had taken place. While before his death he had been the "*man Christ Jesus*," having the form of a servant and perfect human powers, etc., and yet none but human powers, except as the Father's power was operated and manifested through him: (John xiv. 10.) Yet now, since his resurrection he claims *divine powers* not as the Father in him, but as his own, saying—"All power in heaven and in earth is given unto *me*" and he is no longer a natural, but a spiritual body. It was sown a natural body, raised a spiritual body—sown mor-

FOREWORD

IT IS a very responsible thing to translate the Holy Scriptures from their original languages of Hebrew, Aramaic and Greek into modern speech. Translating the Holy Scriptures means rendering into another language the thoughts and sayings of Jehovah God, the heavenly Author of this sacred library of sixty-six books that holy men of long ago were inspired to write down for our benefit today.

That is a very sobering thought. The translators of this work, who fear and love the Divine Author of the Holy Scriptures, feel toward Him a special responsibility to transmit his thoughts and declarations as accurately as possible. They also feel a responsibility toward the searching readers who depend upon a translation of the inspired Word of the Most High God for their everlasting salvation.

It was with such a sense of solemn responsibility that over the course of many years this committee of dedicated men have produced the *New World Translation of the Holy Scriptures*. The entire work was originally released in six volumes, from 1950 to 1960. From the start it was the desire of the translators to have all these volumes brought together into one book, inasmuch as the Holy Scriptures are in actuality one book by the One Author. While the original volumes contained marginal references and footnotes, the revised one-volume edition, released in 1961, contained neither footnotes nor marginal references. A second revision was released in 1970 and a third revision with footnotes followed in 1971. In 1969 the committee released *The Kingdom Interlinear Translation of the Greek Scriptures*—which presented under the Greek text revised by Westcott and Hort (1948 Reprint) a literal word-for-word translation into English. During the past 34 years the *New World Translation* has been translated in part or in its entirety into ten other languages, with a total printing and distribution surpassing 39 million.

This new edition is not just a refinement of the translated text beyond its already previous revisions, but it has been expanded to include a complete updating and revision of the marginal (cross) references that were initially presented in English, from 1950 to 1960.

This 1984 revision has been released by us to the Watch Tower Bible and Tract Society of Pennsylvania for printing, translation into other leading languages and distribution. We thus make it available with a deep sense of gratitude to the Divine Author of the Holy Scriptures, who has so privileged us and in whose spirit we have trusted in producing this revision. We pray for his blessing upon those who use this translation for spiritual advancement.

New World Bible Translation Committee

June 1, 1984, New York, N.Y.

5

PUBLISHERS
WATCHTOWER BIBLE AND TRACT SOCIETY
OF NEW YORK, INC.
International Bible Students Association
Brooklyn, New York, U.S.A.

Complete editions published in Czech, Danish, Dutch, English (also Braille), French, German, Italian, Japanese, Portuguese (also Braille), Slovak, Spanish, and Swedish
(Also in part in Cebuano, Finnish, Greek, Iloko, Norwegian, and Tagalog)

Total complete *New World Translations* printed of all editions:
74,200,000 Copies

New World Translation of the Holy Scriptures
English (*bi12-E*)

Made in the United States of America

53

COURT OF SESSION, SCOTLAND.

A   LORD STRACHAN.

P R O O F

B   I.C.

DOUGLAS WALSH

v.

C   THE RIGHT HONOURABLE JAMES
LATHAM CLYDE, M.P., P.C., as
representing the Minister of
Labour and National Service.

Tuesday, 23rd November, 1954.

D

Counsel for the Pursuer:-   The Dean of Faculty,
(Sir John Cameron, Q.C.), Mr. Emslie, and Miss
Clark Hutchison.

E   Counsel for the Defender:-   Mr. Leslie, Q.C., and
Mr. Kissen.

P U R S U E R ' S   P R O O F

F   FREDERICK WILLIAM FRANZ (61)

EXAMINED:- I reside at Brooklyn, King's County,

New/   54

83

F.W.Franz

A Q. Have you also made yourself familiar with Hebrew? A.
Yes. Q. Do you also know and speak Spanish Portuguese
and French A. Spanish Portuguese and German, but I
have a reading knowledge of French. Q. So that you have
a substantial linguistic apparatus at your command? A.

B Yes, for use in my biblical work. Q. I think you are able
to read and follow the Bible in Hebrew, Greek. Latin,
Spanish. Portuguese. German and French? A. Yes. Q. It
is the case, is it not, that in 1950 there was prepared
and issued what is called the New World Translation of

C the Christian Greek Scriptures? A. Yes. (Shown No. 41
of Process) I recognise that as an authentic copy of the
New World Translation of the Christian Greek Scriptures
issued in the summer of 1950. Q. That. as it shows,
bears to be the New World Translation of the Christian

D Greek Scriptures rendered from the original language by
the New World Biblical Translation Committee, A.D. 1950?
A. Yes. Q. That is on the flyleaf? A. Yes. Q. And
I see that it is copyrighted by the Watchtower Bible and
Tract Society and published by the Watchtower Bible and

E Tract Society Incorporated, and made in the U.S.A.? A.
Yes. Q. And I think you have a foreword. Are you
responsible yourself for the foreword? A. That is
is prepared by the Translation Committee as the
signature will show. Q. And are the Christian Greek

F Scriptures referred to there what are usually called
the/   55   DOUGLAS WALSH TRIAL, 1954

84

A   tho Now Toatamont? A. That is truo. Q. I think that
it was your duty, was it not, before tho issuo of that
NEW World Translation by your Society to shock that
translation for accuracy? A. That is truo. Q. In light
of your studios and in light of your knowledge? A. That

B   is truo. Q. And did you do so? A. I did so. Q. I think,
as tho book shows, that there was a substantial printing
of that translation? The first edition was 480,000 copios
and tho second edition was 1.000,000? A. Yes. Q. So
that at least one and a half million copies have been issued;

C   is that right? A. That is true. Q. And have these
been issued in connection with the work of the Sociaty all
over the world? A. Yes, particularly in English-speaking
countries. Q. I should ask you this: has that version
been translated into any other language than English? A.

D   No. Q. It is an English translation? A. Yes. Q. So
may I take it in round figures that you have published
and disseminated something like one and a half million
copies of that translation under the authority of your
Society? A. Yes. Q. And does the Society regard

E   it as an authoritative translation of the New Testament
Scriptures? A. Yes. Q. And as the foundation of
Bible study in English-speaking lands amongst members
of the Society with regard to the New Testamont? A.
Yes. Q. In 1952 was there a similar translation of

F   the/

DOUGLAS WALSH TRIAL, 1954
56

9   F.W. Franz

A   the Hebrew Scriptures issued by and on behalf of the

Society? A. In 1953. Q. Would you look at No. 42

of proofs. Is that a first volume of the New World

Translation of the Hebrew Scriptures? A. Yes, that is.

Q. And that is a translation of the books of the Old

B   Testament up to and including the Book of Ruth? A. Yes,

known as the pentatouch. Q. And was it your duty on

behalf of the society to check the translation into

English from the original Hebrew of that first volume of

the Old Testament Scriptures? A. Yes. Q. I think that the

C   flyleaf shows that the first edition of half a million

copies was printed and published? A. Yes. Q. And has

that been distributed? A. I could not say. Q. You

cannot say about that? A. No. Q. Anyway that would be

the published edition? A. Yes. Q. Have you in fact

D   received favourable comments on these two volumes? A.

We have. Q. From scholars and theologians who are wholly

unconnected with the Society? A. That is true. Q. I

want to ask you now some of the simple and fundamental

matters about the Association which is now called

E   Jehovah's Witnesses. In the first place are Jehovah's

Witnesses an association of Christian people? A. Yes.

Q. Is it an international Association? A. Yes. Q.

Have you congregations all over the world? A. Yes.

Q. Perhaps you would look at the Year Book for 1954

F   No. 38 of Process. Is that one of the most recent of

the/   DOUGLAS WALSH TRIAL, 1954
57

86

published in English.   Q. In so far as translation of
the Bible itself is undertaken, are you responsible for
that?   A. I have been authorised to examine a translation and determine its accuracy and recommend its acceptance in the form in which it is submitted.   Q Are the
translators members of the Editorial Committee?   A. That
is a question which I, as a member of the Board of Directors,
am not authorised to disclose, because when the translation
was donated to the Society at a meeting of the Board of
Directors there, the Translation Committee made it known
that they did not wish their names to be disclosed, and
the Board of Directors, acting for the Society, accepted
the translation upon that basis, that the names would not
be revealed now or after death.   Q. Are the translators
all members of Jehovah's Witnesses?   A. That again is
part and parcel of the agreement that their names shall
not be revealed.   They are consecrated men as the foreword
to the translation discloses.   Q. It is awfully important,
isn't it, to beware of false prophets?   A. That is right.
Q. Is it the view of your theocratic organisation that the
qualifications of translators and interpreters of the
Scriptures should be kept secret?   A. That is the business
of the Translation Committee.   They can make a donation on
their own terms and we can accept it.   The Society can
accept it on their terms.   Q. You are speaking now of
donations /   DOUGLAS WALSH TRIAL, 1954
                58

91.   F.W.Frunz
                                        (Cross)

A   and treasurer? A. Yes. Q. You yourself are multi-
     lingual? A. Yes. Q. At what age did you go to
     Cincinnati University? A. I entered the University
     in 1913, after graduating from Woodward High School
     and I continued there until April 1914. Q. When did you
B   go to the University? A. In 1911, and I continued there
     until April 1914. Q. Did you graduate? A. No, I
     did not. I left the University in 1914 because I realised,
     according to the Scriptures, that that was the crucial
     year which was to be marked by the outbreak of a great
C   trouble, and I realised that the ministerial work was
     the most important thing in the world to do and I wanted
     to get into the ministerial work before the great trouble
     broke, and so I wanted to get in earlier but my father
     refused to permit me to leave the University, because I
D   was still under 21.   In April of 1914 he acceded to
     my wishes and allowed me to leave the University, and
     I immediately entered full time ministerial service
     as a pioneer. Q. What subjects were you studying
     at Cincinnati University? A. I was studying in the
E   Liberal Arts College and among other things taking up
     Chemistry, English, Latin, Greek and German. Q. Had
     you done any Hebrew in the course of your University
     work? A. No, I had not, but in the course of my
     editorial work, my special research work for the president
F   of/

          DOUGLAS WALSH TRIAL, 1954
               59

88

92.   F.W. Franz
        (Cross)

A   of the Society, I found it was very necessary to have a
knowledge of Hebrew, and so I undertook a personal
study of that.   Q.   What subjects did you hold passes-
in when at Cincinna'i University?   A. Passes?   Q.
I do not know whether you work there the same as we do
B   here, but after the anguish of examination you got a
certificate saying you have passed certain subjects.
Do you work that way in America?   A. Well I passed the
junior year of the University, and I did not complete the
third year.   I left in April and the term terminated at the
C   beginning of June.   Q.   What subjects did you have
passes when you left the University?   A.   I had passed
through Greek and Latin and I had also taken two terms
in German.   Q.   Did you do Hellenic Greek?   A. Yes,
as well as cdined Greek, the Greek of the New Testament.
D   Q.   Were you yourself responsible for the translation
of the Old Testament?— A. Again I cannot answer that
question, in harmony with the gentleman's agreement
made by the Board of Directors and the Translation
Committee.   Q.   Why the secrecy?   A.   Because the
E   Committee of Translation wanted it to remain anonymous
and not seek any glory or honour at the making of a
translation, and having any names attached thereto.
Q.   Writers of books and translators do not always get
glory and honour for their efforts, do they?   A.   But
F   �) DOUGLAS WALSH TRIAL, 1954

60

102.   F.W. Franz.
                                 (Cross.)

Wednesday, 24th November, 1954.

PURSUER'S PROOF CONTINUED

FREDERICK WILLIAM FRANZ (61)

CROSS CONTINUED: Q. First, I just wanted to
get from you the Officers of the various societies.
Of the Watch Tower Bible and Tract Society,
Pennsylvania, the Officers are, President, Mr. Knorr?
A. Yes.   Q. Vice-President yourself?   A. Yes.
Q. And Secretary and Treasurer, Mr. Grant Souter?
A. Yes.   Q. These sa me three are the Officers of
the Watch Tower Bible and Tract Society Incorporated of
New York? A. The Year Book shows that.   Q. Then
for the International Bible Students Association in
London, the Officers are, President, Mr. Knorr,
Vice-President, Mr. A. Pryce Hughes, Secretary E.C.
Chitty, and Mr. Grant Souter is t he Assistant Secretary
and Treasurer.   Would you look, please, at No. 42 of
Process, which is the New World translation of the
Hebrew Scriptures.   I think we come to the name
Jehovah in the fourth verse, don't we, of the Second
Chapter of Genesis, Page 34?   A. Yes.   Q. You,
yourself, read and speak Hebrew, do you?   A. I do
not speak Hebrew.   Q. You do not? A. No.   Q. Can
you, yourself, translate that into Hebrew?   A. Which?
Q. That fourth verse of the Second Chapter of Genesis?
A. You mean here?   Q. Yes?   A. No. I won't
attempt/   DOUGLAS WALSH TRIAL, 1954
                        61

90

·103·   F.W. Franz.
                                     (Cross.)

A   <u>attempt to do that.</u> Q. As the footnote there shows, and I understand correctly, the name Jehova. in the original Hebrew consisted simply of consonants? A. That is right. Q. It was called the Tetragrammaton? A. Yes. Q. Do you subscribe to the view that in Ancient Hebrew it was the ineffable name which was not to be pronounced?

B   A. According to the Jewish tradition which developed later on after the closing of the Calan that was not to be pronounced. Q. But you follow later manuscripts, do you, in inserting vowels to make it a word which may be pronounced? A. Yes. The Masseritic text contains the

C   vowels. That is the traditional text. Q. Do you, yourself, speak Aramaic? A. No. Q. The Book of Daniel is partly in Hebrew and partly in Aramaic in the original, isn't it? A. That is correct. Q. I think we get the same thing, don't we, in the Prophets such as

D   Ezra and Nehemiah? A. In Ezra, yes, and there are Aramaic words scattered throughout various Books of the Bible. Q. Did you O.K., as you put it yesterday, the text of the translations of the Books of Ezra and of Daniel in No. 42 of Process? A. No. Q. You said yesterday, I think, that the Society had modified its views in various respects as time passed? A. That is right. Q. I may assume, may I, that you, yourself, have anxiously and carefully studied the whole

E   literature of your movement from the beginning? A. Yes. Q. Am I right that you put what is described as the end of/   62 DOUGLAS WALSH TRIAL, 1954

The Kingdom Interlinear Translation of the Greek Scriptures

Presenting a literal word-for-word translation into English under the Greek text as set out in "The New Testament in the Original Greek—The Text Revised by Brooke Foss Westcott D.D. and Fenton John Anthony Hort D.D." (1948 Reprint)

together with the

New World Translation of the Christian Greek Scriptures, Revised Edition, a modern-language translation of the Westcott and Hort Greek Text, first published by them in the year 1881 C.E., with which are included the valuable Foreword and the Appendix of the said translation, with numerous footnotes and an Explanation of the Symbols Used in the Marginal References

PRODUCED BY

New World Bible Translation Committee

—1969 C.E.—

"OUR FATHER IN THE HEAVENS, LET YOUR NAME BE SANCTIFIED. LET YOUR KINGDOM COME. LET YOUR WILL TAKE PLACE, AS IN HEAVEN, ALSO UPON EARTH."—Matthew 6:9, 10, *NW*.

63

92

BY WAY OF EXPLANATION

The Christian Greek Scriptures, completed near the end of the first century of our Common Era, are an indispensable part of the Sacred Scriptures inspired by the Creator of heaven and earth. In fact, the original Greek Scriptures give us the key to the proper understanding of the first and larger part of the Holy Bible, that is, the inspired Hebrew Scriptures, commonly called "The Old Testament." Comparatively few persons in this latter half of the 20th century have studied the original language of the inspired Greek Scriptures so as to be able to enjoy directly the basic thoughts of the original written text. The inspired Greek Scriptures were written in *koi-ne'* (common) Greek of the first century of our Common Era, the international language of that period of time.

Sincere searchers for eternal, life-giving truth desire an accurate understanding of the faith-inspiring Greek Scriptures, an understanding that is fortified by the knowledge of what the original language says and means. The purpose behind the publishing of *The Kingdom Interlinear Translation of The Greek Scriptures* is to aid such seekers of truth and life. Its literal Interlinear English translation is specially designed to open up to the student of the Sacred Scriptures what the original *koi-ne'* Greek basically or literally says.

In the broad left-hand column of the pages will be found the Greek text edited by B. F. Westcott and F. J. A. Hort, and published in 1881. Between the lines of the Greek text will be found the word-for-word English translation of 1969. In the narrower right-hand column of the pages will be found the 20th-century *New World Translation of the Holy Scriptures*, Matthew to Revelation, in its 1984 revision. The word-for-word interlinear translation and the *New World Translation* are arranged in parallel on the page, so that comparisons can be made between the two readings. Thus, the accuracy of any modern translation can be determined.

The interlinear word-for-word rendering has not been made by taking the English word or phrase from the modern translation in the right-hand column and transferring it to a position under the Greek word to which it corresponds. Rather, the translation under each Greek word sets out what the Greek word itself says according to its root meanings (where the Greek word is made up of two or more particles) and according to its grammatical form. So in many cases the reading in the English word-for-word interlinear translation is not the same as that found in the right-hand column. This helps one to determine what the Greek text actually, basically says. In using these interlinear readings, one will find a greater demand for scrutiny than when reading the

5

ness have been insinuated into the teachings of the inspired writings.

The Son of God taught that the traditions of creed-bound men made the commandments and teachings of God to be without power or effect. The endeavor of the New World Bible Translation Committee has been to avoid this snare of religious traditionalism. This very effort distinguishes this work as a translation of the "Christian Greek Scriptures." It is a traditional mistake to divide God's written Word into two sections and call the second section, from Matthew to Revelation (or Apocalypse), "The New Testament".—See Appendix 5D.

No uninspired translator or committee of translators can claim any direct command from the Most High God to engage in translating the divine Word into another language. But translation of it is necessary, and that into many languages, if Christ's command for this momentous day is to be fulfilled: "This good news of the kingdom will be preached in all the inhabited earth for a witness to all the nations; and then the end will come." (Matthew 24:14) So, to do the work of translating is a privilege. In presenting this translation of the Christian Greek Scriptures, our confidence has been in the help of the great Author of The Book. Our primary desire has been to seek not the approval of men but that of God, by rendering the truth of his inspired Word as purely and as consistently as our dedicated abilities make possible. There is no benefit in self-deception. More than that, those who provide a translation for the spiritual instruction of others come under a special responsibility as teachers before the Divine Judge. Hence, we are aware of the need to be careful.

*

GREEK TEXT: The Greek text that we have used as the basis for the New World Translation is the widely accepted

Westcott and Hort text (1881), by reason of its acknowledged excellence.* But we have also taken into consideration other texts, including those prepared by D. Eberhard Nestle," the Spanish Jesuit scholar José Maria Bover,^ and another Jesuit scholar, A. Merk." The UBS text of 1975 and the Nestle-Aland text of 1979 were consulted to update the critical apparatus of this edition.

We have disposed of archaic language altogether, even in using the now-sanctimonious formal pronouns *thou, thy, thine, thee,* and *ye,* with their corresponding verb inflections. The original Bible was written in the living languages of the people of the day, Hebrew, Aramaic, and Greek; and so the Bible characters addressed God and prayed to him in the same everyday language that they employed in speaking to their fellow creatures on earth. The translation of the Scriptures into a modern language should be rendered in the same style, in the speech forms current among the people. We offer no paraphrase of the Scriptures. Our endeavor throughout has been to give as literal a translation as possible where the modern English idiom allows for it or wardness in the literal rendition. In this way, we can best meet the desire of those who are scrupulous for getting, as nearly as possible word for word, the exact statement of the original. We realize that sometimes the use of so small a thing as the definite or indefinite article or the omission of such may alter the correct sense of the original passage.

* Besides using the 1948 Macmillan Company edition of this text, we have availed ourselves of the two exhaustive volumes on Matthew and Mark, prepared under the supervision of S. C. E. Legg, A.M., and published by the Oxford Clarendon Press, *Novum Testamentum Graece Secundum Textum Westcotto-Hortianum—Evangelium Secundum Matthaeum* (1940) and *Evangelium Secundum Marcum* (1935).

" The 18th edition of *Novum Testamentum Graece* by D. Eberhard Nestle, elaborated by D. Erwin Nestle, published in 1948 by the Württemberg Bible Society, Stuttgart, Germany.

^ *Novum Testamenti Biblia Graeca et Latina* by José M. Bover, S.J., dated 1943 and published at Barcelona, Spain.

" The 1948 printing of the sixth edition of *Novum Testamentum Graece et Latina* by Augustinus Merk, S.J., and printed at Rome, Italy.

Close watch has been kept against taking liberties with texts merely for the sake of brevity or shortcuts and against substitution of a modern parallel where the rendering of the original idea makes good sense. To each major word we have assigned one meaning and have held to that meaning as far as the context permitted. This, indeed, has imposed a restriction upon our diction, yet it makes for good cross-reference work and for a more reliable comparison of related texts or verses. At the same time, in order to bring out the richness and variety of the language of the inspired writers, we have avoided the rendering of two or more Greek words by the same English word, for this hides the distinction in shade of meaning between the several words thus rendered. Attention has been given to the tenses of verbs to bring out the intended description of the action, position, or state. As the reader becomes familiar with our translation he will discern more and more the harmony and interagreement of our renderings in all these respects.

CHAPTER AND VERSE NUMBERING: This follows that of the *King James Version*, thus making possible easy comparison. But, instead of making each verse a separate paragraph in itself, we have grouped verses into paragraphs for the proper development of a complete thought in all its context. Mindful of the Hebrew background of the Christian Greek Scriptures, we have followed mainly the Hebrew spelling of the names of persons and places, rather than that of the Greek text, which imitates the Greek *Septuagint* translation (*LXX*) of the Hebrew Scriptures.

RESTORING THE DIVINE NAME, JEHOVAH: The evidence is that the original text of the Christian Greek Scriptures has been tampered with, the same as the text of the *LXX* has been. (See App 1A, B.) Sometime during the second or third centuries C.E., the Tetragrammaton (*YHWH*, or *JHVH*) was eliminated from the Greek text by copyists who did not understand or appreciate the divine name or who developed an aversion to it, possibly under the influence of anti-

Semitism. Instead of *YHWH* (or, *JHVH*) they substituted the words *Ky'ri·os*, "Lord," and *The·os'*, "God."

In view of this, what is the modern translator to do? Is he justified or authorized in entering the divine name, Jehovah, into a translation of the Christian Greek Scriptures? In the *LXX* the Greek words *Ky'ri·os* and *The·os'* have been used to crowd out the distinctive name of the Supreme Deity. Every comprehensive Greek-English dictionary states that these two Greek words have been used as equivalents of the divine name.* Hence, the modern translator is warranted in using the divine name as an equivalent of those two Greek words, that is, at places where the writers of the Christian Greek Scriptures quote verses, passages, and expressions from the Hebrew Scriptures or from the *LXX* where the divine name occurs.

Throughout the centuries many translations of parts or of all the Christian Greek Scriptures have been made into Hebrew. Such translations, designated in this work by "J" with a superior number, have restored the divine name to the Christian Greek Scriptures in various places. They have restored the divine name not only when coming upon quotations from the Hebrew Scriptures but also in other places where the texts called for such restoration.

How may modern translators determine when to render the Greek words *Ky'ri·os* and *The·os'* as the divine name? By determining where the inspired Christian writers have quoted from the Hebrew Scriptures. Then they must refer

_____
* *A Greek and English Lexicon to the New Testament*, by J. Parkhurst, revised ed. of 1845, says, on p. 347, under ΚΥΡΙΟΣ: "III. In LXX it answers frequently to יהוה: ... In the N. T. likewise Κύριος, when used as a name of God, though it sometimes answers to יהוה, yet it most usually corresponds to יהוה—*Jehovah*, and in this sense is applied."

A Greek-English Lexicon of the New Testament, by J. H. Thayer, 1889 ed., p. 365, says under ... universe (so the Sept. for יהוה, יהוה, and Jah]), ... Op. 281 it says, under θεός; "Sept. for ... 'c. this title is given α. to God, the ruler of the universe ... 'elo·him', Jehovah, and Jah]). ... Says *A Greek-English Lexicon*, by Liddell and Scott, 1968 ed., on p. 1013, under κύριος: "B....4. ὁ Κύριος,=Hebr. *Yahweh*, Lxx *Ge.*11.5, al."

Colossians 1:28—2:5 (882)

ὅ ἐστιν Χριστὸς ἐν ὑμῖν, ἡ ἐλπὶς τῆς
which is Christ in you, the hope of the

δόξης· 28 ὃν ἡμεῖς καταγγέλλομεν
glory; whom we are announcing down

νουθετοῦντες πάντα ἄνθρωπον καὶ
putting mind into every man and

διδάσκοντες πάντα ἄνθρωπον ἐν πάσῃ σοφίᾳ,
teaching every man in all wisdom,

ἵνα παραστήσωμεν πάντα ἄνθρωπον
in order that we might present every man

τέλειον ἐν Χριστῷ· 29 εἰς ὃ καὶ
perfect in Christ; into which also

κοπιῶ ἀγωνιζόμενος κατὰ τὴν
I am laboring struggling according to the

ἐνέργειαν αὐτοῦ τὴν ἐνεργουμένην ἐν
operation within of him the operating within in

ἐμοὶ ἐν δυνάμει.
me in power.

2 Θέλω γὰρ ὑμᾶς εἰδέναι ἡλίκον
I am willing for you to have known how great

ἀγῶνα ἔχω ὑπὲρ ὑμῶν καὶ τῶν
struggle I am having over you and of the (ones)

ἐν Λαοδικείᾳ καὶ ὅσοι οὐχ ἑόρακαν
in Laodicea and as many as not have seen

τὸ πρόσωπόν μου ἐν σαρκί, 2 ἵνα
the face of me in flesh, in order that

παρακληθῶσιν αἱ καρδίαι αὐτῶν,
might be comforted the hearts of them,

συμβιβασθέντες ἐν ἀγάπῃ καὶ
having been made to go together in love and

εἰς πᾶν πλοῦτος τῆς πληροφορίας τῆς
into all riches of the fully being borne of the

συνέσεως, εἰς ἐπίγνωσιν τοῦ
comprehension, into accurate knowledge of the

μυστηρίου τοῦ θεοῦ, Χριστοῦ, 3 ἐν ᾧ
mystery of the God, of Christ, in whom

εἰσὶν πάντες οἱ θησαυροὶ τῆς σοφίας
are all the treasures of the wisdom

καὶ γνώσεως ἀπόκρυφοι.
and of knowledge hidden away.

4 Τοῦτο λέγω ἵνα μηδεὶς ὑμᾶς
This I am saying in order that no one you

παραλογίζηται ἐν πιθανολογίᾳ. 5 εἰ γὰρ
may be deluding in persuasive saying. If for

καὶ τῇ σαρκὶ ἄπειμι, ἀλλὰ τῷ
even to the flesh I am absent, but to the

πνεύματι σὺν ὑμῖν εἰμι, χαίρων καὶ
spirit together with you I am, rejoicing and

Translation: It is Christ in union with you, the hope of [his] glory. 28 He is the one we are publicizing, admonishing every man and teaching every man in all wisdom, that we may present every man complete in union with Christ. 29 To this end I am indeed working hard, exerting myself in accordance with the operation of him and which is at work in me with power.

2 For I want you to realize how great a struggle I am having in behalf of you and of those at La-odi-ce'a and of all those who have not seen my face in the flesh, 2 that their hearts may be comforted, that they may be harmoniously joined together in love and with a view to all the riches of the full assurance of [their] understanding, with a view to an accurate knowledge of the sacred secret of God, namely, Christ. 3 Carefully concealed in him are all the treasures of wisdom and of knowledge. 4 This I am saying that no man may delude you with persuasive arguments. 5 For though I am absent in the flesh, all the same I am with you in the spirit, rejoicing and

Colossians 2:6—12 (883)

βλέπων ὑμῶν τὴν τάξιν καὶ τὸ στερέωμα
seeing of you the line-up and the firmness

τῆς εἰς Χριστὸν πίστεως ὑμῶν.
of the into Christ faith of you.

6 Ὡς οὖν παρελάβετε τὸν
As therefore you received alongside the

Χριστὸν Ἰησοῦν τὸν κύριον, ἐν αὐτῷ
Christ Jesus the Lord, in him

περιπατεῖτε, 7 ἐρριζωμένοι καὶ
be you walking, having been rooted and

ἐποικοδομούμενοι ἐν αὐτῷ καὶ βεβαιούμενοι
being built upon in him and being stabilized

τῇ πίστει καθὼς ἐδιδάχθητε,
to the faith according as you were taught,

περισσεύοντες ἐν αὐτῇ ἐν εὐχαριστίᾳ.
abounding in it in thanksgiving.

8 Βλέπετε μή τις ὑμᾶς ἔσται
Be you looking at not someone you will be

ὁ συλαγωγῶν διὰ τῆς
(the one) leading as booty through the

φιλοσοφίας καὶ κενῆς ἀπάτης κατὰ
philosophy and empty seduction according to

τὴν παράδοσιν τῶν ἀνθρώπων, κατὰ
the tradition of the men, according to

τὰ στοιχεῖα τοῦ κόσμου καὶ οὐ
the elementary things of the world and not

κατὰ Χριστόν· 9 ὅτι ἐν αὐτῷ
according to Christ; because in him

κατοικεῖ πᾶν τὸ πλήρωμα τῆς θεότητος
is dwelling down all the fullness of the divinity

σωματικῶς, 10 καὶ ἐστὲ ἐν αὐτῷ
bodily, and you are in him

πεπληρωμένοι, ὅς ἐστιν ἡ κεφαλὴ
(ones) having been filled, who is the head

πάσης ἀρχῆς καὶ ἐξουσίας, 11 ἐν ᾧ
of all government and of authority, in whom

καὶ περιετμήθητε περιτομῇ
also you were circumcised to circumcision

ἀχειροποιήτῳ ἐν τῇ ἀπεκδύσει τοῦ
not done by hand in the stripping off of the

σώματος τῆς σαρκός, ἐν τῇ περιτομῇ
body of the flesh, in the circumcision

τοῦ Χριστοῦ, 12 συνταφέντες
of the Christ, having been jointly buried

αὐτῷ ἐν τῷ βαπτίσματι, ἐν ᾧ καὶ
to him in the baptism, in whom also

συνηγέρθητε διὰ τῆς πίστεως
you were jointly raised up through the faith

Translation: beholding your good order and the firmness of youa faith toward Christ.

6 Therefore, as you have accepted Christ Jesus the Lord, go on walking in union with him, 7 rooted and being built up in him and being stabilized in the faith, just as you were taught, overflowing with [faith] in thanksgiving.

8 Look out: perhaps there may be someone who will carry you off as his prey through the philosophy and empty deception according to the tradition of men, according to the elementary things of the world and not according to Christ; 9 because it is in him that all the fullness of the divine quality dwells bodily. 10 And so you are possessed of a fullness by means of him, who is the head of all government and authority. 11 By relationship with him you were also circumcised with a circumcision performed without hands by the stripping off of the body of the flesh, by the circumcision that belongs to the Christ, 12 for you were buried with him in [this] baptism, and by relationship with him you were also raised up together through [your] faith

67

The New Thayer's GREEK ENGLISH LEXICON OF THE NEW TESTAMENT, 1974

COLOSSIANS 1:16—21   880

the image of the invisible God, the first-born of all creation; 16 because by means of him all [other] things were created in the heavens and upon the earth, the things visible and the things invisible, no matter whether they are thrones or lordships or governments or authorities. All [other] things have been created through him and for him. 17 Also, he is before all [other] things and by means of him all [other] things were made to exist, 18 and he is the head of the body, the congregation. He is the beginning, the firstborn from the dead, that he might become the one who is first in all things; 19 because [God] saw good for all fullness to dwell in him, 20 and through him to reconcile again to himself all [other] things by making peace through the blood [he shed] on the torture stake, no matter whether they are the things upon the earth or the things in the heavens. 21 Indeed, you who were once alienated and enemies because YOUR minds were on the works that were

16° All [other], as in Luke 11:41, 42.   20° See App 3C.

881   COLOSSIANS 1:22—27

wicked, 22 he now has again reconciled by means of that one's fleshly body through [his] death, in order to present YOU holy and unblemished and open to no accusation before him, 23 provided, of course, that YOU continue in the faith, established on the foundation and steadfast and not being shifted away from the hope of that good news which YOU heard, and which was preached in all creation that is under heaven. Of this [good news] I Paul became a minister. 24 I am now rejoicing in my sufferings for YOU, and I, in my turn, am filling up what is lacking of the tribulations of the Christ in my flesh on behalf of his body, which is the congregation. 25 I became a minister of this [congregation] in accordance with the stewardship from God which was given me in YOUR interest to preach the word of God fully, 26 the sacred secret that was hidden from the past systems of things and from the past generations. But now it has been made manifest to his holy ones, 27 to whom God has been pleased to make known what are the glorious riches of this sacred secret among the nations.

69

GALATIANS 2:20—3:6 — 830

νόμῳ ἀπέθανον ἵνα
law I died In order that

Χριστῷ συνεσταύρωμαι. ζῶ δὲ
to Christ I have been put on stake together. I am living but

20 Χριστῷ δὲ ἐν ἐμοὶ
to Christ but in me

... Indeed, the life that I now live in flesh I live by the faith that is toward the Son of God, who loved me and handed himself over for me.

21 I do not shove aside the undeserved kindness of God; for if righteousness is through law, Christ actually died for nothing.

3 O senseless Galatians, who is it that brought you under evil influence, you before whose eyes Jesus Christ was openly portrayed impaled? 2 This alone I want to learn from you: Did you receive the spirit due to works of law or due to a hearing by faith? 3 Are you so senseless? After starting in spirit are you now being completed in flesh? 4 Did you undergo so many sufferings to no purpose? If it really was to no purpose. 5 He, therefore, who supplies you the spirit and performs powerful works among you, does he do it owing to works of law or owing to a hearing by faith? 6 Just as

831 — GALATIANS 3:7—13

Ἀβραάμ ἐπίστευσεν τῷ Θεῷ, καὶ
Abraham believed to the God, and

ἐλογίσθη αὐτῷ εἰς δικαιοσύνην.
it was reckoned to him into righteousness.

7 Γινώσκετε ὅτι οἱ ἐκ
Are you knowing that the the (ones) out of

πίστεως, οὗτοι υἱοί εἰσιν Ἀβραάμ.
faith, these sons are of Abraham.

8 προϊδοῦσα δὲ ἡ γραφὴ ὅτι
Having seen before but the scripture that

10 Ὅσοι γὰρ ἐξ ἔργων νόμου εἰσὶν
As many as for out of works of law they are

...

13 Χριστὸς ἡμᾶς ἐξηγόρασεν ἐκ τῆς
Christ us bought out out of the

νόμου κατάρας γενόμενος
of the Law curse having become

Abraham "put faith in Jehovah," and it was counted to him as righteousness." 7 Surely you know that those who adhere to faith are the ones who are sons of Abraham. 8 Now the Scripture, seeing in advance that God would declare people of the nations righteous due to faith, declared the good news beforehand to Abraham, namely: "By means of you all the nations will be blessed." 9 Consequently those who adhere to faith are being blessed together with faithful Abraham.

10 For all those who depend upon works of law are under a curse; for it is written: "Cursed is every one that does not continue in all the things written in the scroll of the Law in order to do them." 11 Moreover, that by law no one is declared righteous with God is evident, because "the righteous one will live by reason of faith." 12 Now the Law does not adhere to faith, but "he that does them shall live by means of them." 13 Christ by purchase released us from the curse of the Law by becoming

6* Jehovah, J7,8 (compare Romans 4:3); God, P46אABJ13,14,17,18VgSyp

2 CORINTHIANS 13:1-7   822

13 This is the third time I am coming to YOU. "At the mouth of two witnesses or of three every matter must be established". 2 I have said previously and, as if present the second time and yet absent now, I say in advance to those who have sinned before and to all the rest, that if ever I come again I will not spare, 3 since YOU are seeking a proof of Christ speaking in me, [Christ] who is not weak toward YOU but is powerful among YOU. 4 True, indeed, he was impaled owing to weakness, but he is alive owing to God's power. For, indeed, we are weak with him, but we shall live together with him owing to God's power toward YOU.

5 Keep testing whether YOU are in the faith, keep proving what YOU yourselves are. Or do YOU not recognize that Jesus Christ is in union with YOU? Unless YOU are disapproved. 6 I truly hope YOU will come to know we are not disapproved. 7 Now we pray to God that YOU may do nothing wrong, not that we ourselves may appear approved, but that

823   **2 CORINTHIANS 13:8-14**

YOU may be doing what is fine, though we ourselves may appear disapproved. 8 For we can do nothing against the truth, but only for the truth. 9 We certainly rejoice whenever we are weak but YOU are powerful; and for this we are praying, YOUR being readjusted. 10 That is why I write these things while absent, that, when I am present, I may not act with severity according to the authority that the Lord gave me, to build up and not to tear down.

11 Finally, brothers, continue to rejoice, to be readjusted, to be comforted, to think in agreement, to live peaceably; and the God of love and of peace will be with YOU. 12 Greet one another with a holy kiss. 13 All the holy ones send YOU their greetings.

14 The undeserved kindness of the Lord Jesus Christ and the love of God and the sharing in the holy spirit be with all of YOU.

PHILIPPIANS 3:4-10 — 872

have our boasting in Christ Jesus and do not have our confidence in the flesh, 4 though I, if anyone, do have grounds for confidence also in the flesh.

If any other man thinks he has grounds for confidence in the flesh, I the more so: 5 circumcised the eighth day, out of the family stock of Israel, of the tribe of Benjamin, a Hebrew [born] from Hebrews; as respects law, a Pharisee; 6 as respects zeal, persecuting the congregation; as respects righteousness that is by means of law, one who proved himself blameless. 7 Yet what things were gains to me, these I have considered loss on account of the Christ. 8 Why, for that matter, I do indeed also consider all things to be loss on account of the excelling value of the knowledge of Christ Jesus my Lord. On account of him I have taken the loss of all things and I consider them as a lot of refuse, that I may gain Christ 9 and be found in union with him, having, not my own righteousness, which results from law, but that which is through faith in Christ, the righteousness that issues from God on the basis of faith, 10 so as to know him and the power of his resurrection and a sharing of his sufferings, submitting myself to a death like his,

873 — PHILIPPIANS 3:11-18

11 [to see] if I may by any means attain to the earlier resurrection from the dead. 12 Not that I have already received it or am already made perfect, but I am pursuing to see if I may also lay hold on that for which I have also been laid hold on by Christ Jesus. 13 Brothers, I do not yet consider myself as having laid hold on it; but there is one thing about it: Forgetting the things behind and stretching forward to the things ahead, 14 I am pursuing down toward the goal for the prize of the upward call of God by means of Christ Jesus. 15 Let us, then, as many of us as are mature, be of this mental attitude; and if you are mentally inclined otherwise in any respect, God will reveal the above [attitude] to you. 16 At any rate, to what extent we have made progress, let us go on walking orderly in this same routine.

17 Unitedly become imitators of me, brothers, and keep YOUR eye on those who are walking in a way that accords with the example YOU have in us. 18 For there are many, I used to mention them often but now I mention them also with weeping, who are walking as the enemies of the torture stake"

12* Jesus, P⁴⁶אAVg; omitted by BD. 18* See App 3c.

PHILIPPIANS 1:30—2:8 (page 868)

οὐ μόνον τὸ εἰς αὐτὸν πιστεύειν ἀλλὰ	not only the into him to be believing but
καὶ τὸ ὑπὲρ αὐτοῦ πάσχειν, 30 τὸ τὸν	also the over him to be suffering, the the
αὐτὸν ἀγῶνα ἔχοντες οἷον εἴδετε ἐν ἐμοί,	very struggle having of what sort YOU saw in me,
καὶ νῦν ἀκούετε ἐν ἐμοί.	and now YOU are hearing in me.
2 Εἴ τις οὖν παράκλησις ἐν Χριστῷ,	If any therefore encouragement in Christ,
εἴ τι παραμύθιον ἀγάπης, εἴ τις κοινωνία	if any consolation of love, if any sharing
πνεύματος, εἴ τις σπλάγχνα καὶ οἰκτιρμοί,	of spirit, if any bowels and compassions,
2 πληρώσατέ μου τὴν χαρὰν ἵνα τὸ	make full of me the joy in order that the
αὐτὸ φρονῆτε, τὴν αὐτὴν	very (thing) YOU may be minding, the very
ἀγάπην ἔχοντες, σύμψυχοι, τὸ ἓν	love having, together in soul, the one
φρονοῦντες, 3 μηδὲν κατ'	(thing) minding, nothing according to
ἐριθείαν μηδὲ κατὰ κενοδοξίαν, ἀλλὰ	contentiousness nor according to vainglory, but
τῇ ταπεινοφροσύνῃ ἀλλήλους	to the lowly-mindedness one another
ἡγούμενοι ὑπερέχοντας ἑαυτῶν, 4 μὴ	considering (ones) having over of selves, not
τὰ ἑαυτῶν ἕκαστοι σκοποῦντες, ἀλλὰ	the (things) of selves each (ones) looking at, but
καὶ τὰ ἑτέρων	also the (things) of different (ones)
ἕκαστοι. 5 τοῦτο φρονεῖτε ἐν ὑμῖν ὃ καὶ	each (ones). This be YOU minding in YOU which also
ἐν Χριστῷ Ἰησοῦ, 6 ὃς ἐν μορφῇ θεοῦ	in Christ Jesus, who in form of God
ὑπάρχων οὐχ ἁρπαγμὸν ἡγήσατο τὸ εἶναι	existing not snatching he considered the to be
ἴσα θεῷ, 7 ἀλλὰ ἑαυτὸν ἐκένωσεν	equal (things) to God, but himself he emptied
μορφὴν δούλου λαβών, ἐν ὁμοιώματι	form of slave having taken, in likeness
ἀνθρώπων γενόμενος· 8 καὶ σχήματι	of men having become; and to fashion
εὑρεθεὶς ὡς ἄνθρωπος ἐταπείνωσεν	having been found as man he made lowly
ἑαυτὸν γενόμενος ὑπήκοος μέχρι θανάτου,	himself having become obedient until death,

NWT translation (868): not only to put YOUR faith in him, but also to suffer in his behalf. 30 For YOU have the same struggle as YOU saw in my case and as YOU now hear about in my case.

2 If, then, there is any encouragement in Christ, if any consolation of love, if any sharing of spirit, if any tender affections and compassions, 2 make my joy full in that YOU are of the same mind and have the same love, being joined together in soul, holding the one thought in mind, 3 doing nothing out of contentiousness or out of egotism, but with lowliness of mind considering that the others are superior to YOU, 4 keeping an eye, not in personal interest upon just YOUR own matters, but also in personal interest upon those of the others. 5 Keep this mental attitude in YOU that was also in Christ Jesus, 6 who, although he was existing in God's form, gave no consideration to a seizure, namely, that he should be equal to God. 7 No, but he emptied himself and took a slave's form and came to be in the likeness of men. 8 More than that, when he found himself in fashion as a man, he humbled himself and became obedient as far as death,

PHILIPPIANS 2:9—16 (page 869)

θανάτου δὲ σταυροῦ. 9 διὸ καὶ ὁ	of death but of stake. through which also the
θεὸς αὐτὸν ὑπερύψωσεν, καὶ	God him put high up over, and
ἐχαρίσατο αὐτῷ τὸ ὄνομα τὸ ὑπὲρ	he graciously gave to him the name the over
πᾶν ὄνομα, 10 ἵνα ἐν τῷ ὀνόματι	every name, in order that in the name
Ἰησοῦ πᾶν γόνυ κάμψῃ ἐπουρανίων	of Jesus every knee should bend of those in heaven
καὶ ἐπιγείων καὶ καταχθονίων,	and of those on earth and of those underground,
11 καὶ πᾶσα γλῶσσα ἐξομολογήσηται ὅτι	and every tongue should confess out that
Κύριος Ἰησοῦς Χριστὸς εἰς δόξαν θεοῦ	Lord Jesus Christ into glory of God
πατρός. 12 Ὥστε, ἀγαπητοί μου, καθὼς	Father. And so, loved (ones) of me, according as
πάντοτε ὑπηκούσατε, μὴ ὡς ἐν τῇ παρουσίᾳ	always YOU obeyed, not as in the presence
μου μόνον ἀλλὰ νῦν πολλῷ μᾶλλον ἐν τῇ	of me only but now much rather in the
ἀπουσίᾳ μου, μετὰ φόβου καὶ τρόμου τὴν	absence of me, with fear and trembling the
ἑαυτῶν σωτηρίαν κατεργάζεσθε, 13 θεὸς	of selves salvation be YOU working down, God
γάρ ἐστιν ὁ ἐνεργῶν ἐν ὑμῖν καὶ τὸ	for is the (one) working within in YOU both the
θέλειν καὶ τὸ ἐνεργεῖν	to be willing and the to be working within
ὑπὲρ τῆς εὐδοκίας· 14 πάντα	over the well-thinking; all (things)
ποιεῖτε χωρὶς γογγυσμῶν	be YOU doing apart from murmurings
καὶ διαλογισμῶν, 15 ἵνα	and divided reckonings; in order that
γένησθε ἄμεμπτοι καὶ ἀκέραιοι,	YOU may become blameless and unblended,
τέκνα θεοῦ ἄμωμα μέσου	children of God unblemished (in) midst
γενεᾶς σκολιᾶς καὶ διεστραμμένης, ἐν	of generation crooked and turned through, in
οἷς φαίνεσθε ὡς φωστῆρες ἐν κόσμῳ,	whom YOU are shining as illuminators in world,
16 λόγον ζωῆς ἐπέχοντες, εἰς καύχημα ἐμοὶ	word of life having upon, into boasting to me

* See App 3c.

NWT translation (869): yes, death on a torture stake. 9 For this very reason also God exalted him to a superior position and kindly gave him the name that is above every [other] name, 10 so that in the name of Jesus every knee should bend of those in heaven and those on earth and those under the ground, 11 and every tongue should openly acknowledge that Jesus Christ is Lord to the glory of God the Father.

12 Consequently, my beloved ones, in the way that you have always obeyed, not during my presence only but now much more readily during my absence, keep working out your own salvation with fear and trembling; 13 for God is the one that, for the sake of [his] good pleasure, is acting within you both to will and to act. 14 Keep doing all things free from murmurings and arguments, 15 that you may come to be blameless and innocent, children of God without a blemish in among a crooked and twisted generation, among whom you are shining as illuminators in the world, 16 keeping a tight grip on the word of life, that I may have cause for exultation

LUKE 24:45—53

400

ψαλμοῖς περὶ ἐμοῦ. 45 τότε διήνοιξεν αὐτῶν τὸν νοῦν τοῦ συνιέναι τὰς γραφάς, 46 καὶ εἶπεν αὐτοῖς ὅτι Οὕτως γέγραπται παθεῖν τὸν χριστὸν καὶ ἀναστῆναι ἐκ νεκρῶν τῇ τρίτῃ ἡμέρᾳ, 47 καὶ κηρυχθῆναι ἐπὶ τῷ ὀνόματι αὐτοῦ μετάνοιαν εἰς ἄφεσιν ἁμαρτιῶν εἰς πάντα τὰ ἔθνη, — ἀρξάμενοι ἀπὸ Ἰερουσαλήμ· 48 ὑμεῖς μάρτυρες τούτων. 49 καὶ ἰδοὺ ἐγὼ ἐξαποστέλλω τὴν ἐπαγγελίαν τοῦ πατρός μου ἐφ' ὑμᾶς· ὑμεῖς δὲ καθίσατε ἐν τῇ πόλει ἕως οὗ ἐνδύσησθε ἐξ ὕψους δύναμιν.

50 Ἐξήγαγεν δὲ αὐτοὺς ἕως πρὸς Βηθανίαν, καὶ ἐπάρας τὰς χεῖρας αὐτοῦ εὐλόγησεν αὐτούς. 51 καὶ ἐν τῷ εὐλογεῖν αὐτὸν αὐτοὺς διέστη ἀπ' αὐτῶν [καὶ ἀνεφέρετο εἰς τὸν οὐρανόν]. 52 καὶ αὐτοὶ [προσκυνήσαντες αὐτὸν] ὑπέστρεψαν εἰς Ἰερουσαλὴμ μετὰ χαρᾶς μεγάλης, 53 καὶ ἦσαν διὰ παντὸς ἐν τῷ ἱερῷ εὐλογοῦντες τὸν θεόν.

Psalms about me must be fulfilled." 45 Then he opened up their minds fully to grasp the meaning of the Scriptures, 46 and he said to them: "In this way it is written that the Christ would suffer and rise from among the dead on the third day, 47 and on the basis of his name repentance for forgiveness of sins would be preached in all the nations—starting out from Jerusalem. 48 You are to be witnesses of these things. 49 And, look! I am sending forth upon you that which is promised by my Father. You, though, abide in the city until you become clothed with power from on high.

50 But he led them out as far as Beth'any, and he lifted up his hands and blessed them. 51 As he was blessing them he was parted from them and began to be borne up to heaven. 52 And they did obeisance to him and returned to Jerusalem with great joy. 53 And they were continually in the temple blessing God.

ΚΑΤΑ ΙΩΑΝΗΝ

ACCORDING TO JOHN

1 Ἐν ἀρχῇ ἦν ὁ λόγος, καὶ ὁ λόγος ἦν πρὸς τὸν θεόν, καὶ θεὸς ἦν ὁ λόγος. 2 Οὗτος ἦν ἐν ἀρχῇ πρὸς τὸν θεόν. 3 πάντα δι' αὐτοῦ ἐγένετο, καὶ χωρὶς αὐτοῦ ἐγένετο οὐδὲ ἕν. ὃ γέγονεν 4 ἐν αὐτῷ ζωὴ ἦν, καὶ ἡ ζωὴ ἦν τὸ φῶς τῶν ἀνθρώπων· 5 καὶ τὸ φῶς ἐν τῇ σκοτίᾳ φαίνει, καὶ ἡ σκοτία αὐτὸ οὐ κατέλαβεν. 6 Ἐγένετο ἄνθρωπος ἀπεσταλμένος παρὰ θεοῦ, ὄνομα αὐτῷ Ἰωάνης· 7 οὗτος ἦλθεν εἰς μαρτυρίαν, ἵνα μαρτυρήσῃ περὶ τοῦ φωτός, ἵνα πάντες πιστεύσωσιν δι' αὐτοῦ. 8 οὐκ ἦν ἐκεῖνος τὸ φῶς, ἀλλ' ἵνα μαρτυρήσῃ περὶ τοῦ φωτός. 9 Ἦν τὸ φῶς τὸ ἀληθινὸν ὃ φωτίζει πάντα ἄνθρωπον ἐρχόμενον εἰς τὸν κόσμον. 10 ἐν

1 In [the] beginning the Word was, and the Word was with God, and the Word was a god.* 2 This one was in [the] beginning with God. 3 All things came into existence through him, and apart from him not even one thing came into existence.

What has come 4 by means of him was life, and the life was the light of men. 5 And the light is shining in the darkness, but the darkness has not overpowered it.

6 There arose a man that was sent forth as a representative of God: his name was John.* 7 This [man] came for a witness, in order to bear witness about the light, that people of all sorts might believe through him. 8 He was not that light, but he was meant to bear witness about that light.

9 The true light that gives light to every sort of man was about to come into the world. 10 He

401

1* "A god," in contrast with "the God." See App 2x. 6* See Matthew 3:1 footnote. 9* World (κόσμον, ko'smon), אABД; עוֹלָם, 'oh·lam', Jⁿ·¹ᴴ·ᴹᴬᴮ.

JOHN 8:47—54 · 450

λέγω, διὰ τί ὑμεῖς οὐ πιστεύετέ
I am saying, through what you not are believing
μοι; 47 ὁ ὢν ἐκ τοῦ θεοῦ τὰ
to me? The (one) being out of the God the
ῥήματα τοῦ θεοῦ ἀκούει· διὰ τοῦτο
sayings of the God is hearing; through this
ὑμεῖς οὐκ ἀκούετε, ὅτι ἐκ τοῦ θεοῦ
you not are hearing, because out of the God
οὐκ ἐστέ.
not you are.
48 Ἀπεκρίθησαν οἱ Ἰουδαῖοι καὶ
Answered the Jews and
εἶπαν αὐτῷ Οὐ καλῶς λέγομεν
they said to him Not finely we are saying
ἡμεῖς ὅτι Σαμαρείτης εἶ σὺ καὶ δαιμόνιον
we that Samaritan are you and demon
ἔχεις; 49 ἀπεκρίθη Ἰησοῦς Ἐγὼ
you are having? Answered Jesus I
δαιμόνιον οὐκ ἔχω, ἀλλὰ τιμῶ
demon not am having, but I am honoring
τὸν πατέρα μου, καὶ ὑμεῖς ἀτιμάζετέ με.
the Father of me, and you are dishonoring me.
50 ἐγὼ δὲ οὐ ζητῶ τὴν δόξαν μου·
I but not am seeking the glory of me;
ἔστιν ὁ ζητῶν καὶ κρίνων. 51 ἀμὴν
is the (one) seeking and judging. Amen
ἀμὴν λέγω ὑμῖν, ἐάν τις τὸν ἐμὸν
amen I am saying to you, If ever anyone the my
λόγον τηρήσῃ, θάνατον οὐ μὴ
word should observe, death not not
θεωρήσῃ εἰς τὸν αἰῶνα. 52 εἶπαν αὐτῷ
he should behold into the age. Said to him
οἱ Ἰουδαῖοι Νῦν ἐγνώκαμεν ὅτι
the Jews Now we have known that
δαιμόνιον ἔχεις. Ἀβραὰμ ἀπέθανεν
demon you are having. Abraham died
καὶ οἱ προφῆται, καὶ σὺ λέγεις Ἐάν
and the prophets, and you are saying If ever
τις τὸν λόγον μου τηρήσῃ, οὐ μὴ
anyone the word of me should observe, not not
γεύσηται θανάτου εἰς τὸν αἰῶνα. 53 μὴ
he should taste of death into the age. Not
σὺ μείζων εἶ τοῦ πατρὸς ἡμῶν
you greater you are of the father of us
Ἀβραάμ, ὅστις ἀπέθανεν; καὶ οἱ προφῆται
Abraham, who died? And the prophets
ἀπέθανον· τίνα σεαυτὸν ποιεῖς;
died. whom yourself are you making?
54 ἀπεκρίθη Ἰησοῦς Ἐὰν ἐγὼ δοξάσω
Answered Jesus If ever I should glorify

Translation: why is it YOU do not believe me? 47 He that is from God listens to the sayings of God. This is why YOU do not listen, because YOU are not from God." 48 In answer the Jews said to him: "Do we not rightly say, You are a Samaritan and have a demon?" 49 Jesus answered: "I do not have a demon, but I honor my Father, and YOU dishonor me. 50 But I am not seeking glory for myself; there is One that is seeking and judging. 51 Most truly I say to YOU, If anyone observes my word, he will never see death at all." 52 The Jews said to him: "Now we do know you have a demon. Abraham died, also the prophets; but you say, 'If anyone observes my word, he will never taste death at all.' 53 You are not greater than our father Abraham, who died, are you? Also, the prophets died. Who do you claim to be?" 54 Jesus answered: "If I glorify

451 · JOHN 8:55—9:2

ἐμαυτόν, ἡ δόξα μου οὐδέν ἐστιν·
myself, the glory of me nothing is;
ὁ πατήρ μου ὁ δοξάζων με, ὃν
the Father of me the (one) glorifying me, whom
ὑμεῖς λέγετε ὅτι θεὸς ὑμῶν ἐστιν, 55 καὶ
you are saying that God of you is, and
οὐκ ἐγνώκατε αὐτόν, ἐγὼ δὲ οἶδα
not you have known him, I but have known
αὐτόν· κἂν εἴπω ὅτι οὐκ
him; and if ever I should say that not
οἶδα αὐτόν, ἔσομαι ὅμοιος ὑμῖν
I have known him, I shall be like you
ψεύστης· ἀλλὰ οἶδα αὐτὸν καὶ
liar; but I have known him and
τὸν λόγον αὐτοῦ τηρῶ. 56 Ἀβραὰμ ὁ
the word of him I am observing. Abraham the
πατὴρ ὑμῶν ἠγαλλιάσατο ἵνα
father of you exulted in order that
ἴδῃ τὴν ἡμέραν τὴν ἐμήν, καὶ εἶδεν
he might see the day the mine, and he saw
καὶ ἐχάρη. 57 εἶπαν οὖν οἱ Ἰουδαῖοι
and rejoiced. Said therefore the Jews
πρὸς αὐτόν Πεντήκοντα ἔτη οὔπω
toward him Fifty years not yet
ἔχεις καὶ Ἀβραὰμ ἑώρακας; 58 εἶπεν
you are having and Abraham you have seen? Said
αὐτοῖς Ἰησοῦς Ἀμὴν ἀμὴν
to them Jesus Amen amen
λέγω ὑμῖν, πρὶν Ἀβραὰμ γενέσθαι
I am saying to you, Before Abraham to become
ἐγὼ εἰμί. 59 ἦραν οὖν λίθους ἵνα
I am. They lifted up therefore stones in order that
βάλωσιν ἐπ' αὐτόν· Ἰησοῦς δὲ
they might throw upon him; Jesus but
ἐκρύβη καὶ ἐξῆλθεν ἐκ τοῦ ἱεροῦ.
hid and went out of the temple.
9 Καὶ παράγων εἶδεν ἄνθρωπον τυφλὸν
And going beside he saw man blind
ἐκ γενετῆς. 2 καὶ ἠρώτησαν αὐτὸν οἱ
out of birth. And questioned him the
μαθηταὶ αὐτοῦ λέγοντες Ῥαββεί, τίς
disciples of him saying Rabbi, who
ἥμαρτεν, οὗτος ἢ οἱ γονεῖς αὐτοῦ,
sinned, this (one) or the parents of him,
ἵνα τυφλὸς γεννηθῇ;
in order that blind he should be generated?

Translation: myself, my glory is nothing. It is my Father that glorifies me, he who YOU say is YOUR God; 55 and yet YOU have not known him. But I know him. And if I said I do not know him, I should be like YOU, a liar. But I do know him and am observing his word. 56 Abraham YOUR father rejoiced greatly in the prospect of seeing my day, and he saw it and rejoiced." 57 Therefore the Jews said to him: "You are not yet fifty years old, and still you have seen Abraham?" 58 Jesus said to them: "Most truly I say to YOU, Before Abraham came into existence, I have been." 59 Therefore they picked up stones to hurl [them] at him; but Jesus hid and went out of the temple.
9 Now as he was passing along he saw a man blind from birth. 2 And his disciples asked him: "Rabbi, who sinned, this man or his parents, so that he was born blind?"

57* Has Abraham seen you? P75*,Sᶜ. 58* "I have been" (ἐγὼ εἰμί, e·go' ei·mi'). The action expressed by this verb began in the past, is still in progress, and is properly translated by the perfect indicative. See App 2c.

75

JOHN 9:3-9   452

3 Jesus answered: "Neither this man sinned nor his parents, but it was in order that the works of God might be made manifest in his case. 4 We must work the works of him that sent me while it is day; the night is coming when no man can work. 5 As long as I am in the world, I am the world's light." 6 After he said these things, he spit on the ground and made a clay with the saliva, and put his clay upon the [man's] eyes 7 and said to him: "Go wash in the pool of Si·lo′am"" (which is translated 'Sent forth'). And so he went off and washed, and came back seeing.

8 Therefore the neighbors and those who formerly used to see he was a beggar began to say: "This is the man that used to sit and beg, is it not?" 9 Some would say: "This is he." Others would say: "Not at all, but he is like him." The man would say: "I am [he]."

7* Si·lo′am, אAB; Shi·lo′ah, J⁷,¹⁴,¹⁶,¹⁷,²². See Isaiah 8:6 in LXX.

453   **JOHN 9:10—17**

10 Consequently they began to say to him: "How, then, were your eyes opened?" 11 He answered: "The man called Jesus made a clay and smeared [it] on my eyes and said to me, 'Go to Si·lo′am and wash.' I therefore went and washed and gained sight." 12 At this they said to him: "Where is that [man]?" He said: "I do not know."

13 They led the once-blind man himself to the Pharisees. 14 Incidentally it was Sabbath on the day that Jesus made the clay and opened his eyes. 15 This time, therefore, the Pharisees also took up asking him how he gained sight. He said to them: "He put a clay upon my eyes, and I washed and have sight."

16 Therefore some of the Pharisees began to say: "This is not a man from God, because he does not observe the Sabbath." Others began to say: "How can a man that is a sinner perform signs of that sort?" So there was a division among them. 17 Hence they said to the blind man

76

105

JOHN 14:14—21

I will do this, in order that the Father may be glorified in connection with the Son. 14 If you ask anything in my name, I will do it.

15 "If you love me, you will observe my commandments; 16 and I will request the Father and he will give you another helper to be with you forever, 17 the spirit of the truth, which the world cannot receive, because it neither beholds it nor knows it. You know it, because it remains with you and is in you. 18 I shall not leave you bereaved. I am coming to you. 19 A little longer and the world will behold me no more, but you will behold me, because I live and you will live. 20 In that day you will know that I am in union with my Father and you are in union with me and I am in union with you. 21 He that has my commandments and observes them, that one is he who loves me. In turn he that loves me will be loved by my Father, and I will love him and will plainly show myself to him."

JOHN 14:6—13

6 Jesus said to him: "I am the way and the truth and the life. No one comes to the Father except through me. 7 If you men had known me, you would have known my Father also; from this moment on you know him and have seen him.

8 Philip said to him: "Lord, show us the Father, and it is enough for us."

9 Jesus said to him: "Have I been with you men so long a time, and yet, Philip, you have not come to know me? He that has seen me has seen the Father [also]. How is it you say, 'Show us the Father'? 10 Do you not believe that I am in union with the Father and the Father is in union with me? The things I say to you men I do not speak of my own originality; but the Father who remains in union with me is doing his works. 11 Believe me that I am in union with the Father and the Father is in union with me; otherwise, believe on account of the works themselves. 12 Most truly I say to you, He that exercises faith in me, that one also will do the works that I do; and he will do works greater than these, because I am going my way to the Father. 13 Also, whatever it is that you ask in my name,

APPENDIX

John 1:1 — "a god"

(θεός [the‧os'], Greek)

THE KINGDOM INTERLINEAR TRANSLATION OF THE GREEK SCRIPTURES, 1969

A GROSSLY MISLEADING TRANSLATION

John 1: 1, which reads "In the beginning was the Word and the Word was with God and the Word was God", is shockingly mistranslated, "Originally the Word was, and the Word was with God, and the Word was a god," in a New World Translation of the Christian Greek Scriptures, published under the auspices of Jehovah's Witnesses.

Since my name is used and our Manual Grammar of the Greek New Testament is quoted on page 744 to seek to justify their translation I am making this statement.

The translation suggested in our Grammar for the disputed passage is, "the Word was deity." Moffatt's rendering is "the Word was divine." William's translation is, "the Word was God Himself." Each translation reflects the dominant idea in the Greek. For, whenever an article does not precede a noun in Greek, that noun can either be considered as emphasizing the character, nature, essence or quality of a person or thing, as theos (God) does in John 1: 1, or it can be translated in certain contexts as indefinite, as they have done. But of all the scholars in the world, as far as we know, none have translated this verse as Jehovah's Witnesses have.

If the Greek article occurred with both Word and God in John 1: 1 the implication would be that they are one and the same person, absolutely identical. But John affirmed that "the Word was with (the) God" (tha definite article preceding each noun), and in so writing he indicated his belief that they are distinct and separate personalities. Then John next stated that the Word was God, i.e., of the same family or essence that characterizes the Creator. Or, in other words, that both are of the same nature, and that nature is the highest in existence, namely divine.

Examples where the noun in the predicate does not have an article, as in the above verse, are: John 4: 24, "God is spirit". (not a spirit); I John 4: 16, "God is love", (not a love); I John 1: 5, "God is light", (not a light); and Matthew 13: 39, "the reapers are angels," i.e. they are the type of beings known as angels. In each instance the noun in the predicate was used to describe some quality or characteristic of the subject, whether as to nature or type.

The apostle John in the context of the introduction to his gospel is pulling all the stops out of language to portray not only the deity of Christ but also His equality with the Father. He states that the Word was in the beginning, that He was with God, that He was God and that all creation came into existence through Him and that not even one thing exists which was not created by Christ. What else could be said that John did not say? In John 1: 18 he explained that Christ had been so intimate with the Father that He was in His bosom and that He came to earth to exhibit or portray God. But if we had no other statement from John except that which is found in John 14: 9, "He that has seen me has seen the Father," that would be enough to satisfy the seeking soul that Christ and God are the same in essence and that both are divine and equal in nature.

79

2/25/83 DJ-40

-2-

Besides, the whole tenor of New Testament revelation points in this direction. Compare Paul's declaration in Colossians 1: 19, for instance: "that all the divine fullness should dwell in Him," or the statement in Hebrews 1: 3, "He is the reflection of God's glory and the perfect representation of His being, and continues to uphold the universe by His mighty word." (Williams translation). And note the sweeping, cosmic claim recorded in Matthre 28: 19, "All authority has been given to me in heaven and earth."

And, if we contrast with that the belittling implication that Christ was only a god, do we not at once detect the discord? Does not such a conception conflict with the New Testament message both in whole and in part? Why, if John, in the midst of the idolartry of his day, had made such a statement would not the first century hearers and readers have gotten a totally inadequate picture of Christ, who we believe, is the Creator of the universe and the only Redeemer of humanity?

Julius Robert Mantey, A.B., Thd.D., Ph.D., D.D.
Professor of Greek and New Testament
Northern Baptist Theological Seminary
Chicago, Illinois

80

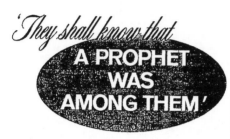

'They shall know that **A PROPHET WAS AMONG THEM**'

JEHOVAH GOD is interested in having people know him. Though he is invisible to human eyes, he provides various ways by which they can know his personality. They can know what to expect from him and what he expects of them.

One can come to understand that Jehovah is a God of surpassing wisdom by observing creation. This also reveals the loving care with which he designed things for man's welfare and enjoyment. A second way to know God is through his Word of truth, the Bible. Herein one finds the full expression of Jehovah's purpose toward mankind—why man is on the earth and the blessings that God has in store.

A third way of coming to know Jehovah God is through his representatives. In ancient times he sent prophets as his special messengers. While these men foretold things to come, they also served the people by telling them of God's will for them at that time, often also warning them of dangers and calamities. People today can view the creative works. They have at hand the Bible, but it is little read or understood. So, does Jehovah have a prophet to help them, to warn them of dangers and to declare things to come?

IDENTIFYING THE "PROPHET"

These questions can be answered in the affirmative. Who is this prophet? The cler-

gy of the so-called "Christian" nations hold themselves before the people as being the ones commissioned to speak for God. But, as pointed out in the previous issue of this magazine, they have failed God and failed as proclaimers of his kingdom by approving a man-made political organization, the League of Nations (now the United Nations), as "the political expression of the Kingdom of God on earth."

However, Jehovah did not let the people of Christendom, as led by the clergy, go without being warned that the League was a counterfeit substitute for the real kingdom of God. He had a "prophet" to warn them. This "prophet" was not one man, but was a body of men and women. It was the small group of footstep followers of Jesus Christ, known at that time as International Bible Students. Today they are known as Jehovah's Christian witnesses. They are still proclaiming a warning, and have been joined and assisted in their commissioned work by hundreds of thousands of persons who have listened to their message with belief.

Of course, it is easy to say that this group acts as a "prophet" of God. It is another thing to prove it. The only way that this can be done is to review the record. What does it show?

During the World War I period this group, the International Bible Students, was very active in preaching the good news of God's kingdom, as their Leader Jesus Christ had set this work before them in his prophecy at Matthew 24:14. They took literally Jesus' words to the Roman governor Pontius Pilate: "My kingdom is no part of this world." (John 18:36) They also took to heart Jesus' words to his fol-

197

obtained the dominion (Dan. 2: 37, 38). Medo-Persia existed before it conquered Babylon; and so with all kingdoms: they must first have existed and have received superior power before they could conquer others. So, too, with God's Kingdom: it has existed in an embryo form for eighteen centuries; but it, with the world at large, was made subject to "the powers that be," "ordained of God." Until their "seven times" shall end, the Kingdom of God cannot come into universal dominion. However, like the others, it must obtain power adequate to the overthrow of these kingdoms before it shall break them in pieces.

So, in this "Day of Jehovah," the "Day of Trouble," our Lord takes his great power (hitherto dormant) and reigns, and this it is that will cause the trouble, though the world will not so recognize it for some time. That the saints shall share in this work of breaking to pieces present kingdoms, there can be no doubt. It is written, "This honor have all his saints—to execute the judgments written, to bind their kings with chains, and their nobles with fetters of iron,"—of strength. (Psa. 149:8, 9.) "He that overcometh, and keepeth my works unto the end, to him will I give power over the nations, and he shall rule them with a rod of iron; as the vessels of a potter shall they [the empires] be broken to shivers."—Rev. 2:26, 27; Psa. 2:8, 9.

But our examination, in the preceding volume, of the great difference in character between the Kingdom of God and the beastly kingdoms of earth, prepares us to see also a difference in modes of warfare. The methods of conquest and breaking will be widely different from any which have ever before overthrown nations. He who now takes his great power to reign is shown in symbol (Rev. 19:15) as the one whose sword went forth out of his mouth, "that with it he should smite the nations; and he shall rule them with a rod of iron." That sword is the TRUTH (Eph. 6:17);

and the living saints, as well as many of the world, are now being used as the Lord's soldiers in overthrowing errors and evils. But let no one hastily infer a *peaceable immersion* of the nations to be here symbolized; for many scriptures, such as Rev. 11:17, 18; Dan. 12:1; 2 Thes. 2:8; Psalms 149 and 47, teach the very opposite.

Be not surprised, then, when in subsequent chapters we present proofs that the setting up of the Kingdom of God is already begun, that it is pointed out in prophecy as due to begin the exercise of power in A.D. 1878; and that the "battle of the great day of God Almighty" (Rev. 16:14,) which will end in A.D. 1914 with the complete overthrow of earth's present rulership, is already commenced. The gathering of the armies is plainly visible from the standpoint of God's Word.

If our vision be unobstructed by prejudice, when we get the telescope of God's Word rightly adjusted we may see with clearness the character of many of the events due to take place in the "Day of the Lord"—that we are in the very midst of those events, and that "the Great Day of His Wrath is come."

"The sword of truth, already sharpened, is to smite every evil system and custom—civil, social and ecclesiastical. Nay, more, we can see that the smiting is commenced. Freedom of thought, and human rights, civil and religious, long lost sight of under kings and emperors, popes, synods, councils, traditions and creeds, are being appreciated and asserted as never before. The internal conflict is already fomenting; it will ere long break forth as a consuming fire, and human systems, and errors, which for centuries have fettered truth and oppressed the groaning creation, must melt before it. Yes, truth—and widespread and increasing knowledge of it—is the sword which is perplexing and wounding the heads over many countries. (Psa. 110:6.)

THE TIME IS AT HAND (Studies In the Scriptures vol. 2) 1889

82

The Time is at Hand.

obtained the dominion (Dan. 2:37, 38); Medo-Persia existed before it conquered Babylon; and so with all kingdoms: they must first have existed and have received superior power before they could conquer others. So, too, with God's Kingdom: it has existed in an embryo form for eighteen centuries; but it, with the world at large, was made subject to "the powers that be," "ordained of God." Until their "seven times" shall end, the Kingdom of God cannot come into universal dominion. However, like the others, it must obtain power adequate to the overthrow of these kingdoms before it shall break them in pieces.

So, in this "Day of Jehovah," the "Day of Trouble," our Lord takes his great power (hitherto dormant) and reigns, and this it is that will cause the trouble, though the world will not so recognize it for some time. That the saints shall share in this work of breaking to pieces present kingdoms, there can be no doubt. It is written, "This honor have all his saints—to execute the judgments written, to bind their kings with chains, and their nobles with fetters of iron"—of strength. (Psa. 149:8, 9.) "He that overcometh, and keepeth my works unto the end, to him will I give power over the nations, and he shall rule them with a rod of iron; as the vessels of a potter shall they [the empires] be broken to shivers."—Rev. 2:26, 27; Psa. 2:8, 9.

But our examination, in the preceding volume, of the great difference in character between the Kingdom of God and the beastly kingdoms of earth, prepares us to see also a difference in modes of warfare. The methods of conquest and breaking will be widely different from any which have ever before overthrown nations. He who now takes his great power to reign is shown in symbol (Rev. 19:15) as the one whose sword went forth out of his mouth, that with it he should smite the nations; and he shall rule them with a rod of iron." That sword is the TRUTH (Eph. 6:17).

Times of the Gentiles.

and the living saints, as well as many of the world, are now being used as the Lord's soldiers in overthrowing errors and evils. But let no one hastily infer a *peaceable conversion* of the nations to be here symbolized; for many scriptures, Such as Rev. 11:17, 18; Dan. 12:1; 2 Thes. 2:8; Psalms 149 and 47, teach the very opposite.

Be not surprised, then, when in subsequent chapters we present proofs that the setting up of the Kingdom of God is already begun, that it is pointed out in prophecy as due to begin the exercise of power in A.D. 1878, and that the "battle of the great day of God Almighty" (Rev. 16:14), which will end in A.D. 1915, with the complete overthrow of earth's present rulership, is already commenced. The gathering of the armies is plainly visible from the standpoint of God's Word.

If our vision be unobstructed by prejudice, when we get the telescope of God's Word rightly adjusted we may see with clearness the character of many of the events due to take place in the "Day of the Lord"—that we are in the very midst of those events, and that the Great Day of His Wrath is come."

The sword of truth, already sharpened, is to smite every evil system and custom—civil, social and ecclesiastical. Nay, more, we can see that the smiting is commenced: freedom of thought, and human rights, civil and religious, long lost sight of under kings and emperors, popes, synods, councils, traditions and creeds, are being appreciated and asserted as never before. The internal conflict is already fomenting: it will ere long break forth as a consuming fire, and human systems, and errors, which for centuries have fettered truth and oppressed the groaning creation, must melt before it. Yes, truth—and widespread and increasing knowledge of it—is the sword which is perplexing and wounding the heads over many countries. (Psa. 110:6.)

THE TIME IS AT HAND (1889) 1917 edition

83

484   The Finished Mystery   EZEK. 7

24:18. So I spake unto the people in the morning; and at even my wife died; and I did in the morning as I was commanded.—He continued his addresses and writings to the Lord's people; his wife became to him as one dead and he continued uninterruptedly in the work of the ministry.

24:19. And the people said unto me, Wilt thou not tell us what these things are to us, that thou doest so?—Why was Pastor Russell caused by his Father to endure the fiery trials and ecclesiastical falsehoods in connection with this incident of his life?

THE CHURCHES TO CEASE TO BE

24:20, 21. Then I answered them, The word of the Lord came unto me, saying, Speak unto the house of Israel. Thus saith the Lord God; Behold, I will profane My Sanctuary, the excellency of your strength, the desire of your eyes, and that which your soul pitieth; and your sons and your daughters whom ye have left shall fall by the sword.—God gives the reason. It was as a picture or parable of what is to happen to Christendom. Until 1878 the nominal church had been in a sense God's sanctuary or Temple; but He was from then on, culminating in 1918, to remove it with a stroke or plague of erroneous doctrines and deeds Divinely permitted. The Church was the strength of Christendom, that about which its life centered, and around which its institutions were built. It was the desire of the eyes of the people, that which all Christians loved. Nevertheless, God was to make manifest the profanation which ecclesiasticism had made of the Christian Church, and to cause the church organizations to become to Him as one dead, an unclean thing, not to be touched, or mourned. And the "children of the church" shall perish by the sword of war, revolution and anarchy, and by the Sword of the Spirit be made to see that they have lost their hope of life on the spirit plane—that "the door is shut."

24:22. And ye shall do as I have done: ye shall not cover your lips, nor eat the bread of men.—So universal and dreadful will be the troubles that the dead will literally lie unburied and unwept. There can be no mourning for the dead in a period when the living are overwhelmed by troubles worse than death.

24:23. And your tires shall be upon your heads; and your shoes upon your feet: ye shall not mourn nor weep; but ye shall pine away for your iniquities, and mourn one toward another.—The mourning will be an inner sorrow of a people stupefied by terrible experiences, who pine

485   The Boiling Caldron

away and without outward expression sink together into the fellowship of helpless grief.

24:24. Thus Ezekiel is unto you a sign; according to all that he hath done shall ye do: and when this cometh, ye shall know that I am the Lord God.—Thus the silent sorrow at Pastor Russell's heart was to be a sign to Christendom. The sorrowful experiences of Pastor Russell in this connection shall later on be those of all Christendom; "and when this cometh" they shall know that Jehovah God is supreme, and back of all the judgments of the trouble time.

PASTOR RUSSELL DEAD, BUT SPEAKING AGAIN

24:25, 26. Also, thou son of man, shall it not be in the day when I take from them their strength, the joy of their glory, the desire of their eyes, and that whereupon they set their minds, their sons and their daughters. That he that escapeth in that day shall come unto thee, to cause thee to hear it with thine ears?—Also, in the year 1918, when God destroys the churches wholesale and the church members by millions, it shall be that any that escape shall come to the works of Pastor Russell to learn the meaning of the downfall of "Christianity".

24:27. In that day shall thy mouth be opened to him which is escaped, and thou shalt speak, and be no more dumb; and thou shalt be a sign unto them; and they shall know that I am the Lord.—Pastor Russell's voice has been stilled in death; and his voice is, comparatively speaking, dumb to what it will be. In the time of revolution and anarchy he shall speak, and be no more dumb to those that escape the destruction of that day. Pastor Russell shall "be a sign unto them," shall tell them the truth about the Divine appointment of the trouble, as they consult his books, scattered to the number of ten million throughout Christendom. His words shall be a sign of hope unto them, enabling them to see the bright side of the cloud and to look forward with anticipation to the glorious Kingdom of God to be established. Then "they shall know the Lord."

"Build thee more stately mansions, O my soul,
    As the swift seasons roll!
Leave thy low-vaulted past!
Let each new temple, nobler than the last,
Shut thee from heaven with a dome more vast,
    Till thou at length art free,
Leaving thine outgrown shell by life's unresting sea."

THE FINISHED MYSTERY, 1917

in due time after the establishment of the kingdom. Then it shall come to pass that every one who will keep the saying of the Lord shall never see death. This promise would not have been made by Jesus if he did not intend to carry it into full force and effect in due time.

Again he said: "Whosoever liveth and believeth in me shall never die". (John 11:26) Do we believe the Master's statement? If so, when the time comes for the world to know, then they who believe and, of course, render themselves in obedience to the terms have the absolute and positive statement of Jesus that they shall never die.

Based upon the argument heretofore set forth, then, that the old order of things, the old world, is ending and is therefore passing away, and that the new order is coming in, and that 1925 shall mark the resurrection of the faithful worthies of old and the beginning of reconstruction, it is reasonable to conclude that millions of people now on the earth will be still on the earth in 1925. Then, based upon the promises set forth in the divine Word, we must reach the positive and indisputable conclusion that millions now living will never die.

Of course, it does not mean that every one will live; for some will refuse to obey the divine law; but those who have been evil and turn again to righteousness and obey righteousness shall live and not die. Of this we have the positive statement of the Lord's prophet, as follows:

that a plan of redemption exists and that the way is open for him to accept the terms of it and live. Knowledge being essential, it precedes the reception of blessings from the Lord; and knowing this fact, it is easy to be seen why the adversary, the devil, and his agencies so diligently strive to prevent the people from knowing the truth. But when Messiah's kingdom is established we are definitely informed [Revelation 20:1-4] that Satan will be restrained of his power that he might deceive the nations no more; and then the people shall know the truth and nothing shall hinder them from knowing it.

POSITIVE PROMISE

The words of Jesus must be given full force and effect because he spake as never man spake. His speech was with absolute authority. And in God's due time his words must have a fulfillment; and they cannot have a fulfillment until that due time. Jesus plainly said: "Verily, verily, I say unto you, If a man keep my saying, he shall never see death". (John 8:51) As above stated, no one could keep the saying of Jesus until he hears it, until he has a knowledge of God's arrangement. Throughout the Gospel age none but Christians have had this knowledge and all who have kept this saying and keep it faithfully until the end will receive life everlasting on the divine plane. (Revelation 2:10) The remainder of mankind have not heard it; therefore could not keep it. They will hear, however,

85

the generations of the sons of Noah: Shem, Ham, and Japheth; and unto them were sons born after the flood." (Gen. 10: 1) "These are the generations of Shem: Shem was an hundred years old, and begat Arphaxad two years after the flood; and Shem lived after he begat Arphaxad five hundred years, and begat sons and daughters."—Genesis 11: 10, 11.

⁵ There is no evidence that any children were taken into the ark, but, on the contrary, the Scriptural record is that Noah and his wife and his three sons and their wives, that is, eight persons in all, were taken into the ark: "And the Lord said unto Noah, Come thou and all thy house into the ark; for thee have I seen righteous before me in this generation. And Noah went in, and his sons, and his wife, and his sons' wives, with him, into the ark, because of the waters of the flood." (Gen. 7: 1, 7) "And Noah went forth, and his sons, and his wife, and his sons' wives with him." (Gen. 8: 18) "The ark . . . wherein few, that is, eight souls, were saved by water." (1 Pet. 3: 20) These scriptures support the conclusion that the beginning of the 'filling of the earth' is not due before Armageddon; and in further support thereof mark the words of Jesus, which definitely seem to discourage the bearing of children immediately before or during Armageddon: "And woe unto them that are with child, and to them that give suck in those days!" —Matt. 24: 19.

⁶ There are Jonadabs now who are fully devoted to God and his kingdom and many of which now have children; what must be expected for them? The obligation is upon the parents to teach their children the truth of and concerning Jehovah and his kingdom under Christ and thus to lead them that they may 'seek righteousness and meekness', and, so doing, the divine promise will apply to such children, to wit: "Seek righteousness, seek meekness: it may be ye shall be hid in the day of the Lord's anger." (Zeph. 2: 3) Children born before Armageddon are brought into the world while Satan's wicked, oppressive organization affects the lives of all on the earth, and there is but one way of finding protection and safety for such children, as well as others, and that is to devote themselves to God and his kingdom and find refuge in the organization of Jehovah under Christ. They must seek to learn the truth and conform themselves to God's expressed will. Therefore the Jonadabs should see to it that their children are properly taught and afforded an opportunity to place themselves fully under the protection of the kingdom of God. It would therefore appear that there is no reasonable or Scriptural injunction to bring children into the world immediately before Armageddon, where we now are. If children are born, then the parents should see to it that such children are properly instructed concerning the Lord and his kingdom until the child reaches the age when it must freely exercise intelligently its own will and bear its own responsibility. While it is not

the obligation of the remnant to seek out children not their own and to give them instruction, yet all children who accompany their parents or foster parents or those friendly to them, and who desire to attend and do attend study meetings with the grownups and there seek righteousness and meekness, should be given aid and encouragement. Such aid and encouragement can be given by having the children sit quietly at such study meetings and listen to the instructions that are given. At the "feast of weeks" those other than Israelites were permitted to attend, concerning which God there gave the commandment, to wit: "And thou shalt rejoice before the Lord thy God, thou, and thy son, and thy daughter, and thy manservant, and thy maidservant, and the Levite that is within thy gates, and the stranger, and the fatherless, and the widow, that are among you, in the place which the Lord thy God hath chosen to place his name there." (Deut. 16: 11) At the "feast of tabernacles", when his people assembled at the temple, God commanded thus: "Gather the people together, men, and women, and children, and thy stranger that is within thy gates, that they may hear, and that they may learn, and fear the Lord your God, and observe to do all the words of this law." —Deut. 31: 12.

⁷ Separate meetings called "Sunday schools", which are used for the juveniles, are not Scriptural, but the children should accompany their parents to the place of study of God's Word, the place of worship; and when other children come with them that they too might learn, such should be required to sit quietly in the meeting and learn. (For a more complete consideration of instruction of children see *The Watchtower* of April 15 and May 1, 1938.)

AFTER ARMAGEDDON

⁸ Adam and his wife Eve were commanded to "multiply and fill the earth". They were then righteous. Adam and Eve failed to raise up a righteous generation because they both sinned before beginning to exercise the function of bringing children into the world. After Armageddon the willful violators of God's law will all be gone from the earth, and the survivors, being righteous, by God's grace, and being thus counted by him, may then fulfill the divine mandate. The Devil will then be bound, so that he cannot interfere with or influence the upbringing of the children of the Jonadabs. (Rev. 20: 1-3) The degenerate or wicked offspring of Adam will then be dead, so that they cannot exercise any influence over children of the great multitude, such as Nimrod exercised over the generation of Noah's sons. (Gen. 10: 8-10) The kingdom of God then in full operation being unto life for the obedient, the children of the great multitude conceived under the kingdom would be conceived unto life by the grace of God through Christ Jesus. Lucifer, as man's overlord, failed in the performance of the commission given to him because he rebelled and then

November 1, 1938

HOW ARE YOU USING YOUR LIFE?

IS IT not apparent that most of mankind are living their lives for themselves? They are using their lives as *they* see fit, without concern for others. But what about us? The apostle Paul wrote to fellow servants of Jehovah, saying: "None of us, in fact, lives with regard to himself only, and no one dies with regard to himself only; for both if we live, we live to Jehovah, and if we die, we die to Jehovah. Therefore both if we live and if we die, we belong to Jehovah."—Rom. 14:7, 8.

This is something for all of us to give serious thought to: It would be entirely inappropriate for us, while professing to be Jehovah's people, to try to live our lives with regard to ourselves only. As the apostle Paul wrote: "You do not belong to yourselves, for you were bought with a price. By all means, glorify God."—1 Cor. 6:19, 20.

Are we not thankful that Jehovah God has purchased us and that we now belong to Him? He has bought us with the life of his own dear Son so that eternal death does not have to be our lot, but we have before us the opportunity to enjoy everlasting life. (John 3:16, 36) How are you affected by this loving provision of God? Does it not cause you to want to show Jehovah your deep appreciation? The apostle Peter noted that if we have the proper mental disposition we will be moved to "live the remainder of [our] time in the flesh, no more for the desires of men, *but for God's will.*"—1 Pet. 4:2.

Is that what you are doing? Are you living no longer simply to satisfy personal ambitions or desires, but to do God's will? Are there ways in which you could share more fully in doing the will of God?

God's Will for Us

Jehovah makes clear in his Word that his will for us today includes accomplishing a great work of Kingdom-preaching before the end of this system comes. (Matt. 24:14) Jesus Christ did a similar work. He said: "Also to other cities I must declare the good news of the kingdom of God, *because for this I was sent forth.*"—Luke 4:43.

KINGDOM MINISTRY, MAY 1974

Jesus did not hold back, but was wholesouled in his service to God. When we read the historical accounts of his ministry in the Gospels, how impressed we are with his energy and zeal in doing the Kingdom-preaching! Jesus knew that he had only a short time, and he did not spare himself in finishing his assignment. Should we not today be imitating his example, especially since we have such a short time left now in which to complete the Kingdom-preaching?

Yes, the end of this system is so very near! Is that not reason to increase our activity? In this regard we can learn something from a runner who puts on a final burst of speed near the finish of a race. Look at Jesus, who apparently stepped up his activity during his final days on earth. In fact, over 27 percent of the material in the Gospels is devoted to just the last week of Jesus' earthly ministry!—Matt. 21:1–27:50; Mark 11:1–15:37; Luke 19:29–23:46; John 11:55–19:30.

By carefully and prayerfully examining our own circumstances, we also may find that we can spend more time and energy in preaching during this final period before the present system ends. Many of our brothers and sisters are doing just that. This is evident from the rapidly increasing number of pioneers.

Yes, since the summer of 1973 there have been new peaks in pioneers every month. Now there are 20,394 regular and special pioneers in the United States, an all-time peak. That is 5,190 more than there were in February 1973! A 34-percent increase! Does that not warm our hearts? Reports are heard of brothers selling their homes and property and planning to finish out the rest of their days in this old system in the pioneer service. Certainly this is a fine way to spend the short time remaining before the wicked world's end.—1 John 2:17.

Circumstances such as poor health or responsibilities in connection with your family may limit what you can do in the field ministry. And yet, the pioneer ranks include many who have health limitations, as well as some persons with families. But these broth-

3

87

evidence that application of Bible counsel transforms lives, that it can make people honest and morally upright, that it can enable people of all races and nationalities to live and work together in a spirit of genuine brotherhood.

Are works really necessary if a person has faith?

Jas. 2:17, 18, 21, 22, 26: "Faith, if it does not have works, is dead in itself. Nevertheless, a certain one will say: 'You have faith, and I have works. Show me your faith apart from the works, and I shall show you my faith by my works.' Was not Abraham our father declared righteous by works after he had offered up Isaac his son upon the altar? You behold that his faith worked along with his works and by his works his faith was perfected. Indeed, as the body without spirit is dead, so also faith without works is dead."

Illustration: A young man may court a young lady, telling her that he loves her. But if he never asks her to marry him, is he really demonstrating that his love is thorough? Likewise, works are a means of demonstrating the genuineness of our faith and our love. If we do not obey God we do not really love him or have faith in the rightness of his ways. (1 John 5:3, 4) But we cannot *earn* salvation no matter what works we do. Eternal life is a *gift* from God through Jesus Christ, not payment for our works.—Eph. 2:8, 9.

False Prophets

Definition: Individuals and organizations proclaiming messages that they attribute to a superhuman source but that do not originate with the true God and are not in harmony with his revealed will.

How can true prophets and false ones be identified?

True prophets make known their faith in Jesus, but more is required than claiming to preach in his name

1 John 4:1-3: "Test the inspired expressions to see wheth-

er they originate with God, because many false prophets have gone forth into the world. You gain the knowledge of the inspired expression from God by this: Every inspired expression that confesses Jesus Christ as having come in the flesh originates with God, but every inspired expression that does not confess Jesus does not originate with God."

Matt. 7:21-23: "Not everyone saying to me, 'Lord, Lord,' will enter into the kingdom of the heavens, but the one doing the will of my Father who is in the heavens will. Many will say to me in that day, 'Lord, Lord, did we not prophesy in your name ...?' And yet then I will confess to them: I never knew you! Get away from me, you workers of lawlessness."

True prophets speak in the name of God, but merely claiming to represent him is not enough

Deut. 18:18-20: "A prophet I shall raise up for them from the midst of their brothers, like you [like Moses]; and I shall indeed put my words in his mouth, and he will certainly speak to them all that I shall command him. And it must occur that the man who will not listen to my words that he will speak in my name, I shall myself require an account from him. However, the prophet who presumes to speak in my name a word that I have not commanded him to speak or who speaks in the name of other gods, that prophet must die." (Compare Jeremiah 14:14; 28:11, 15.)

Jesus said: "I do nothing of my own initiative; but just as the Father taught me I speak these things." (John 8:28) He said: "I have come in the name of my Father." (John 5:43) Jesus also said: "He that speaks of his own originality is seeking his own glory."—John 7:18.

If any individuals or organizations claim to represent God but decline to use God's personal name, and make it a practice to express their own opinions on matters, are they measuring up to this important qualification of a true prophet?

Ability to perform "great signs," or "miracles," is not necessarily proof of a true prophet

Matt. 24:24: "False Christs and false prophets will arise

REASONING FROM THE SCRIPTURES

What characterizes their way of life? "The works of the flesh are . . . fornication, uncleanness, loose conduct, idolatry, practice of spiritism, enmities, strife, jealousy, fits of anger, contentions, divisions, sects, envies, drunken bouts, revelries, and things like these. . . . Those who practice such things will not inherit God's kingdom. On the other hand, the fruitage of [God's] spirit is love, joy, peace, long-suffering, kindness, goodness, faith, mildness, self-control."—Gal. 5: 19-23; see also 2 Peter 2:1-3.

Have not Jehovah's Witnesses made errors in their teachings?

Jehovah's Witnesses do not claim to be inspired prophets. They have made mistakes. Like the apostles of Jesus Christ, they have at times had some wrong expectations.—Luke 19:11; Acts 1:6.

The Scriptures provide time elements related to Christ's presence, and Jehovah's Witnesses have studied these with keen interest. (Luke 21:24; Dan. 4:10-17) Jesus also described a many-featured sign that would tie in with the fulfillment of time prophecies to identify the generation that would live to see the end of Satan's wicked system of things. (Luke 21:7-36) Jehovah's Witnesses have pointed to evidence in fulfillment of this sign. It is true that the Witnesses have made mistakes in their understanding of what would occur at the end of certain time periods, but they have not made the mistake of losing faith or ceasing to be watchful as to fulfillment of Jehovah's purposes. They have continued to keep to the fore in their thinking the counsel given by Jesus: "Keep on the watch, therefore, because you do not know on what day your Lord is coming."—Matt. 24:42.

Matters on which corrections of viewpoint have been needed have been relatively minor when compared with the vital Bible truths that they have discerned and publicized. Among these are the following: Jehovah is the only true God. Jesus Christ is not part of a Trinitarian godhead but is the only-begotten Son of God. Redemption from sin is possible only through faith in Christ's ransom sacrifice. The holy spirit is not a person but is Jehovah's active force, and its

fruitage must be evident in the lives of true worshipers. The human soul is not immortal, as the ancient pagans claimed; it dies, and the hope for future life is in the resurrection. God's permission of wickedness has been because of the issue of universal sovereignty. God's Kingdom is the only hope for mankind. Since 1914 we have been living in the last days of the global wicked system of things. Only 144,000 faithful Christians will be kings and priests with Christ in heaven, whereas the rest of obedient mankind will receive eternal life on a paradise earth.

Another factor to consider regarding the teachings of Jehovah's Witnesses is this: Have these truly uplifted people morally? Are those who adhere to these teachings outstanding in their communities because of their honesty? Is their family life beneficially influenced by applying these teachings? Jesus said that his disciples would be readily identified because of having love among themselves. (John 13:35) Is this quality outstanding among Jehovah's Witnesses? We let the facts speak for themselves.

If Someone Says—

'My minister said that Jehovah's Witnesses are the false prophets'

You might reply: 'May I ask, Did he show you anything in the Bible that describes what we believe or do and that says people of that sort would be false prophets? . . . May I show you how the Bible describes false prophets? (Then use one or more of the points outlined on pages 132-136.)'

Or you could say: 'I'm sure you'll agree that specific evidence should back up such a serious charge. Did your minister mention any specific examples? (If householder refers to some claimed "predictions" that did not come to pass, use material on page 134, and from the bottom of page 135 to the top of 137.)'

Another possibility: 'I'm sure that if someone accused you of something similar, you would welcome the opportunity at least to explain your position or point of view, wouldn't you? . . . So may I show you from the Bible . . .?'

REASONING FROM THE SCRIPTURES

89

was it possible for imperfect men to produce a record that is actually God's message?

⁹ It was because they did not write of their own impulse, but were inspired by God. What is here meant by the word "inspired"? It means that God, the Creator of heaven and earth, moved these men by his spirit or invisible empowering force, putting into their minds what they should write down as his "word," or message, for mankind. For example, the psalm writer David said:

"The spirit of Jehovah [God] it was that spoke by me, and his word was upon my tongue." (2 Samuel 23:2)

And concerning prophetic messages, the apostle Peter wrote:

"No prophecy of Scripture springs from any private interpretation. For prophecy was at no time brought by man's will, but men spoke from God as they were borne along by holy spirit."—2 Peter 1: 20, 21.

¹⁰ It was no problem for God, the Supreme Being and Creator of all the universe, to convey messages to faithful men on earth. In modern times men have traveled to the moon, and the messages they sent back from there to earth by radio came through clearly and understandably from over 400,000 kilometers out in space. Also, TV pictures were transmitted over all that distance, so that men on earth could actually sit in their homes and watch astronauts walking about on the moon. If man can transmit messages in this way, how easy must it be for the Creator of

9. How could imperfect men produce a perfect message for mankind?
10. (a) Why would it be easy for God to transmit messages to faithful man? (Exodus 34:27, 28; Jeremiah 1:1, 2, 9; Ezekiel 11:1; Daniel 7:1) (b) What directed the assembling of the complete Bible, and what is this called? (Revelation 22:18, 19)

all things to transmit messages and visions to men on earth, even from beyond "the heaven of the heavens"! (1 Kings 8:27) As God conveyed his thoughts to the minds of Bible scribes, they wrote these down as "the word of God"—his message. (Hebrews 4:12) God, by his spirit, also directed men to assemble these sixty-six "little books," and these only, to make up the complete Bible, known as the Bible "canon."

AN ACCURATE AND RELIABLE RECORD

¹¹ An amazing thing about the Bible is the carefulness with which it records details, and also its complete harmony. For example, in Genesis, chapters 5 and 10, it sets out the family lists from the time of the first man Adam to that of the sons of Noah, covering a period of more than 2,000 years. Later, the priest Ezra wrote First Chronicles and devoted the first nine chapters to repeating and enlarging on these previous family lists, bringing the record down through another 1,500 years of ancient history to the time when the Israelites returned from captivity in Babylonia. Still later, both Matthew and Luke, in their Gospels, repeated essential parts of these earlier records, and extended the Bible family lists down to Jesus Christ. (Matthew 1:1-17; Luke 3:23-38) Thus, under the direction of God's spirit, the Bible writers made a permanent record of the line of descent from our first ancestor, Adam, down through more than 4,000 years to Jesus, the "Son of man." Of his own Gospel account, the physician Luke wrote:

"I have traced all things from the start with accuracy, to write them in logical order." (Luke 1:3) The record is indeed accurate and logical.

11. Illustrate the accuracy and logical arrangement of the Bible.

90

ison. (1Pe 3:19;
abyss in which
sand years is a
aint or confine-

PROCESSION.

ossibly from a
before in a cho-
nen full of spirit
equal treatment
the first-century
em.—Ac 6:1-6.

administrator of
upervision of the

us of Rome took
i the presence of
ers as senatorial
if the latter was
. The proconsuls
(those who had
insul), who were
l and ex-praetors.
. and ex-praetors,
inces.

bility to direct the
ake judicial deci-
er. His jurisdiction
though his actions
oman senate. The
ir a quaestor. The
y dress or carry a

s is mentioned at
ne a Christian. He
: Acts 18:12, Gallio
l of the province of
ng the term "pro-
ia was a senatorial
E., and again after
senatorial province
us has been found
idius (in Latin) on
Arminius Proclus,
Greek) on the re-

nessage; a revela-
e or the proclama-
: an inspired moral
ivine command or
something to come.
diction, or foretell-
inveyed by the root

verbs in the original languages (Heb., *na·vaʼ*; Gr., *pro·phe·teuʼo*); yet it forms an outstanding feature of Bible prophecy.

Illustrating the sense of the original words are these examples: When Ezekiel in a vision was told to "prophesy to the wind," he simply expressed God's command to the wind. (Eze 37:9, 10) When individuals at Jesus' trial covered him, slapped him, and then said, "Prophesy to us, you Christ. Who is it that struck you?" they were not calling for prediction but for Jesus to identify the slappers by divine revelation. (Mt 26:67, 68; Lu 22:63, 64) The Samaritan woman at the well recognized Jesus as "a prophet" because he revealed things about her past that he could not have known except by divine power. (Joh 4:17-19; compare Lu 7:39.) So, too, such Scriptural portions as Jesus' Sermon on the Mount and his denunciation of the scribes and Pharisees (Mt 23:1-36) may properly be defined as prophecy, for these were an inspired 'telling forth' of God's mind on matters, even as were the pronouncements by Isaiah, Jeremiah, and other earlier prophets.—Compare Isa 55:13-16 and Lu 6:20-25.

Examples of foretelling, or prediction, are, of course, very numerous throughout the entire Bible, some earlier examples being found at Genesis 3:14-19; 9:24-27; 27:27-40; 49:1-28; Deuteronomy 18:15-19.

The Source of all true prophecy is Jehovah God. He transmits it by means of his holy spirit or, occasionally, by spirit-directed angelic messengers. (2Pe 1:20, 21; Heb 2:1, 2) The Hebrew prophecies frequently begin, "Hear the word of Jehovah" (Isa 1:10; Jer 2:4), and by the expression 'the word' is often meant an inspired message, or prophecy.—Isa 44:26; Jer 21:1; Eze 33:30-33; compare Isa 24:3.

In what way did 'the bearing witness to Jesus inspire prophesying'?

In the apostle John's vision he was told by an angel that "the bearing witness to Jesus is what inspires [literally, "is the spirit of"] prophesying." (Re 19:10) The apostle Paul calls Christ "the sacred secret of God" and says that "carefully concealed in him are all the treasures of wisdom and of knowledge." (Col 2:2, 3) This is because Jehovah God assigned to his Son the key role in the outworking of God's grand purpose to sanctify His name and restore earth and its inhabitants to their proper place in His arrangement of things, doing this by means of "an administration at the

full limit of the appointed times, namely, to gather all things together again in the Christ, the things in the heavens and the things on the earth." (Eph 1:9, 10; compare 1Co 15:24, 25.) Since the fulfillment of God's great purpose is all bound up in Jesus (compare Col 1:19, 20), then all prophecy, that is, all inspired messages from God proclaimed by his servants, pointed toward his Son. Thus, as Revelation 19:10 states, the entire "spirit" (the whole inclination, intent, and purpose) of prophecy was to bear witness to Jesus, the one Jehovah would make "the way and the truth and the life." (Joh 14:6) This would be true not only of prophecy that preceded Jesus' earthly ministry but also of prophecy subsequent thereto.—Ac 2:16-36.

At the very time rebellion arose in Eden, Jehovah God started off this "witness to Jesus" by his prophecy regarding the "seed" that would eventually 'crush the head of the serpent,' God's Adversary. (Ge 3:15) The Abrahamic covenant was prophetic of that Seed, of its blessing all the families of earth, and of its victory over the Adversary and his "seed." (Ge 22:16-18; compare Ga 3:16.) It was foretold that the promised Seed, called "Shiloh" (meaning "He Whose It Is; He To Whom It Belongs"), would come from the tribe of Judah. (Ge 49:10) By means of the nation of Israel, Jehovah revealed his purpose to have "a kingdom of priests and a holy nation." (Ex 19:6; compare 1Pe 2:9, 10.) The sacrifices of the Law given to Israel foreshadowed the sacrifice of God's Son, and its priesthood pictures his royal heavenly priesthood (with associate priests) during his Thousand Year Reign. (Heb 9:23, 24; 10:1; Re 5:9, 10; 20:6) Consequently the Law became a "tutor leading to Christ."—Ga 3:23, 24.

Of events marking the history of the nation of Israel, the apostle says: "Now these things went on befalling them as examples [or, "for a typical purpose"], and they were written for a warning to us [followers of Christ Jesus] upon whom the ends of the systems of things have arrived." (1Co 10:11) David, the nation's most prominent king, became a prophetic figure of God's Son, and God's covenant with David for an everlasting kingdom was inherited by Jesus Christ. (Isa 9:6, 7; Eze 34:23, 24; Lu 1:32; Ac 13:32-37; Re 22:6) The various battles fought by faithful kings (usually guided and encouraged by God's prophets) prefigured the war to be waged by God's Son against enemies of his Kingdom, and the victories God gave them thus prefigured Christ's victory over all of Satan's forces, bringing deliverance to God's people.—Ps 110:1-5; Mic 5:2-6; Ac 4:24-28; Re 16:14, 16; 19:11-21.

INSIGHT ON THE SCRIPTURES, Vol 2, 1988

91

⁴ Consider, too, the fact that <u>Jehovah's organization alone, in all the earth, is directed by God's holy spirit or active force.</u> (Zech. 4:6) Only this organization functions for Jehovah's purpose and to his praise. To it alone God's Sacred Word, the Bible, is not a sealed book. Many persons of the world are very intelligent, capable of understanding complex matters. They can read the Holy Scriptures, but they cannot understand their deep meaning. Yet God's people can comprehend such spiritual things. Why? Not because of special intelligence on their part, but as the apostle Paul declared: "For it is to us God has revealed them through his spirit, for the spirit searches into all things, even the deep things of God." (1 Cor. 2:10) Jesus Christ praised his heavenly Father for 'hiding such things from the wise and intellectual ones but revealing them to babes.' (Matt. 11:25) How very much true Christians appreciate associating with the only organization on earth that understands the "deep things of God"!

⁵ Direction by God's spirit enables Jehovah's servants to have divine light in a world of spiritual darkness. (2 Cor. 4: 4) For instance, long ago they understood that 1914 C.E. would mark the end of the Gentile Times or "appointed times of the nations," during which the Gentile nations were allowed uninterrupted rulership of the earth. (Luke 21:24) This 2,520-year period began with the destruction of Jerusalem and its temple by the Babylonians in the late seventh century B.C.E. For example, *Zion's Watch Tower* of March 1880 had declared: " 'The Times of the Gentiles' extend to 1914, and the heavenly kingdom will not have full sway till then." Only God by his holy spirit could have revealed this to those early Bible students so far in advance.

⁶ Another reason to appreciate the organization of Jehovah's Christian witnesses is that it aids us to understand God's provisions for blessing obedient ones, and then to bring our lives into harmony with the divine will. (Matt. 24:45-47) This brings us happiness now despite world gloom, for it is truly satisfying to know that one is pleasing God. By its publications and through other means, the true Christian organization keeps prominently before us the Biblical prospect of endless, happy life under the rule of God's kingdom. (Rev. 21:3-5) What a blessing! How much we should appreciate God's earthly organization and our opportunities to praise Jehovah with his people!

⁷ Furthermore, this organization alone is supplied with "gifts in men," such as evangelizers, shepherds and teachers, who serve God's purpose in connection with the spiritual development and welfare of his people. (Eph. 4:7-16) Appointed overseers or elders and ministerial servants meet Scriptural requirements for their responsible places in Jehovah's organization. Among other things, they welcome honest-hearted people into the Christian congregation and help to educate them in Jehovah's ways. (1 Tim. 3:1-10, 12, 13; Titus 1:5-9) Under the influence of God's holy spirit, you can share in this grand work of finding, welcoming and educating those who will become fellow praisers of Jehovah. What a blessed privilege!

⁸ Think of the people themselves—those praising Jehovah as part of his earthly organization. They are indeed "the desirable things of all the nations." (Hag. 2:7) True Christians have many spiritual brothers, sisters, mothers and children.

---

4. Why can those in Jehovah's earthly organization understand spiritual things?
5. Direction by God's spirit enabled Jehovah's servants long ago to understand what about 1914 C.E.?
6. As to life, what prospect does the Christian organization set before us?
7. What purpose is served by "gifts in men"?
8. Persons of what kind make up Jehovah's earthly organization?

(Mark 10:2
such moral,
live accord
something 1

GRATE

⁹ No wonc
grateful to
earthly org
God with 1
said:

I just wa
happy I am :
I am so grat
me about th
tion in the ;
to be able to
that I am or

¹⁰ After th
one Christia:
fellow believ
wrote:

Let me ass
Jehovah has
brothers and
us. Through
vah's spirit ;
eyes. We are :
these that Je
from the nati

We hope t
to a small d
have brothers
vah's organiz
God's spirit ;
joy cannot b

¹¹ A man wl
years at the ;
vah's witnessc
lyn, New Yor

In the year
have come to
. . . Bethel ca
the crossroads

9. How did one fi
association with Gc
10. Jehovah's organ
bereaved family?
11. How was Bethe
for many years?

2. They had
ctations. As
tainly they
2 lie, steal,
ther wrong-
might well
to them at
0-13) They
d promises.
2 surmount
to God. We
g Christian
y. Also, by
her "to love
. 25.

Jehovah's
remain loyal
ation is his.
e else could
organization
or that is
sting. When
t, he asked
t to go also,
whom shall
ngs of ever-
elieved and
he Holy One
ithful early
persecution
d and to his
ongregation.
aristians in
city's cata-
eas. Family
d places for
Christians
ed and the
couragement
required go-
way. If we
ve, too, will
ization, his
e difficulties

hovah's organi-

[17] You can also show appreciation for God's earthly organization by joining wholeheartedly in the Christian ministry, taking God's Word to other people. Thus you further the educational work that the organization carries on. There is need to participate in that work with a sense of urgency, too, for the end of this wicked system of things is drawing near. The time is short. The harvest is great and the workers are few. (Matt. 9:37, 38) What a privilege it is to be one of the industrious modern-day harvest workers and to do a lifesaving preaching work! By all means, keep busy in the Christian ministry, "always having plenty to do in the work of the Lord, knowing that your labor is not in vain in connection with the Lord." —1 Cor. 15:58.

[18] Faithful, appreciative ones wish to offer a fine "sacrifice of praise" to God. (Heb. 13:15) But how can this be done? Seek Jehovah's help in prayer. Guidance by his holy spirit is needed to aid sheeplike persons and to do one's best in the ministry. So pray for God's spirit to rest upon you. Jehovah graciously grants it to his dedicated servants who make this plea. Jesus Christ stated: "Therefore, if you, although being wicked, know how to give good gifts to your children, how much more so will the Father in heaven give holy spirit to those asking him!"—Luke 11:13.

[19] The holy angels also play their part. Yielding to angelic direction and the influence of Jehovah's holy spirit, Philip the evangelizer found the Ethiopian eunuch and "declared to him the good news about Jesus." The results were immediate. Promptly the Ethiopian was baptized.

---

17. Why engage in the Christian ministry with a sense of urgency?
18. To do well in the ministry, how important are prayer and God's holy spirit?
19, 20. (a) What connection did God's spirit and the holy angels have with the Christian ministry in the past? (b) Do God's holy spirit and angelic direction still affect Christian preaching activities?

Thereafter "Jehovah's spirit quickly led Philip away" and soon he was caring for another ministerial assignment. (Acts 8: 26-40) God's holy spirit and angelic direction also played their part in the preaching work done by the apostle Peter at the home of the Gentile Cornelius. —Acts chapter 10.

[20] That same holy spirit and angelic direction still affect the preaching activities of Christian ministers. The aged apostle John envisioned an "angel flying in mid-heaven" with "everlasting good news" to declare to earth's inhabitants. (Rev. 14: 6, 7) No, today you cannot behold such an angel flying in the sky, or literally hear him speak. But you can hear his message, for it is being delivered on earth by Jehovah's worshipers. In essence, they say of Jehovah: "Look! This is our God. We have hoped in him, and he will save us. This is Jehovah. We have hoped in him. Let us be joyful and rejoice in the salvation by him." (Isa. 25:9) How very much one should appreciate being influenced by God's holy spirit and having angelic direction while bearing the name and declaring the purposes and praises of the Most High as one of Jehovah's Christian witnesses!—Isa. 43:10.

[21] Such an awesome privilege calls for the Christian's best efforts in the ministry. If you are a Christian minister, how can you be effective in your field service? For one thing, keep a good record of ministerial activity. Then it will be possible to make prompt return visits. Furthermore, make these especially effective by thinking in advance about the person's problems, interests or needs. Locate Bible texts that will help the individual. Thereafter, where possible, start and conduct *good* home Bible studies with the person. In this the aid of Jehovah's holy spirit is essential and will be evident. Among oth-

---

21. How can one make effective return visits and conduct good home Bible studies?

heaven-sent messenger, his guide. The vision is a very intimate one of the Lord to his servant, but the remnant whom Ezekiel pictured are commanded to tell others of God's people about it. In obedience to this commandment the faithful have been telling others about the temple of Jehovah.

It was in the spring of 1918 that the Lord Jesus, as the representative of Jehovah, appeared at the temple, and from that time forward the glory of Jehovah has been there. "And I heard him speaking unto me out of the house; and the man stood by me." (43:6) When Ezekiel heard the Lord speaking to him the man stood by him. "The man" was the heavenly messenger, and this pictures the heavenly messengers or angels of the Lord now used by the Lord in behalf of the remnant. These angels are invisible to human eyes and are there to carry out the orders of the Lord. No doubt they first hear the instruction which the Lord issues to his remnant and then these invisible messengers pass such instruction on to the remnant. The facts show that the angels of the Lord with him at his temple have been thus rendering service unto the remnant since 1919. The Lord from his holy temple speaks: "Hear, all ye people; hearken, O earth, and all that therein is: and let the Lord God be witness against you, the Lord from his holy temple." (Mic. 1:2) The faithful remnant in 1922 began to hear and to respond: "Also I heard the voice of the Lord, saying, Whom shall I send, and who will go for us? Then said I, Here am I; send me. And he said, Go and tell this people; Hear ye indeed, but understand not; and see ye indeed, but perceive not." —Isa. 6:8, 9.

That the temple company will have part in the vindication of Jehovah's name, and glorify his holy name, is shown by the words of the Lord spoken to Ezekiel: "And he said unto me, Son of man, the place of my throne, and the place of the soles of my feet, where I will dwell in the midst of the children of Israel for ever, and my holy name, shall the house of Israel no more defile, neither they, nor their kings, by their whoredom, nor by the carcases of their kings in their high places [in their death, A.R.V., margin]." (43:7) The temple of which Ezekiel had a vision is a representation of God's royal house, his kingly organization. Here at the temple Jehovah makes the faithful anointed members of his organization to be kings and priests with Christ. (Rev. 1:6) Jehovah's organization is the place of his rest. (Ps. 132:13,14) It is therefore 'the place of the soles of his feet'. His entire organization is subject to him, as it is written: "The head of Christ is God." (1 Cor. 11:3) His organization is his dwelling place. This corresponds with Revelation 21:3.

The prophetic house of Israel defiled the name of Jehovah, but the real or royal house after the spirit will never defile his holy name. "Christendom" by her ruling factors has greatly defiled the name of Jehovah God. That wicked organization has tried to make Christ to have concord with Satan's organization and to make the temple of God have agreement with idols. (2 Cor. 6:15,16; Rev. 17:1,2) The kings of the earth and their allies, the faithless "Christendom", have at all times of their existence been no better than dead carcasses, because they were dead in trespasses and in sins. The hypocritical claims of such

1971

56   "THE NATIONS SHALL KNOW THAT I AM JEHOVAH",   Ezekiel 2:3-5

4 "And he went on to say to me: 'Son of man, I am sending you to the sons of Israel, to rebellious nations that have rebelled against me. They themselves and their forefathers have transgressed against me down to this selfsame day. And the sons insolent of face and hard of heart—I am sending you to them, and you must say to them, "This is what the Sovereign Lord Jehovah has said." And as for them, whether they will hear or will refrain—for they are a rebellious house—they will certainly know also that a prophet himself happened to be in the midst of them.'"—Ezekiel 2:3-5.

5 "There Ezekiel is definitely told that he is henceforth to serve as a prophet. He is commissioned to speak in the divine name, saying: 'This is what the Sovereign Lord Jehovah has said.' Just as Jehovah had sent Moses as his prophet nine hundred years previously, so now he was sending Ezekiel. Ezekiel was not raising himself up as a prophet and presuming to speak in the divine name. He was really a prophet sent by the Most High God. The fact that Jehovah appeared to Ezekiel in vision and spoke from his throne on his celestial chariot and directly sent Ezekiel on a definite mission with a definite message proves that Ezekiel was a true prophet, sent by God, and that what he spoke under inspiration was the real word of God. The fact, too, that he was sent on such a difficult mission adds to the proof that he did not assume to be a prophet speaking in Jehovah's name, but that the Highest Authority in all existence sent him to speak in the divine name. He was thus, in an outstanding way, made a witness of Jehovah.

6 "Not alone were the inspired words of Ezekiel prophetic, but he himself was a prophetic figure in his action, as is later shown on occasions, (Ezekiel 24:24) Since Ezekiel himself was a "portent," or "sign" (AV), of someone to come, and since he was not a type or

4. To whom was Ezekiel told that he was sent, and after he spoke Jehovah's saying to them, what would they certainly know?
5. Therefore, what proves that Ezekiel did not presume or himself assume to be a prophet speaking in the divine name?
6. Not only were Ezekiel's words prophetic, but what was he himself at the same time?

Ezekiel 2:3-5   COMMISSIONED TO SPEAK IN THE DIVINE NAME   57

prophetic figure of Jesus Christ, whom did the prophet Ezekiel typify in carrying out his divine commission?

7 "Although Ezekiel did not know it at the time that he was commissioned to be Jehovah's prophet, the city of Jerusalem was to be destroyed by the Babylonians just six years later, in 607 B.C.E. Ever since Ezekiel's former acquaintance, Jeremiah the son of Hilkiah the priest, was raised up back there in Jerusalem in the year 647 B.C.E., in the thirteenth year of the reign of King Josiah of Jerusalem, that city and the nation of Judah had been in their fear of the end. (Jeremiah 1:1-3; 25:10, 11) In the right timing of things we today should look for the modern-day counterpart of Ezekiel as a type or prophetic figure in the "time of the end" in which we now find ourselves. Modern historians are agreed that an era ended in the year 1914 C.E., the year in which World War I began its violent, destructive course of more than four years and three months. What those historians do not take into account is that, according to the Holy Bible, the "times of the Gentiles" ended in early autumn of that very year of 1914. (Luke 21:24, AV) Since then we have been in the world's "time of the end."

8 "While the prophet Ezekiel was still an exile in Babylon, those Gentile Times began, in 607 B.C.E., when the armies of the king of Babylon brought destruction upon Jerusalem and, two months later, complete desolation came upon the whole land of Judah, including Jerusalem. (2 Kings 25:1-26; Jeremiah 39:1 to 43:7; 52:1-27) Ezekiel's fellow exile, the prophet Daniel, was used to indicate that those Gentile Times would continue for a period of seven prophetic "times," or for 2,520 years. (Daniel 4:1-28) A count of 2,520 years from the desolation of the land of Judah in the year 607 B.C.E. proves that these years of uninterrupted rule of the whole earth by the Gentile nations ended

7. We should look for the antitype of Ezekiel in what period of time, and since when have we been in that time period?
8. During whose exile in Babylon did those Gentile Times begin, and how, and did the time for us to look for Ezekiel's modern counterpart begin when?

in 1914 C.E. Since that date the Gentile nations, including the nations of Christendom, have been in their "time of the end." Do not world events and developments since then indicate this to be true? (Matthew 24:3-44) Here, then, since 1914, and particularly since the year 1919, after World War I had ended, we should look for the modern-day counterpart of the prophet Ezekiel.

⁹ Who is Ezekiel's present-day counterpart, whose message and conduct correspond with that of that ancient prophet of Jehovah? Of whom today was he a "sign" or "portent"? Not of some individual man, but of a group of people. Being made up of a unified company of persons, the modern Ezekiel is a composite personage, made up of many members, just the same as the human body is. This reminds us of what the onetime persecutor, the Christian apostle Paul, wrote to fellow Christians in Rome, Italy, saying: "Just as we have in one body many members, but the members do not all have the same function, so we, although many, are one body in union with Christ, but members belonging individually to one another." (Romans 12:4, 5) Using the same illustration, Paul said in his letter to the congregation in Corinth, Greece: "Just as the body is one but has many members, and all the members of that body, although being many, are one body, so also is the Christ. For truly by one spirit we were all baptized into one body, whether Jews or Greeks, whether slaves or free, and we were all made to drink one spirit."—1 Corinthians 12:12, 13.

¹⁰ So it is with the modern-day counterpart of Ezekiel: it is, not one person's body, but a composite body, made up of many members. All these members were together to do the will of Jehovah, who is the Creator of this modern "Ezekiel." Who, then, are the group of persons who, toward the beginning of this "time"

9. Is the modern-day Ezekiel an individual person, and how does the apostle Paul illustrate how Ezekiel's counterpart could be?
10. In order to determine which group is Ezekiel's modern counterpart, what do we have to do?

of the end," were commissioned to serve as the mouthpiece and active agent of Jehovah? In order to determine this, check the history of 1919, the first postwar year after the first world war.

¹¹ We do not look among the natural circumcised Jews, for they had actively taken part in World War I, the famous Zionist leader, Chaim Weizmann, lending his services as a discoverer in the chemical field to the British Government during that world conflict. In 1919 they were mainly interested in establishing a National Homeland for the Jews in Palestine, rather than in fulfilling any religious commission like that of ancient Ezekiel. But what about religious Christendom? Her appearance before Jehovah was also gruesomely bloodstained, for World War I was mainly her war, twenty-four of the twenty-eight participants in carnal warfare claiming to be Christian nations. When this first world conflict ended in 1918 (November 11), victorious Great Britain and her allies were interested in establishing a peace arrangement with the conquered nations, besides dealing with the newly arisen Communist State in Russia. Playing the modern-day role of the Bible "Ezekiel" was far from their thoughts.

¹² The churches of Christendom had taken no courageous Christian steps to prevent World War I. They had split into two great camps over the nationalistic war issues. The end of the war found them disunited, needing to get reconciled and to become religious friends again. According to the Treaty of London that had been signed on May 9, 1915, by Italy, Great Britain, France and Russia, "the Holy See [the pope of Rome] was not to be permitted to intervene by diplomatic action in regard to peace or questions arising from the war."* So the pro-German Vatican was not allowed to have any part in drawing up the Peace

* Quoted from The Encyclopedia Americana, Volume 17, edition of 1929, page 633.

11. When we look at natural Jewry and then at Christendom for the proper group, wherein lies unsatisfactoriness; do we find?
12. When we look at the churches of Christendom, including the Vatican, for the proper group, what do we find?

96

1971

²³ Why, though, are all these facts of history brought to our attention? It is to show the fulfillment of prophecy. Jehovah has found and commissioned his modern-day "Ezekiel." It is a composite Ezekiel. It is composed of those dedicated, baptized proclaimers of God's kingdom, who have been anointed with His spirit for their work. (Isaiah 61:1-3) It is manifest that in the year 1919 the invisible heavenly organization of Jehovah, like the celestial chariot seen in Ezekiel's vision, rolled up and stopped, not before Christendom's advocates of the League of Nations, but before the anointed proclaimers of the heavenly kingdom of God in the hands of Jesus Christ. From atop this celestial chariotlike organization Jehovah commissioned this dedicated, baptized, anointed class of servants to speak to all the nations in His name. Thus, like Ezekiel, they became Jehovah's witnesses. It was most fitting that, after twelve years of worldwide activity as such, they embraced the distinguishing name Jehovah's witnesses in the summer of 1931, and that in connection with the publishing of the book *Vindication*.

WHO COMMISSIONED THE MODERN-DAY "EZEKIEL"?

²⁴ Let not the rabbis of Judaism and the clergy of Christendom say, "We did not ordain and commission these witnesses of Jehovah to be the modern antitype of the prophet Ezekiel." But what does that matter? Whoever made those rabbis and sectarian clergymen a religious body for the appointment of the official servants of the Most High God? Any ordination and commission proceeding from those religionists would be of no value and of no force in this regard. What is all-essential is for a person or group of persons to have an appointment and a commission from the Most High God, Jehovah, himself. This is what counts. As the

24. Our attention to these facts of history helps us to identify whom today, and what name was embraced at the time when the book *Vindication* was released?
25. Of what concern is it, that Jewish rabbis and Christendom's clergy have not appointed Jehovah's witnesses as an antitypical Ezekiel, and what is it that counts, and why?

Supreme Being he can go over the heads of those religionists and determine for Himself who qualifies for the special work that He desires to be done in this "time of the end."

²⁵ Back in the year 613 B.C.E. Jehovah went over the head of the High Priest, Seraiah, and of the second priest, Zephaniah, at the temple in Jerusalem, and appointed Ezekiel the son of Buzi an underpriest to be his prophet in the land of Babylon, to speak in His name and to bear witness to Him. (2 Kings 25:18) From atop his celestial chariot Jehovah said to Ezekiel: "Son of man, I am sending you to the sons of Israel, to rebellious nations that have rebelled against me." (Ezekiel 2:3) So it was with the anointed, dedicated witnesses of Jehovah back there in the year 1919 C.E. The facts from then on down to this date prove that they received their ordination and appointment and commission for their work in this "time of the end" from Jehovah himself through his heavenly chariotlike organization. Hence they have taken their divine commission very seriously as being a real Biblical thing, and they have tried to carry it out faithfully in spite of the criticism and objections of the clergy of Christendom.

²⁶ Who, then, are the "sons of Israel,... rebellious nations that have rebelled against [Jehovah]," to whom the modern-day antitypical Ezekiel is sent in this "time of the end"? They are not the natural, circumcised "sons of Israel," who were seeking a National Jewish Homeland back in the year 1919 C.E, with Chaim Weizmann as their Zionist leader. No, but there is a modern-day counterpart of those ancient "sons of Israel,...rebellious nations."

²⁷ That counterpart is Christendom, which claims

26. Who were disregarded in the appointment of Ezekiel to be prophet and witness, and from whom do Jehovah's anointed witnesses of today receive their appointment as coming?
27. What question arises as to the "sons of Israel, ...rebellious nations," to whom the modern-day Ezekiel was sent, and what about the natural Jews back in 1919 C.E.?
28. What is the modern-day counterpart of the "sons of Israel,...rebellious nations," according to what religious claim?

97

was sent were "insolent of face and hard of heart." At the time, they might not view or appreciate him as a prophet of Jehovah. Nevertheless, whether they paid attention to him or refrained, the occasion was to come when these rebellious people would "know also that a prophet himself happened to be in the midst of them." Jehovah would confirm him as a prophet then by causing what Ezekiel prophesied to come true. (Ezek. 2:3-5) Ezekiel was further told:

> "And you, O son of man, do not be afraid of them; and of their words do not be afraid, because there are obstinate ones and things pricking you and it is among scorpions that you are dwelling. Of their words do not you be afraid, and at their faces do not you be struck with terror, for they are a rebellious house. And you must speak my words to them, regardless of whether they hear or they refrain, for they are a case of rebellion." —Ezek. 2:6, 7.

Since the year 1919 C.E. Jehovah's witnesses have found circumstances to be just like that as they have made the widest possible declaration of the good news of the Kingdom in 207 lands of the earth.

To Ezekiel, in his vision, and, symbolically to the modern-day "prophet," the spirit-begotten, anointed ones who are the nucleus of Jehovah's witnesses today, God gave something to eat. Ezekiel says:

> "And I began to see, and, look! there was a hand thrust out to me, and, look! in it there was the roll of a book. And he gradually spread it out before me, and it was written upon in front and on the back; and there were written in it dirges and moaning and wailing." —Ezek. 2:8-10.

No space on the scroll being wasted, it being written upon on both sides, it was a full message, containing a great deal of gloomy messages of calamity, back there to Jewry, and today to Christendom. Why so? Because in both instances Jehovah's professed people were so rebellious and set in their ungodly way that Jehovah had to pronounce judgment upon them.

The scroll was doubtless delivered to Ezekiel by the hand of one of the cherubs in the vision. This would indicate that Jehovah's witnesses today make their declaration of the good news of the Kingdom under angelic direction and support. (Rev. 14:6, 7; Matt. 25:31, 32) And since no word or work of Jehovah can fail, for he is God Almighty, the nations will see the fulfillment of what these witnesses say as directed from heaven.

Yes, the time must come shortly that the nations will have to know that really a "prophet" of Jehovah was among them. Actually now more than a million and a half persons are helping that collective or composite "prophet" in his preaching work and well over that number of others are studying the Bible with the "prophet" group and its companions.

So Jehovah has made every provision for individuals to know him and to receive his loving-kindness and life. Thus there is no excuse for Christendom's people not to know Jehovah. More than that, Jehovah is interested not only in the vindication of his own name but also in vindicating his "prophet." Through another of his ancient prophets, Isaiah, he said to Jewry just as he says to Christendom today: "Look! My own servants will cry out joyfully because of the good condition of the heart, but you yourselves will make outcries because of the pain of heart and you will howl because of sheer breakdown of spirit." —Isa. 65:14.

Even today we hear complaints from Christendom's churches about dwindling church attendance and see many young men abandoning the priesthood and the ministerial profession. Yet at the same time we see spiritual prosperity and contentment among those proclaiming Jehovah's Messianic kingdom. We may look for an even more marked fulfillment of Isaiah's words in the near future.

...entire picture shows that what is there de-...ed is fulfilled when the Lord Jesus is at the tem-...of Jehovah for judgment, and this fixes the time ...the work of scattering the fire by the man in ...must be done. 'Jehovah is in his holy temple, ...ovah's throne is in heaven; his eyes behold, his ...lids try, the children of men. Jehovah trieth the ...teous; but the wicked, and him that loveth vio-...his soul hateth. Upon the wicked he shall rain ...fire and brimstone, and an horrible tempest; ...shall be the portion of their cup.' (Ps. 11:4-6; ...14:15; Mal. 3:1-3) When the Lord is at the ...ple for judgment, the glory of Jehovah is over the ...When Jehovah shall build up Zion, he shall ...pear in his glory.' (Ps. 102:16) The vision of ...kiel discloses the Lord Jesus Christ at the temple ...judgment, accompanied by his corps of officers ...up of cherubim, seraphim and angels, and em-...ing both animate and inanimate parts of the great ...organization to carry forward God's purposes; and ...are symbolized by wheels and the cherubim and ...living creatures.

...foregoing scriptures lay the foundation for the ...clusion that, following the year 1918, which marks ...coming of the Lord to his temple, the prophetic ...on of Ezekiel here described began to be fulfilled, ...until that time the prophecy could not be under-...

...commandment to the man clothed in linen was ...in between the wheels, under the cherubim, thus ...ing that the "servant" class on earth is under ...direction of the higher officers of God's organi-...tion and are to work with both animate and inani-...parts of the organization in obedience to the ...commandments. "And it came to pass, that when ...had commanded the man clothed in linen, saying, ...ke fire from between the wheels, from between the ...rubims; then he went in, and stood beside the ...els. And one cherub stretched forth his hand from ...ween the cherubims unto the fire that was between ...cherubims, and took thereof, and put it into the ...hands of him that was clothed with linen; who took ...and went out." (Ezek. 10:6,7) This shows that ...d makes all provision necessary to carry out all his ...judgments of fiery indignation upon Satan's organi-...tion. It is thrilling and awesome for the "servant" ...class of Jehovah to realize that they are permitted ...work under the guiding hand of God's great officers ...are invisible to their eyes. This helps them to ap-...ciate the fact that, the "servant", trusting im-...licitly in Jehovah and not following his own selfish ...course, but being always joyfully obedient to Jehovah, ...ways are directed of Jehovah and therefore cannot ...l. (Prov. 3:5,6) "The steps of a good man [God's ...al man, the 'faithful servant'] are ordered by the ...d; and he delighteth in his way."—Ps. 37:23.

...actual burning or destruction by fire is done ...the officers of Jehovah that are invisible to human

eyes, that is, the cherubim, seraphim and angels; but it seems clear that the cherubim have charge over fire or that which destroys. These invisible ones Jehovah uses to put in the hands of his "faithful servant" class, that is, the man clothed with linen, the fiery message from his Word, or judgments written, and which is to be used as directed. The resolutions adopted by conventions of God's anointed people, booklets, magazines, and books published by them, contain the message of God's truth and are from the Almighty God, Jehovah, and provided by him through Christ Jesus and his underofficers. This shows the grand and glorious organization working in exact harmony, as indeed it must work. These instruments being provided by Jehovah, and placed in the hand of the remnant, the remnant or "servant" class is commanded to use the same.

The interpretation of prophecy, therefore, is not from man, but is from Jehovah; and Jehovah causes events to come to pass in fulfillment of the prophecy in due time. It is his truth, and not man's; and when men attempt to give the honor and glory for the message of truth to a man or men, such make fools of themselves. Jehovah provides the machinery, the printing presses, and all material for the purpose of preparing his fiery message that must be poured out or scattered upon "Christendom", and this is done by his "faithful servant" class. The Devil tries to induce men to believe that the Watch Tower Bible and Tract Society is engaging in a bookselling scheme. Only the Devil is capable of manufacturing such a lie. God's "servant" class, pictured by the man in linen, is commanded to do the work of declaring the vengeance of Jehovah, and only those who obey this commandment can and will maintain their integrity toward God. The "servant", or remnant class, will not be deceived or discouraged by the slanderous statements of enemies that they are engaged in a bookselling scheme. They carry the message of truth to the people in printed form; and this is done under the commandment of Jehovah, and is the greatest privilege that has ever been granted the followers of Christ on earth. The remnant delights to do this work and continually sings the praises of Jehovah while doing it.

It is easy to be seen that the remnant must do a twofold work, as pictured by the work of Ezekiel, in this: They go from house to house, carrying the message of truth in printed form of books and magazines and by phonograph with discs; they first deliver an introductory message to the one whom they address; they do not open their testimony with a denunciation of the wicked, but first speak of the message of the goodness of God that gives hope to those who will hear, and comfort those that mourn. This is the commission of the remnant.

At the same time the remnant must declare or tell the people of God's judgment of fiery indignation

99

over his household, to give them meat in due season? Blessed is that servant, whom his lord when he cometh shall find so doing. Verily I say unto you, that he shall make him ruler over all his goods." (Matt. 24: 45-47; see also Luke 12: 42-44) Whom do the facts of our day prove to be that "faithful and wise servant"?

Aside from Christ Jesus, divine prophecy foretells no individual man. In times past prophetic figures such as Elijah, Elisha, and others, were used to foreshadow a company or society of faithful, devoted servants of God, who should be Jehovah's witnesses at the end of the world, where we are at present. Likewise, the expression "faithful and wise servant" does not picture any man or individual on earth now, but means the faithful remnant of Jehovah's witnesses who are begotten of His spirit and gathered into a unity unto Him and His service. They are part of his Theocratic organization and are subject to Theocratic rule, which means, the divine will as to organization and work. They act as a unit or society, together doing Jehovah's "strange work" as he reveals it to them. (Isa. 54: 13; Ps. 65: 14) Such "society" is not a legal society or corporation, chartered according to the laws of some state or nation, but is a society or association formed by the Creator, Jehovah God, and composed of his spiritual remnant approved by Christ Jesus at the temple judgment. Such society, however, may use as their earthly instrumentality or servant a legal corporation, such as the Watch Tower Bible and Tract Society; and they do so, since A.D. 1884. Christ Jesus is the Chief Servant of Jehovah God, and he is the invisible or heavenly Head of the "faithful and wise servant" class.—Isa. 42: 1; Matt. 12: 15-21.

To such remnant of faithful servants of Jehovah God Christ Jesus has entrusted all "his goods", or earthly interests of the Kingdom. This does not signify that the faithful remnant or society of Jehovah's anointed witnesses are an earthly tribunal of interpretation, delegated to interpret the Scriptures and its prophecies. No; Christ Jesus the King has not entrusted that office to them. THE SUPREME COURT STILL INTERPRETS, thank God; and Christ Jesus, the Court's official mouthpiece of interpretation, reserves to himself that office as Head of Jehovah's "faithful and wise servant" class. He merely uses the "servant" class to publish the interpretation after the Supreme Court by Christ Jesus reveals it. How does the Lord God make known the interpretation? By causing the facts to come to pass visibly which are in fulfillment of the prophecy or dark saying or misunderstood scripture. Thereafter "in due season" he calls such

fulfillment or clarification of prophecy and scripture to the attention of his "faithful and wise servant" class. Thereby he makes them responsible to make known the meaning of such scriptures to all members of the household of faith and to all persons of good-will. This constitutes giving them the "meat in due season".

In bygone days those now composing the "faithful and wise servant" class or remnant of Jehovah's witnesses have believed many things which were not strictly correct according to the Scriptures. They continued to hold on to such beliefs even for some time after A.D. 1918, when Christ Jesus arrived at the temple. Today they see and understand differently, with Scripture backing. Does this mean that God is the Author of confusion or that they are not of His Theocratic organization? No; Jehovah God is not the author of confusion, but is the remover of confusion from his devoted people who both pray and seek to know his truth. Although the understanding of his "servant" class has cleared up and has been corrected, yet the text of God's infallible Word has not changed and its information has been there all the time from days of old.

After Jehovah's royal Associate Judge came to the temple for judgment and the purification of his people, Jehovah God used his Messenger and Interpreter to cleanse away, little by little and point by point, any misunderstanding, which misunderstanding was due to their having been in contact with religion in the past or due to not having the fulfilled facts at hand because it was not yet God's due time. Thus Jehovah by Christ Jesus continues to this day to lead them in the path of truth, and they follow the revealed decisions of the Supreme Court of Interpretation and walk on in the light. Such increase of light is in fulfillment of God's promise: "The path of the just is as the shining light, that shineth more and more unto the perfect day." (Prov. 4: 18) The light continues to grow brighter, and the perfect day is at hand, as we walk on where our Guide and Interpreter leads us.—Ps. 25: 9.

Thus the great Supreme Interpreter magnifies now his infallible Word. Shortly, at the battle of Armageddon, Jehovah by his Associate Judge and Executioner will vindicate that Word. He will also magnify his holy name and destroy all opposing kings of this world. For that reason his faithful remnant, who are in line to be "kings and priests" with Christ Jesus, bow toward Jehovah God, who is representatively in his holy temple by Christ Jesus. Their beloved earthly companions bow with them,

---

36. (a) Whom does that "faithful and wise servant" picture? (b) Is a legal corporation meant, or what part does a legal corporation play therein? (a) The Lord's entrusting "all his goods" to the "servant" class has what connection with interpretation of the Scriptures? (b) How does the Lord God make known the interpretation, and what responsibility thereafter falls upon the "servant" class?

37. Why does difference of understanding today from that held previously not prove God the author of confusion or prove that the remnant of Jehovah's witnesses are not of His organization?
38. How, then, do we explain Scripturally the change of understanding since the Lord's coming to the temple?
39. What is the Supreme Interpreter thereby doing respecting his Word? and for that cause what do the remnant and their faithful companions do respecting Jehovah God?

APRIL 15, 1943   *The*WATCHTOWER   127

Joshua to that of David Jehovah fought their battles for them and ultimately the accursed Canaanites were subjugated. Some served the priests at the temple as "hewers of wood and drawers of water". (Josh. 9:23) During the peaceful reign of Solomon all the Canaanites who had not been destroyed or driven out of the promised land were subject to a tribute of bond-service. "And all the people that were left of the Amorites, Hittites, Perizzites, Hivites, and Jebusites, which were not of the children of Israel, their children that were left after them in the land, whom the children of Israel also were not able utterly to destroy, upon those did Solomon levy a tribute of bondservice unto this day." (1 Kings 9:20, 21) Thus the descendants of Shem, whose God was Jehovah, possessed the land once occupied by the descendants of Ham and the accursed Canaan, who did not acknowledge Jehovah as their God but worshiped idols and false gods. They were either destroyed or reduced to a condition of servitude.

The name "Shem" means "name, renown, fame", and through his lineage came many men of valor. Their fame as men of faith in Jehovah, the God of Shem, is made known in the eleventh chapter of Hebrews. Another statement concerning Shem which, if true, would greatly enhance his fame and renown, is that made by many scholars that Shem and Melchizedek were one and the same person. Melchizedek is the first one mentioned in the Scriptures as a man who ruled any people by divine right: Undoubtedly he was of Shem's line, and it is quite probable that he was Shem. Shem was living at the time Abraham met Melchizedek and paid tithes to him. In fact, he lived up till within twenty-five years of Abraham's death. "Shem was an hundred years old, and begat Arphaxad two years after the flood: and Shem lived after he begat Arphaxad five hundred years."—Gen. 11:10, 11.

If the peoples of earth today would receive the blessings of the Lord, some of which were prophetically foretold through Shem, let them follow a course of action that says, in effect, "Blessed be Jehovah, the God of Shem."

RESOLUTION

We, the Hot Springs (Ark.) company of Jehovah's witnesses, knowing that we must pass through much tribulation before entering the Kingdom, do adopt and make this our resolution:

As Jehovah's witnesses we are commissioned to comfort all that mourn, as stated in Isaiah 61:1, 2; that Jehovah has enthroned Christ Jesus as King of The Theocracy and he has now begun his reign amidst his enemies, and that now is the time to defeat persecution; that the time is now here when the people have a right to hear discussed the great truths concerning the establishment of the great Theocracy as expressed in His Word, the Bible.

That it is our duty to fear only God, and not man, and that we must and will obey His supreme command in preference to man's command the same as the faithful that have gone before us have suffered for and obeyed The Theocracy and rejoiced in that privilege.

Therefore, be it resolved, that we, as Jehovah's witnesses,

will, by His grace, be faithful to our covenant and that we are determined not to slack the hand and therefore not yield to the Devil's side of the issue. We, therefore, will stand unitedly, shoulder to shoulder in the fight for The Theocracy on Jehovah's side and as "fighters for the New World". That we will not break our covenant because of arrests, persecution or imprisonment and will push on in the work Jehovah through Christ Jesus has commissioned us to perform until "the cities be wasted" and Armageddon is on. We rejoice in the opportunity of bearing the reproach that fell on the Perfect One and to be counted worthy to suffer for his name, and that, by God's grace, we will not stop preaching this gospel of the Kingdom, regardless of the fact that we are classed as "peddlers" by some city ordinance passed by men.

Further, be it resolved, that we are united with those at Bethel by the spirit of Jehovah and that we will continue so and to recognize Jehovah's channel to give us "meat in due season".

Unanimously adopted.

(Continued from page 114)

cherished freedoms for preservation of which Jehovah's witnesses are putting up a splendid fight on the "home front" everywhere. *Fighting for Liberty on the Home Front* shows, with much evidence, who is the enemy of liberty, and why the fight therefor must continue on after the global war ends. A copy will be mailed to you, postpaid, on your contribution of 5c.

MEMORIAL

The date Scripturally arrived at for 1943 for celebrating the memorial to Jehovah's name and to the faithful death of his King, Christ Jesus, is Monday, April 19. After 6 p.m., Standard Time, of that date each Christian company should assemble, and the anointed ones thereof celebrate the Memorial, their companions as the Lord's "other sheep" being present as observers. If no competent person is present to deliver a brief discourse immediately before partaking of the emblems, then appropriate paragraphs may be read from the Memorial articles appearing in the March 1 and 15, 1943, issues of *The Watchtower* to those assembled. Since the breaking of the bread and the drinking of the wine both picture Christ's death, in which also his body members partake, it follows that both emblems should be served together at partaking, and not separately. The emblems should be unleavened bread and real red wine. Jesus and his apostles most certainly used real red wine in symbol of his blood, and the anointed remnant should follow their lead. Report your cele-

bration and its total attendance and partakers of the emblems to the Society, as instructed also in the *Informant*.

"THE WATCHTOWER"

The Watchtower is a magazine without equal in the earth, and is conceded this rank by all that have been faithful readers thereof during its more than sixty years of publication. *The Watchtower* has increased in importance with the progress of the years, and never has it been more valuable than today, at this world crisis, when the destiny of each intelligent human creature is being decided. The getting of correct information and instruction, just such as is required for the times, to decide your course wisely to a happy destiny, was never more vital than now, for "where there is no vision, the people perish". Informed persons well acquainted with the consistent contents of *The Watchtower* agree that those who want to gain life in peace and happiness without end should read and study it together with the Bible and in company with other readers. This is not giving any credit to the magazine's publishers, but is due to the great Author of the Bible with its truths and prophecies, and who now interprets its prophecies. He it is that makes possible the material that is published in the columns of this magazine and who gives promise that it shall continue to publish the advancing truths as long as it continues to exist for the service of the interests of his Theocratic Government. Carefully and prayerfully read this issue of *The Watchtower*. Then do not delay to mail in your subscription, that you may receive it regularly, twice a month, twenty-four copies the year. It is $1.00 in the United States; $1.50 elsewhere.

Trust in the Lord, wait patiently for him, and he will bring to pass in his due time and way (the best time and way) all the gracious promises of his Word—including the blessing of all the families of earth.

We see the various inequalities and wrongs of the present system of society more clearly than others, because we see them from the standpoint of the Lord's Word; but we can see also that, if it were within our power to suddenly revolutionize matters, that would be undesirable: it would produce a condition far worse than the present. Far better the present social system than none; and far better, while the present system continues, that the power remain in the hands of men of judgment and moderation than that the lever of power be suddenly transferred into the hands of the rash and inexperienced masses, unused to weighty responsibilities, and mere novices and experimenters upon all questions, social and financial. A thousand times better is a social system in the hands of education and experience, even though selfish, than no social system, or an experimental one in the hands of novices equally selfish, but not equally moderate. We much prefer them to stay as long as we can where we are than to change to any other arrangement that men can originate, or assist in any way to precipitate the trouble, which sooner or later must inevitably involve all nations and all individuals.

Better, far better, *wait on the Lord*,—wait until his time for establishing his kingdom and have it come about in his way. He will eventually restrain the forces of evil and selfishness in both rich and poor and bring in equity and everlasting righteousness.

So, then, although we know that the revolution and anarchy and trouble are surely coming, let *us*, "brethren" of Christ, do nothing to promote or hasten it. Let our advice be to the contrary, to any of our friends who seek our counsel. Especially let us improve the opportunity for pointing out to them the true and only remedy for present distress—Christ's kingdom and its new social order under the law of Love. And, to all who have ears to hear, preach Christ the Redeemer, soon, as the Great Physician, to be the Restorer of all who cheerfully obey him. Point him out as *now* our Saviour, *your* Saviour. Tell them of the joy and peace and blessing which he gives and which he promises shall abide with us in every condition. Tell them that it is for this reason that "*We* will not fear though the earth [society] be removed; though the mountains [governments] be removed and carried into the midst of the sea [the ungovernable masses]; though the waters [the people] thereof roar and be troubled; though the mountains [governments] shake with the swellings [riots, tumults, etc.] thereof."

And if they become interested and willing, lead them to the Lamb of God and the streams of truth that make glad the true people of God,—and if they be converted to God, *seal* them in the forehead (mind, intellect) with the wonderful present truth with which God has caused us to be sealed.—Rev. 7:3.

Remember that now is the time to be active co-workers with God in doing this sealing work, and that the disturbing winds are being held back until the sealing work is done. Therefore, when the present disturbances pass away and another season of comparative calm follows, continue earnest and zealous in the sealing work, knowing that the time is short and that the night [the darker period—cometh when no man *can* work." We must labor while it is called day, and cannot hope for a more favorable opportunity than the present. "Be thou faithful unto death, and I will give thee a crown of life," is the promise.

CAN IT BE DELAYED UNTIL 1914?

Seventeen years ago people said, concerning the time features presented in MILLENNIAL DAWN, They seem reasonable in many respects, but surely no such radical changes could occur between now and the close of 1914: if you had proved that they would come about in a century or two, it would seem much more probable.

What changes have since occurred, and what velocity is gained daily?

"The old is quickly passing and the new is coming in."

Now, in view of recent labor troubles and threatened anarchy, our readers are writing to know if there may not be a mistake in the 1914 date. They say that they do not see how present conditions can hold out so long under the strain.

We see no reason for changing the figures—nor could we change them if we would. They are, we believe, God's dates, not ours. But bear in mind that the end of 1914 is not the date for the *beginning*, but for the *end* of the time of trouble. We see no reason for changing from our opinion expressed in the view presented in the WATCH TOWER of January 15, '92. We advise that it be read again.

TRACT No. 21—DO YOU KNOW?

We published one hundred and fifteen thousand copies of this tract, and have sent samples to all our TOWER readers. It seems to give general satisfaction, and orders from all quarters are large. We advise the circulation of this tract by all of you—on street cars, steam cars, at hotels and depots, and Sundays on the street corners—until every one within your reach has been supplied. Order all that you will *agree* to use. Never mind the money. Many have opportunity for distributing sample copies of Old Theology Tracts who have no money to spare to pay for their printing, etc., but others, again, who have less opportunity for distributing tracts, take delight in meeting the publishing expenses, and thus help to preach the "good tidings of great joy, which shall be unto all people."

The first edition, although large, is already exhausted, but we have another addition of over two hundred thousand under way, which will be ready in about ten days. Send in your order and have a share in this feature of the harvest work. There should be a million of these tracts distributed this year.

"ANGELS WHICH KEPT NOT THEIR FIRST ESTATE."

"The sons of God saw the daughters of men that they were fair, and they took them wives of all, which they chose. . . . And they bear children to them, the same became mighty men, which were of old, men of renown."—Gen. 6:2, 4.

The Scriptures not only point us to the future age and call the spiritual government of Christ which shall then exist a "new heavens," and heavenly society and institutions under it a "new earth;" but the present spiritual rulership [under Satan, "the prince of this world"] and earthly institutions under it are termed "The present evil world," dispensation or epoch. Moreover, we are informed that the present dominion of evil has not lasted forever, but that it was preceded by a still different dispensation or epoch spoken of as "the world that was before the flood," which also had a heavens or spiritual ruling power, and an earth, or condition of men subject to that spiritual dominion.

The three worlds mentioned by Peter (2 Pet. 3:6, 7, 13) designate these three great epochs of time, in each of which, God's plan with reference to men has a distinct and separate outline, yet each is but a part of the one great plan which, when complete, will exhibit the divine wisdom, though considered separately these parts would fail to show their deep design.

Since that first "world" ("heavens and earth," or that *order of things*,) passed away at the time of the flood, it follows that it must have been a *different* order from the present, and hence the prince of this present evil world was not the prince of that which preceded this—of the world or dispensation before the flood.

Several scriptures seem to throw light on God's dealings during that first dispensation, and we think give a further and clearer insight into his plan and purpose as a whole. The thought suggested by these is, that the first world (the dispensation before the flood) was under the supervision and special ministration of the angels; that these were man's governors and overseers commissioned to communicate God's will and to rule over the fallen and degenerating race, which, because of sin, needed this government.

That angels were the rulers of that epoch is not only indicated by all references to that period, but may be reasonably inferred from the Apostle's remark when contrasting the present dispensation with the past and the future. He endeavors to show both the righteousness and the enduring character of the future rulership of the world, saying, "The world to come hath he not put in subjection to the angels." No, it is put under the control of Jesus and his joint-heirs, and hence it shall not only be more righteous than the present rule of Satan, but it shall be more successful than was the previous rule by the angels.—See Heb. 2:2, 5.

In their original estate all the angels seemed to possess

[1677]
102

world that the great World War would end all wars and make the world safe for democracy; and that the young men who died on the field of battle would die sacrificial deaths as did Jesus and would go to heaven. Their prophecies did not come true. Therefore they are false prophets; and the people should no longer trust them as safe guides, but should look to the Lord through his revealed Word for their instructions as to what is to occur on the earth in the future.

The Apostle Peter warns us of these false prophets in the last days, saying: "But there were false prophets also among the people, even as there shall be false teachers among you, who privily shall bring in damnable heresies, even denying the Lord that bought them." (2 Pet. 2:1) There are many thousands of prominent religious leaders in our day who deny that the blood of Jesus bought the race; they claim that it was not necessary for Jesus to die; they go even further and claim that he did not die, but was really more alive than ever, when he was buried in Joseph's tomb. These are false prophets, because they contradict the Bible and the words of the holy prophets, and thus cast reproach on the Bible and lead people to doubt its truthfulness, and thus turn people away from God.

The words of God's true prophets on this subject are as follows: "Without shedding of blood is no remission." (Heb. 9:22) "Christ died for our sins according to the scriptures." (1 Cor. 15:3) "Ye are bought with a price." (1 Cor. 6:20) "Ye were not redeemed with corruptible things, as silver and gold, . . . but with the precious blood of Christ, as of a lamb without blemish and without spot."—1 Pet. 1:18,19.

Several texts tell us that Jesus was dead, and was raised on the third day. (1 Cor. 15:4) The false teachers claim that Jesus was not dead, and hence did not need a resurrection. These false prophets claim that it is the body that will be resurrected. But Paul, one of God's holy prophets, speaking of the resurrection of the dead, says: "But some man will say, How are the dead raised up? and with what body do they come? Thou fool! . . . that which thou sowest, thou sowest not that body that shall be . . . ; but God giveth it a body as it hath pleased him."—1 Cor. 15:35-38.

The false prophets claim that the earth is to be burned up at some future time; but God's holy prophets emphatically state to the contrary. In Ecclesiastes 1:4 we read: "The earth abideth for ever." Again, in Isaiah 45:18 we read: "God himself . . . formed the earth and made it; he hath established it, he created it not in vain, he formed it to be inhabited." These false prophets tell the people that God has provided a lake of fire and brimstone in which to torture for ever those who do not accept their teach-

ings; others tell the people that many are in purgatory, and that it is possible to pray them out. They teach the people the doctrine of the trinity; namely, that 'God the Father, God the Son, and God the holy ghost are three persons in one, and all three equal in substance, in power and in eternity'. They tell the people that they need not study the Bible, 'because they cannot understand it'; and that if the people will follow the instructions of these false prophets they will not need to study the Bible. Without exception, these things are unscriptural and untrue, and tend to turn the people away from God and from Bible study.

These false prophets claim that the governments of earth, even though very wicked and corrupt, constitute God's kingdom on earth. They claim that all the saved will be in heaven, in face of hundreds of texts which say that the righteous shall inherit the land and dwell therein for ever. (Isa. 60:21) They discourage Bible study by telling the people that the "Bible is an old fiddle on which one can play any tune", that it is a book of mystery, and that God did not intend it to be understood. Such remarks turn people away from God and from the Bible, and brand the authors of such statements as being false prophets.

Why is it that the words of God's holy prophets are discredited, denied and sneered at, while the words of these false prophets are given the widest possible publicity, and approved by all great men of earth? The records of God's holy prophets, found in the Bible, show that Adam was the first man, and that he lived about 6,056 years ago. Quite recently a man found some bones in Nebraska, and broadcast to the world that they were the bones of a man who had lived in Nebraska over 5,000,000 years ago. His statement was wild, unreasonable and foolish; yet it could be published in the best magazines and newspapers and retailed from the best pulpits and platforms in the world.

On the contrary, if any one should try to defend the accuracy of the Bible and prove that its authors were holy men sent of God, his copy would be refused by the best newspapers and magazines, and he would be denied the use of halls or pulpits to put forth his message. Should some paper be liberal enough to publish his defense, it would be so garbled as to discredit the author and hold him up to ridicule. Why is this true? The answer is that the false prophets, financial, political and religious, control the pulpit and the press; and that they desire to hold on to their positions of trust, influence and power. They do not want the truth, namely, that they are false prophets, to get out to the people; and, so they use their power over the pulpit and press to keep the message from the people.

Anyone who will stand up to defend Jehovah God

May 15, 1930

Bible teaching had

itnesses have con-
om. The very first
iat "merit toward
vention sponsored
r Point, Ohio, the
ome! All Believers
of *The Watchtower*
rning the purpose
igning King, Jesus
) gain eternal life."

ll at once. In many
m of truth but did
re willing to learn.
What they learned
they taught; they
y came to appreci-
e details of his pur-
; compare John 16:

oint. If mistakes are
ility is needed. This
h a course strongly
uled by those who
y centuries, though

those who were dil-
rned that when the
ohn 14:3, 19.

t the error of Second
nd teaching that the
urned up in 1873 or
de ideas generally as
r less reproach upon
ing Kingdom. These
nanner of the Lord's
Aanner of Our Lord's

Return.' " This pamphlet was published in 1877. Brother Russell had some 50,000 copies of it printed and distributed.

In that pamphlet, he wrote: "We believe the scriptures to teach, that, at His coming and for a time after
He has come, He will remain invisible; afterward manifesting or showing Himself in judgments and various
forms, so that 'every eye shall see Him.' " In support of
this, he discussed such texts as Acts 1:11 ('he will come
in the same *manner* as you have beheld him go'—that
is, unobserved by the world) and John 14:19 ("a little

> **Progressive Truth**
>
> In 1882, C. T. Russell wrote: "The
> Bible is our only standard, and its
> teachings our only creed, and recog-
> nizing the progressive character of the
> unfolding of Scriptural truths, we are
> ready and prepared to add to or modi-
> fy our creed (faith—belief) as we get
> increase of light from our Standard."
> —"Watch Tower," April 1882, p. 7.

longer and the world will behold me no more"). Brother Russell also referred to the fact that *The Emphatic Diaglott*, which had first been published
in complete form in 1864 with an interlinear word-for-word English translation, gave evidence that the Greek expression *pa·rou·si'a* meant "presence." In analyzing the Bible's use of that term, Russell explained in this
pamphlet: "The Greek word generally used in referring to the second advent—*Parousia*, frequently translated *coming*—invariably signifies *personal
presence*, as having come, arrived and never signifies *to be on the way*, as we
use the word *coming.* "

When discussing the purpose of Christ's presence, Russell made it clear
that this was not something that would be accomplished in a single world-
shattering moment. "The second advent, like the first," he wrote, "covers a
period of time, and is not the event of a moment." During that time, he
wrote, the "little flock" would be given their reward with the Lord as joint
heirs in his Kingdom; others, perhaps billions, would be given opportunity
for perfect life on an earth restored to Edenic beauty.—Luke 12:32.

Within just a few years, on the basis of further study of the Scriptures,
Russell realized that Christ would not only *return* invisibly but also *remain*
invisible, even when manifesting his presence by judgment upon the wicked.

In 1876, when Russell had first read a copy of *Herald of the Morning*, he had learned that there was another group who then believed that
Christ's return would be invisible and who associated that return with
blessings for all families of the earth. From Mr. Barbour, editor of that
publication, Russell also came to be persuaded that Christ's invisible
presence had begun in 1874.* Attention was later drawn to this by the

---

* This was influenced by the belief that the seventh millennium of human history had begun
in 1873 and that a period of divine disfavor (of equal length to a former period considered to be
one of favor) upon natural Israel would end in 1878. The chronology was flawed because of re-
lying on an inaccurate rendering of Acts 13:20 in the *King James Version*, belief that there was a
transcription error at 1 Kings 6:1, and failure to take into account Biblical synchronisms in the
dating of reigns of the kings of Judah and of Israel. A clearer understanding of Biblical chronology was published in 1943, in the book *"The Truth Shall Make You Free,"* and it was then refined
the following year in the book *"The Kingdom Is at Hand,"* as well as in later publications.

1993

subtitle "Herald of Christ's Presence," which appeared on the cover of <u>Zion's Watch Tower.</u>

 Recognition of Christ's presence as being invisible became an important foundation on which an understanding of many Bible prophecies would be built. Those early Bible Students realized that the presence of the Lord should be of primary concern to all true Christians. (Mark 13:33-37) They were keenly interested in the Master's return and were alert to the fact that they had a responsibility to publicize it, but they did not yet clearly discern all the details. Yet, what God's spirit did enable them to understand at a very early time was truly remarkable. One of these truths involved a highly significant date marked by Bible prophecy.

End of the Gentile Times

 The matter of Bible chronology had long been of great interest to Bible students. Commentators had set out a variety of views on Jesus' prophecy about "the times of the Gentiles" and the prophet Daniel's record of Nebuchadnezzar's dream regarding the tree stump that was banded for "seven times."—Luke 21:24, *KJ;* Dan. 4:10-17.

They could see that 1914 was clearly marked by Bible prophecy

 As early as 1823, John A. Brown, whose work was published in London, England, calculated *the "seven times" of Daniel chapter 4 to be 2,520 years in length.* But he did not clearly discern the date with which the prophetic time period began or when it would end. He did, however, *connect these "seven times" with the Gentile Times of Luke 21:24.* In 1844, E. B. Elliott, a British clergyman, drew attention to *1914 as a possible date* for the end of the "seven times" of Daniel, but he also set out an alternate view that pointed to the time of the French Revolution. Robert Seeley, of London, in 1849, handled the matter in a similar manner. At least by 1870, a publication edited by Joseph Seiss and associates and printed in Philadelphia, Pennsylvania, was setting out calculations that *pointed to 1914 as a significant date,* even though the reasoning it contained was based on chronology that C. T. Russell later rejected.

 Then, in the August, September, and October 1875 issues of *Herald of the Morning,* N. H. Barbour helped to harmonize details that had been pointed out by others. Using chronology compiled by Christopher Bowen, a clergyman in England, and published by E. B. Elliott, Barbour identified *the start of the Gentile Times with King Zedekiah's removal from kingship as foretold at Ezekiel 21:25, 26,* and he pointed to *1914 as marking the end of the Gentile Times.*

 Early in 1876, C. T. Russell received a copy of *Herald of the Morning.* He promptly wrote to Barbour and then spent time with him in Philadelphia during the summer, discussing, among other things, prophetic time periods. Shortly thereafter, in an article entitled "Gentile Times: When Do

GROWING IN ACCUR

They End?", Ru
and stated that t
A.D. 1914." This
Examiner.* The t
duced in 1877 by I
to the same concl
as the ones dated
1914 C.E. as bein;
prophecy. In 188!
Dawn (later callec
"The Times of the
mean?

 The Bible Stu
They were convinc
and a blotting out
nificant point in re
that date the King:
trol. When that di
that marked the da
had marked only a

 Similarly, they
anarchy (which the
great day of God ti
But then, ten years
turmoil that would
come right *after* the
to mark a significan
said that 'Jerusalem
fulfilled. When the;
humans and been 'c
with earlier expecta
take place at the enc

 As the years pas
their faith in the pr
from stating what th
they endeavored to :
in the Scriptures.

Did the "Alarm C

 Great turmoil ce
outbreak of World

* A magazine published

PROPHECY, 1929

parable as the "wheat" and the "tares," growing in the same field. He declared they must continue thus to grow together until the end of the world. (Matt. 13:24, 30, 39.) Thus growing together, the true followers of Christ were greatly hindered by the false. The teachers in the churches were selfish men interested in political influence and personal flattery. Under the influence and control of the enemy Satan, they caused the truth to become obscure and to be seen very dimly.

Again attention is called to the words of Jesus, the great Prophet, who with authority from Jehovah said to his disciples: "I go to prepare a place for you. And if I go . . . I will come again and receive you unto myself." It should therefore be expected that the coming again of the Lord would mark the beginning of a better understanding of God's Word. In harmony with this, Peter at Pentecost uttered a prophecy saying: "Times of refreshing shall come from the presence [face] of the Lord [Jehovah]; and he shall send Jesus Christ, which before was preached unto you; whom the heaven must receive [retain] until the times of restitution of all things, which God hath spoken by the mouth of all his holy prophets since the world began." (Acts 3:19-21.) In this the apostle clearly foretells a time of refreshing to the people of the Lord, and that the time would be at the second coming of the Lord Jesus.

That would not mean that Jesus must be bodily present again on the earth, because with him distance is no barrier. He is a spirit being of the divine nature, and his power is without limitation, regardless of his actual bodily position. Being clothed with all power in heaven and in earth, he could administer the affairs of the church from one point as well as from another.

The apostle's words mean that, at a stated time and acting in accord with Jehovah's orders, Christ Jesus would begin to minister to those consecrated to God and give them refreshing. What would be the nature of that refreshing?

Peter mentions "restitution", which would mean a restoring of that which had been taken away or hidden, and would necessarily include the truth that was hidden during the "dark ages". On another occasion Jesus said that 'Elijah must first come and restore all things'. (Matt. 17:11.) Elijah was a prophet of God who did a restitution work in his time, in that he restored to the Israelites an understanding of the truth concerning God and their covenant relationship with God. (1 Ki. 18:39.) His work was prophetic and foretold that the Lord would restore his truth to his own people. After Elijah was dead, Malachi prophesied that God would send Elijah the prophet before the great and dreadful day of the Lord. (Mal. 4:5, 6.) That prophecy is proof that another should do a work similar to that done by Elijah, but on a far greater scale and of much more importance.

The restitution or restoring of all things, of which Jesus spoke, and also that mentioned by the Apostle Peter, must begin with the restoring to the people of God the truths that had been hidden during the dark ages. That restitution work would progress during the manifestation of the second presence of Jesus Christ. It would be expected that the days of understanding of the prophecies would begin sometime after the manifestation of the Lord's second presence, and the understanding would continue to increase thereafter.

The Scriptural proof is that the second presence of the Lord Jesus Christ began in 1874 A.D. This proof

106

345.   H.C. Covington.
(Cross)

...ls and got then angry and infuriated in his day.
Today Jehovah's Witnesses are commissioned to do the
same duty, untasty though what we speak may be, we still
must speak the truth, although as Jehovah said, it makes
all men liars. Q.- Is it not vital to speak the truth
on religious matters? A.- It certainly is. Q.- Is
there in your view room in a religion for a change of
interpretation of Holy Writ from time to time? A.- There
is every reason for a change in interpretation as we view
it, of the Bible. Our view becomes more clear as we see
the prophecy fulfilled by time. Q.- You have promulgated
for the word - false prophecy? A.- We have - I do
not think we have promulgated false prophecy, there have
been statements that were erroneous, that is the way I
put it, and mistaken. Q.- Is it a most vital consideration in the present situation of the world to know if
the prophecy can be interpreted into terms of fact, when
Christ's Second Coming was? A.- That is true, and we
have always striven to see that we have the truth before
we utter it. We go on the very best information we have
but we cannot wait until we get perfect, because if we
wait until we get perfect we would never be able to speak.
Q.- Let us follow that up just a little. It was
promulgated as a matter which must be believed by all
members of Jehovah's Witnesses that the Lord's Second
Coming took place in 1874? A.- I am not familiar with
that.

346.   H.C. Covington.
(Cross)

that. You are speaking on a matter that I know nothing
of. Q.- You heard Mr. Franz's evidence? A.- I heard
Mr. Franz testify, but I am not familiar with what he
said on that, I mean the subject matter of what he was
talking about, so I cannot answer any more than you can,
having heard what he said. Q.- Have me out of it? A.-
That is the source of my information, what I have heard in
court. Q.- You have studied the literature of your
movement? A.- Yes, but not all of it. I have not studied
the seven volumes of "Studies in the Scriptures", and I
have not studied this matter that you are mentioning now
of 1874. I am not at all familiar with that. Q.- Assume
from me that it was promulgated as authoritative by the
Society that Christ's Second Coming was in 1874? A.-
Taking that assumption as a fact, it is a hypothetical
statement. Q.- That was the publication of false prophecy?
A.- That was the publication of a false prophecy, it was a
false statement or an erroneous statement in fulfilment
of a prophecy that was false or erroneous. Q.- And that
had to be believed by the whole of Jehovah's Witnesses?
A.- Yes, because you must understand we must have unity,
we cannot have disunity with a lot of people going every
way, an army is supposed to march in step. Q.- You do
not believe in the worldly armies, do you? A.- We believe
in the Christian Army of God. Q.- Do you believe in the
worldly armies? A.- We have nothing to say about that, we
do.

DOUGLAS WALSH TRIAL, Scotland 1954

347.	E.C. Covington.
(Cross)

do not preach against them, we merely say that the worldly armies, like the nations of the world today, are a part of Satan's Organisation, and we do not take part in them, but we do not say that nations cannot have their armies, we do not preach against warfare. We are merely claiming our exemption from it, that is all. Q.- Back to the point now. A false prophecy was promulgated? A.- I agree that. Q.- It had to be accepted by Jehovah's Witnesses? A.- That is correct. Q.- If member of Jehovah's Witnesses took the view himself that that prophecy was wrong and said so he would be disfellowshipped? A.- Yes, if he said so and kept persisting in creating trouble, because if the whole organisation believes one thing, even though it be erroneous, and somebody else starts on his own trying to put his ideas across then there is disunity and trouble, there cannot be harmony, there cannot be marching. When a change comes it should come from the proper source, the head of the organisation, the governing body, not from the bottom upwards, because everybody would have ideas, and the organisation would disintegrate and go in a thousand different directions. Our purpose is to have unity.
Q./

348.	E.C. Covington.
(Cross)

Q.- Unity at all costs? A.- Unity at all costs, because we believe and are sure that Jehovah God is using our organisation, the governing body of our organisation to direct it, even though mistakes are made from time to time. Q.- And unity based upon an enforced acceptance of false prophecy? A.- That is conceded to be true. Q.- And the person who oppressed his views as you say, that it was wrong, and was disfellowshipped, would be in breach of the Covenant, if he was baptised? A.- That is correct. Q.- And as you said yesterday expressly, would be worthy of death? A.- I think - - . Q.- Would you say yes or no ? A.- I will answer yes, unhesitatingly. Q.- Do you call that religion? A.- It certainly is. Q.- Do you call it Christianity? A.- I certainly do. Q.- Would you look please at No. 40 of Process? A.- I have the "Watchtower" but you will have to direct my attention to the reference. Q.- For May 1st, 1950. Do you see there its Mission? A.- Yes. Q.- "It adheres strictly to the bible as authority for its utterances, it is entirely free and separate from all religion, parties, sects, or other worldly organisations." That means what it says, does it not? A.- It means what it says as we understood the term, "Religion" to mean at that time, which was false religion. We have since had light on that subject. Q.- You are a lawyer
A./

DOUGLAS WALSH TRIAL, Scotland 1954

22 — Thy Kingdom Come.

"Thy Kingdom come, Thy will be done on earth," let their prayers be mere mockeries of lip-service, to which mouth will I judge thee," represents one of the most searching and severe reproofs which the Judge will pronounce against some who have professed to be his servants and to long for his Kingdom of love and justice. Let all who thus pray for and believe in the coming reign of righteousness even now square their actions and words by its just precepts, as far as in them lies.

Those who have caught the force of the lessons of the preceding volumes will see that God's Kingdom will not be one of outward, visible, earthly splendor, but of power and divine glory. This Kingdom has already come into executive authority, although it has not yet conquered and displaced the kingdoms of this world, whose lease of power has not yet expired. Hence it has not yet come into full control of earthly dominion. Its establishment is in progress, however, as indicated by the signs of the times, as well as by the prophecies considered in the previous volume and others examined in this volume.

Succeeding chapters will present prophecies marking various stages of the preparation of the nominal church and the world for the Kingdom, and call attention to some of those most momentous changes foretold to take place during the time of its establishment—than which nothing could be more important or more deeply interesting to those living saints who are longing for the promised joint-heirship in this Kingdom, and seeking to be engaged in co-operation with the Master, the Chief-Reaper and King, in the work now due and in progress.

STUDY II.

"THE TIME OF THE END," OR "DAY OF HIS PREPARATION."

—DANIEL XI.—

THE TIME OF THE END—ITS COMMENCEMENT, A. D. 1799.—ITS CLOSE, A. D. 1914.—WHAT IS TO BE PREPARED, AND THE OBJECT—THE WORLD'S HISTORY PROPHETICALLY TRACED THROUGH ITS CHIEF RULERS—FROM B. C. 405 TO THIS DAY OF PREPARATION.—THE BEGINNING OF THE TIME OF THE END DEFINITELY MARKED, YET WITHOUT NAMES OR DATES.

THE "Time of the End," a period of one hundred and fifteen (115) years, from A. D. 1799 to A. D. 1914, is particularly marked in the Scriptures. "The Day of His Preparation," is another name given to the same period, because in it a general increase of knowledge, resulting in discoveries, inventions, etc., paves the way to the coming Millennium of favor, making ready the mechanical devices which will economize labor, and provide the world in general with time and conveniences, which under Christ's reign of righteousness will be a blessing to all and aid in filling the earth with the knowledge of the Lord. And it is a day or period of preparation in another sense also; for by the increase of knowledge among the masses, giving to all a taste of liberty and luxury, before Christ's rule is established to rightly regulate the world, these blessings will gradually become agencies of class-power and will result in the uprising of the masses and the overthrow of corporative Trusts, etc., with which will fall also all the present dominions of earth, civil and ecclesiastical. And thus the pres-

THY KINGDOM COME (1891), 1914 edition

109

230   *The Harp of God,* 1924

for a year, as the Prophet says: "I have appointed thee each day for a year". (Ezekiel 4:6) Here are mentioned, then, three and a half times of 360 prophetic days each, or a total of 1260 prophetic days, equal to 1260 years. The Prophet then was shown that the 1260 years would mark the beginning of the time of the end of this beastly order. Twelve hundred sixty years from A. D. 539 brings us to 1799—another proof that 1799 definitely marks the beginning of "the time of the end". This also shows that it is from the date 539 A. D. that the other prophetic days of Daniel must be counted.

[388]The most important thing to which all the prophecies point and for which the apostles looked forward has been the second coming of the Lord. It is described by the Prophet as a blessed time. Daniel then says: "Blessed is he that waiteth, and cometh to the thousand three hundred and five and thirty [1335] days". (Daniel 12:12) The watchers here, without question, are those who were instructed by the Lord to watch for his return. This date, therefore, when understood, would certainly fix the time when the Lord is due at his second appearing. Applying the same rule, then, of a day for a year, 1335 days after 539 A. D. brings us to A. D. 1874, at which time, according to Biblical chronology, the Lord's second presence is due. If this calculation is correct, from that time forward we ought to be able to find some evidences marking the Lord's presence.

[389]It is not the purpose of this writing to enter into a detailed statement of Biblical chronology. The searcher for truth can find an extensive treatment of this question in Volumes 2 and 3 of STUDIES IN THE SCRIPTURES. The purpose here is to call attention to certain important dates and then see how much, if any, prophecy has been fulfilled within these dates. Chronology, to

---

Our Lord's Return   231

some extent at least, depends upon accurate calculations and there is always some possibility of mistakes. Fulfilled prophecy is the record of physical facts which are actually existent and definitely fixed. Physical facts do not stultify themselves. They stand as silent witnesses whose testimony must be taken as indisputable.

[400]There are two important dates here that we must not confuse, but clearly differentiate, namely, the beginning of "the time of the end" and of "the presence of the Lord". "The time of the end" embraces a period from A. D. 1799, as above indicated, to the time of the complete overthrow of Satan's empire and the establishment of the Kingdom of the Messiah. The time of the Lord's second presence dates from 1874, as above stated. The latter period is within the first named, of course, and at the latter part of the period known as "the time of the end".

[401]The understanding of the prophecies with reference to "the time of the end" and the Lord's presence was purposely concealed by Jehovah until the due time. Daniel desired to know what would be the end of these things, but God said to him: "But thou, O Daniel, shut up the words, and seal the book, even to the time of the end". (Daniel 12:4) It is reasonable to expect that Jehovah would indicate something by which " the time of the end" could be discerned when it arrived. He did not say to Daniel to look for some words emblazoned across the sky that the end had come, but told him to look for such evidences as could be seen and understood by men familiar with the prophecies, and who in the light of the prophecies should be watching for their fulfillment. He did not expect Daniel to understand it in his day, because he said: "Go thy way, Daniel: for the words are closed up and sealed till the time of the end".—Daniel 12:9.

S OF GOD'S KINGDOM

d on the cover of

became an impor-
Bible prophecies
he presence of the
. (Mark 13:33-37)
ere alert to the fact
did not yet clearly
em to understand
truths involved a

at interest to Bible
n Jesus' prophecy
l's record of Neb-
banded for "seven

published in Lon-
pter 4 to be 2,520
e with which the
He did, however,
e 21:24. In 1844,
4 as a possible date
et out an alternate
Robert Seeley, of
. At least by 1870,
rinted in Philadel-
ted to 1914 as a sig-
as based on chro-

5 issues of *Herald*
ails that had been
Christopher Bow-
ott, Barbour iden-
emoval from king-
914 as marking the

ld of the Morning.
h him in Philadel-
s, prophetic time
Times: When Do

GROWING IN ACCURATE KNOWLEDGE OF THE TRUTH

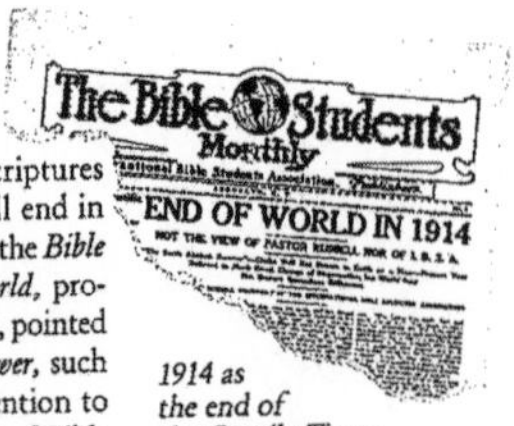

1914 as the end of the Gentile Times was given wide publicity by the Bible Students, as in this I.B.S.A. tract distributed during 1914

They End?", Russell also reasoned on the matter from the Scriptures and stated that the evidence showed that "the seven times will end in A.D. 1914." This article was printed in the October 1876 issue of the *Bible Examiner*.* The book *Three Worlds, and the Harvest of This World*, produced in 1877 by N. H. Barbour in cooperation with C. T. Russell, pointed to the same conclusion. Thereafter, early issues of the *Watch Tower*, such as the ones dated December 1879 and July 1880, directed attention to 1914 C.E. as being a highly significant year from the standpoint of Bible prophecy. In 1889 the entire fourth chapter of Volume II of *Millennial Dawn* (later called *Studies in the Scriptures*) was devoted to discussion of "The Times of the Gentiles." But what would the end of the Gentile Times mean?

The Bible Students were not completely sure what would happen. They were convinced that it would not result in a burning up of the earth and a blotting out of human life. Rather, they knew it would mark a significant point in regard to divine rulership. At first, they thought that by that date the Kingdom of God would have obtained full, universal control. When that did not occur, their confidence in the Bible prophecies that marked the date did not waver. They concluded that, instead, the date had marked only a starting point as to Kingdom rule.

Similarly, they also first thought that global troubles culminating in anarchy (which they understood would be associated with the war of "the great day of God the Almighty") would precede that date. (Rev. 16:14) But then, ten years before 1914, the *Watch Tower* suggested that worldwide turmoil that would result in the annihilating of human institutions would come right *after* the end of the Gentile Times. They expected the year 1914 to mark a significant turning point for Jerusalem, since the prophecy had said that 'Jerusalem would be trodden down' until the Gentile Times were fulfilled. When they saw 1914 drawing close and yet they had not died as humans and been 'caught up in the clouds' to meet the Lord—in harmony with earlier expectations—they earnestly hoped that their change might take place at the end of the Gentile Times.—1 Thess. 4:17.

As the years passed and they examined and reexamined the Scriptures, their faith in the prophecies remained strong, and they did not hold back from stating what they expected to occur. With varying degrees of success, they endeavored to avoid being dogmatic about details not directly stated in the Scriptures.

Did the "Alarm Clock" Go Off Too Soon?

Great turmoil certainly burst forth upon the world in 1914 with the outbreak of World War I, which for many years was called simply the

* A magazine published by George Storrs, Brooklyn, New York.

JEHOVAH'S WITNESSES - PROCLAIMERS OF GOD'S KINGDOM, 1993, p. 135

111

¹⁴"Pentecost, that is, the fiftieth day, or Harvest Feast, or Feast of Weeks, may be regarded as a supplement to the Passover. It lasted only for one day; but the modern Jews extend it over two. The people, having at the Passover presented before God the first sheaf of the harvest, departed to their homes to gather it in, and then returned to keep the harvest-feast before Jehovah. From the sixteenth of Nisan seven weeks were reckoned inclusively, and the next or fiftieth day was the Day of Pentecost, which fell on the sixth of Sivan (about the end of May) (Exodus 23: 16, 34: 22; Leviticus 23: 15-22; Numbers 28: 26-31; Deuteronomy 16: 9-12; 2 Maccabees 12: 32; Acts 2: 1, 20: 16; 1 Corinthians 16: 8). The intervening period included the whole of the grain harvest, of which the wheat was the latest crop. Its commencement is also marked as from the time when 'thou beginnest to put the sickle to the corn.' The Pentecost was the Jewish harvest-home; and the people were especially exhorted to rejoice before Jehovah with their families, their servants, the Levite within their gates, the stranger, the fatherless, and the widow, in the place chosen by God for His name, as they brought a freewill-offering of their hand to Jehovah their God.—Deuteronomy 16: 10, 11."

¹⁵If we assume that the harvest of the wheat class, namely, the saints, began with the beginning of the second presence of our Lord in 1874, then would it be unreasonable to conclude that the harvest must continue for fifty symbolic days, or fifty literal years? If so, then we might expect the harvest to end fifty years after 1874, or with the year 1924. If this be true, what a wonderful incentive for the saints to be watchful, prayerful, active, and rejoicing in their privileges to have a part in the Lord's work in these concluding days of the harvest. That would mean that the selection of the royal family would be completed with the end of 1924. If this be true, then surely with confidence the saints now on earth can announce with the opening of this year, "The kingdom of heaven is at hand," because all the members of the royal line are about completed for the kingdom.

ITS MEANING TO THE CHURCH

¹⁶Surely there is not the slightest room for doubt in the mind of a truly consecrated child of God that the Lord Jesus is present and has been since 1874; that the harvest has been in progress during that time; that most of the saints have now been gathered. Therefore, can there be a reasonable doubt about the early completion of the church and its glorification in view of the fulfilment of prophecy? Do not all the physical facts about us indicate just exactly what we expected during the concluding hours of the church's earthly pilgrimage?

¹⁷Then should we expect the closing days of the harvest work and witnessing for the Lord to be all joy and no trials? To answer this question we must take into consideration the words of Jesus relative to the last work of the church. It seems quite clear that the last work of the church in the flesh is to be that of proclaiming the good news that Satan's empire is falling; that the kingdom of heaven is here, and the blessing that the people will reap from that kingdom. Concerning this Jesus said: "And this gospel of the king-

dom shall be preached in all the world for a witness unto all nations; and then shall the end come." (Matthew 24: 14) The root word from which the word "end" is taken in this text is "*telos*"; and the meaning given to it by Doctor Strong is: "The point aimed at, as a limit, final or uttermost."

¹⁸The Lord's words here then, we would understand, mean to say: The point aimed at, as a limit of the work of the church while in the flesh, the final and uttermost part of that work, is and will be that of proclaiming the good tidings of the end of the old order and that the kingdom of heaven is here and of the blessings it will bring; and this should be done as a witness to the nations; that when this work of witnessing is done, that is, the end or final point aimed at, then will follow the great tribulation that will completely wreck all the nations.

¹⁹Necessarily there must be much joy in the heart of the Christian while proclaiming this blessed message, because it means the bringing to the people that which will comfort and console them in the hour of distress. It means to tell the groaning creation that the time for their deliverance is at hand. At the same time the words of Jesus in the context show that this final work to be done will be accompanied by many severe tests and trials. In verse thirteen he says: "He that endures unto the end, the same shall be saved." Here the word "end" is translated from the same Greek word "*telos*." Therefore we conclude that the endurance must relate to the same time that this message is to be delivered. If those who endure to the end are to be saved, the converse of the statement is true: That those who do not endure to the end will not be of the royal family. Since the endurance to the end and the preaching of the gospel of the kingdom referred to the same time, then it follows that there will be much to endure. The word "endure" means to bear trials, have fortitude, patiently suffer and persevere. Persevere means to persist in any business or enterprise undertaken, to maintain a purpose in spite of counter influences, opposition or discouragement; not to give over or abandon what is undertaken. The inference is, therefore, that there will be a great temptation to relax, to become discouraged, to yield to opposing influences and to give over or abandon the final work.

²⁰The only conclusion to be drawn from these texts is that having put our hand to the plow we must keep on; that since the Lord has committed to his people the interests of his kingdom and commanded that these interests be properly cared for by proclaiming the message of his kingdom, then a failure or refusal to do so would preclude one from being of the royal line. Strange as it may seem, many of these fiery trials, which will tend to discourage, will come from amongst the consecrated. St. Peter concerning this said: "Beloved, think it not strange concerning the fire that is among you to try you, as though some strange thing had happened unto you." Many of these trials will be due to

p 5

124   *Thy Kingdom Come.*

knowledge of his presence will come to the world in another way, and at a later time. None are now prepared to receive this truth, except the consecrated, the Sanctuary class. To the "host," of nominal Christians, as well as to the world, it is foolishness; nor will they be disposed to test the proof set forth in the volumes of this series.

Not only thus has the Lord prepared the hearts of his people and led them by ways which they knew not, but, for this special time, of need, he has furnished wonderful help to Bible study, such as concordances, and varied, and valuable translations of the Scriptures, as well as wonderful facilities for printing, publishing and mailing the truth; and the advantages of general education, so that all can read and study for themselves, and prove, to their own satisfaction all the doctrines advanced; and these under conditions of peace, so that none can molest them or make them afraid to exercise full liberty of conscience in so doing.

After a careful perusal of the foregoing chapters of this and the preceding volume, the thoughtful reader will observe, that, while each of the time-prophecies accomplishes a separate and distinct purpose, the central object of their united and harmonious testimony has been to mark, with definiteness and precision, by either direct or indirect evidence, or corroborative testimony, the date of our Lord's second advent, and of the establishment of his Kingdom in the earth; and also to mark the various stages and means of its establishment, during the harvest period.

In order that we may realize the force of these various lines of prophecy in their bearing on these central truths, let us draw them to a focus, and note how these rays of testimony unitedly and harmoniously blend, clearly revealing the blessed facts, not that the Lord is coming, nor that he will soon come, but that he has come, that he is now present, a spiritual king, establishing a spiritual empire, in

The Times of Harvest.   125

the harvest or end of the Gospel age, which laps upon the new dawning Millennial age. We have seen that there are to come "Times of Restitution of all things." "Times of Refreshing" (Acts 3:19); we have seen also that the Lord Jehovah "*hath appointed a day* [the Millennial age] in the which he will judge the world in righteousness by that man whom he hath ordained, whereof he hath given assurance unto all men; in that he hath raised him from the dead" (Acts 17:31); we have seen that the Gospel age has been the trial time or judgment day of the Church, and that it ends with a harvesting; and the glorification of those who are to live and reign with Christ a thousand years—during the world's judgment day, the Times of Restitution; and we have also seen that the kingdoms of this world, under the prince of this world, Satan, must give place to the Kingdom of God, under the King of glory. All of these great events must tarry until the second advent of our Lord, the King, Bridegroom and Reaper, whose presence and work are to accomplish them, as foretold.

The typical Jubilee cycles pointed out A.D. 1874 as the date of our Lord's return, and yet the date was therein so ingeniously hidden, as to make its discovery impossible until the "Time of the End." And this testimony was made doubly strong by proofs from two standpoints—the Law and the Prophets—the two being entirely independent of each other, and yet equally clear and convincing.

The wonderful parallelism of the Jewish and Gospel dispensations taught us the same truth with additional features. The second advent of our Lord in the end or harvest of the Gospel age, occurring in the fall of 1874, proves to be at a point of time exactly parallel to the time of his first advent, in the end of the Jewish age. (See Table of Correspondencies, Vol. II, pages 246 and 247.) As every prominent feature of the Gospel dispensation is marked by a corre-

THY KINGDOM COME (1891) 1914 ed.

The Time is at Hand.

14.

Paul, "It is high time to awake out of sleep; for now is our salvation nearer than when we believed." The night is far spent, the [Millennial] day is at hand." Yea, it is even at the doors. The kingdom of heaven is now at hand, not in its mere embryotic or incipient stage, as at our Lord's first advent (Matt. 3:2), but in the sense in which he declared it was yet to come (John 18:36, 37)—"in power and great glory."

Only those, however, who have made a careful study of the Plan of the Ages will be prepared to appreciate the teaching of this volume concerning the divinely appointed times and seasons for the development of the various features of that plan, and for its final consummation. It is hoped that none will undertake this study, therefore, before they have thoroughly comprehended the lessons of the preceding volume. Otherwise it will not be meat in due season to them. Truth is only meat in season when we are prepared to receive it. A child is not prepared to solve a mathematical problem until he has first been instructed in the use of figures and of language. So also with 'divine truth; it is built up step by step, and to gain an understanding of it we must ascend by the steps provided—carefully, of course, proving by the Scriptures every advance step we take, yet not fearful to take the steps as we thus find for them sure footing. Only those who have implicit faith in God, and to whom a "Thus saith the Lord" is the end of all doubt and controversy, can be led by the Spirit of God into advanced truth as it becomes due—led into things new, as well as confirmed in things old and proved true by the same authority.

Only such, God proposes so to lead. In the end of the age, which is the harvest time, much truth is due to be uncovered, which God did not make known in times past, even to his most faithful and devoted children. It was in the

Times and Seasons.

15

time of the end that the Prophet Habakkuk (2:3) declared that the vision, concerning 'the glorious consummation of God's plan, should speak and not lie; and that to some of God's children it should speak so plainly that they would be able, as directed, to make it plain on tables; that through their instrumentality others might be enabled to read it clearly; and then Daniel also (12:4, 9, 10) declared that knowledge should be increased, and that the wise (through faith) should understand the vision.

Our object here is not to prophesy out of the abundance of human imagination, nor in any sense to be wise above what is written in the sacred Scriptures. Therefore, discarding all human inventions, we keep close to the fountain of divine truth, endeavoring to read prophecy in the light of prophecy and its manifest fulfilment; and to make plain upon tables that which God said would be sealed up, and which therefore could not be understood before this time of the end, but of which he gave assurance that it should then be understood,

(In this volume we offer a chain of testimony on the subject of God's appointed times and seasons, each link of which we consider Scripturally strong, while the whole of it when viewed together, in the relationship which one part bears to another, gives evidence of a plan so broad and comprehensive, a design so deep, and a harmony so perfect, as to clearly manifest to the studious and reverent inquirer that it is beyond the breadth and depth of human thought, and therefore cannot be of human origin.)

We find that the end of the Gospel age, like the end of the Jewish age, is called a harvest (Matt. 9:37; 13:24, 30, 39); that like that also, it is a period of forty years; and that upon the harvests of the ages the rays of prophetic testimony are specially concentrated, particularly upon the harvest of this age, where even all the light of the Jewish

THE TIME IS AT HAND (1889), 1917 edition

with God, because many false prophets have gone forth into the world." (1 John 4:1) Accordingly, there would be need among the restored remnant of spiritual Israelites to guard against false prophets invading or rising up in the midst of their spiritual estate on earth.

18 How, then, did Jehovah keep their "land" or spiritual estate pure in worship by fulfilling his promise: "Also the prophets and the spirit of uncleanness I shall cause to pass out of the land"? (Zechariah 13:2) It was by causing any wrong understandings of the Bible prophecies that had been entertained before the remnant's reinstatement in their "land" in 1919 C.E. to be corrected. The "time of the end," the "conclusion of the system of things," that began in 1914 at the end of the Gentile Times was God's appointed time for the fulfillment of many prophecies. These could not be understood until they were just about to be fulfilled or after they had been fulfilled. So in the light of all that was taking place since 1914 the reinstated remnant looked anew into the prophecies that God had reserved for the "time of the end" for their fulfillment. (Daniel 12:4; Revelation 10:6, 7) This included a restudy of the books of Ezekiel and Revelation, an explanation of which had been attempted and published in July of 1917 in the book entitled "The Finished Mystery." Thus the restored remnant heeded the words:

19 "We, have the prophetic word made more sure; and you are doing well in paying attention to it as to a lamp shining in a dark place, until day dawns and a daystar rises, in your hearts. For you know this first, that no prophecy of Scripture springs from any private interpretation. For prophecy was at no time brought by man's will, but men spoke from God as they were borne along by holy spirit."—2 Peter 1:19-21.

20 Any attempted interpretation of prophecy, if it proved to be incorrect in the light of historic events and the clearer understanding of the Bible, was cor-

18, 19. (a) What did Jehovah's causing the false prophet to pass out of the land require on the part of the reinstated remnant of spiritual Israel as to do? (b) What purpose of the apostle Peter concerning prophecy did they heed?
20. How, figuratively speaking, did fleshly parents pierce their son through by prophesying falsely?

rected, regardless of who had offered the interpretation. Loyalty to God and to his inspired Word was the issue here to be met. So, as an illustration of the loyalty required, even if a fleshly son should offer a wrong interpretation of divine prophecy and should persist in it, like a false prophet, then his own fleshly parents in their loyalty to God would have nothing further to do with him on a religious basis. Christian parents could not do as under the Mosaic Law covenant, namely, have him put to death; but they could pronounce him spiritually dead to themselves in spite of their parenthood of him physically. In this way, figuratively speaking, they "must pierce him through because of his prophesying." (Zechariah 13:3; compare Deuteronomy 13:1-5.) With their full consent, such a false prophet would be expelled, disfellowshiped, from the Christian congregation. By such loyalty on the part of all members of the restored remnant, the "prophet" of false-hood would be made to pass out of their "land."

21 Yes, too, the "spirit of uncleanness" would thus be made to pass out of their spiritual "land." If that spirit were an inspired expression of uncleanness by a would-be prophet or was any tendency, trend, or inclination to uncleanness, it would be disapproved and resisted by the loyal ones. As a consequence any uncleanness as to religious teaching or as to moral behavior would be forced to pass out, under the driving force of God's holy spirit. The God-given spiritual estate must be maintained as a "land" where clean, Scriptural living is carried on. Persons spiritually and morally unclean must be disfellowshiped therefrom.—2 Corinthians 6:14 to 7:1; compare Deuteronomy 13:6-18.

RELIGIOUS HYPOCRISY EXPOSED

22 Jehovah, the God of the true prophets, will put all false prophets to shame either by not fulfilling the false prediction of such self-assuming prophets or by having

21. How, too, was the "spirit of uncleanness" made to pass out of their spiritual "land"?
22, 23. (a) How does Jehovah put the false prophets to shame? (b) How does Jehovah describe the false prophets trying to hide their reason for feeling shame?

1972

His own prophecies fulfilled in a way opposite to that predicted by the false prophets. False prophets will try to hide their reason for feeling shame by denying who they really are. They will try to avoid being killed or being pronounced spiritually dead by Jehovah's loyal worshipers. He foretold this by having his true prophet Zechariah continue on to say:

23 "And it must occur in that day that the prophets will become ashamed, each one of his vision when he prophesies; and they will not wear an official garment of hair for the purpose of deceiving. And he will certainly say, 'I am no prophet, I am a man cultivating the soil, because an earthling man himself acquired me from my youth on.' And one must say to him, 'What are these wounds on your person between your hands?' And he will have to say, 'Those with which I was struck in the house of my intense lovers.'"—Zechariah 13:4-6, NW; JB; NE; NAB; contrast Amos 7:14-17.

24 Thus Jehovah foretold that his people, in their "land" of restoration, would be so well instructed with his Word and would be so loyal to Him and His true prophecies that they would refuse to be friends and intense lovers of any false prophet. If they did not kill him, then they would discipline him and strike him so hard in their indignation that visible wounds and scars would result. Such marks on his person, yes, on his breast which would be partly exposed, would betray his identity in spite of the fact that he had discarded official garments that he had assumed to wear as a bona fide prophet of Jehovah God. From whom had he got such scar-producing wounds? From his intense lovers, whether these were his own fleshly parents or his intimate associates. However, their intense loyalty to Jehovah as the God of true prophecy would be stronger than their till-then intense love for a deceptive prophet. They would place love of God and his inspired Word above personal friendships with fleshly relatives or associates. Such a course would cause "the prophets"

24. The scar-producing wounds on the deceptive prophet were admitted by him to be inflicted by what would this indicate as to loyalty to God in comparison with attachment to fleshly loved ones?

and the spirit of uncleanness" to pass out of the "land" of Jehovah's repatriated people.

25 This course of supreme loyalty to the Sovereign Lord Jehovah has been the one adopted by the anointed remnant since 1919 C.E. This has resulted in the disfellowshiping or excommunicating of religious apostates or rebels from the theocratic organization that Jehovah the heavenly Theocrat has established among his obedient remnant. The loyal remnant have found out that it is not the mere "official garment of hair," not a professional uniform or type of dress, that makes a true prophet of the one living and true God. That is why they have left Babylon the Great, including Christendom, with its distinctively garbed religious priests, preachers, monks and nuns. What makes a true prophet of Jehovah today is his true Christian personality as Word and its prophecies. It is no wonder, then, that Jehovah's witnesses while acting as ministers of God's Word wear plain business suits or the regular attire of the common people. So the loyal remnant are willing to brush aside intense love for close associates and to inflict spiritual "wounds" upon these in disapproval and rejection of apostates. This has kept their theocratic "land" a spiritual realm of clean godly living.

STRIKING THE SHEPHERD CAUSES A SCATTERING

26 Jehovah's greatest prophet on earth was struck and wounded to the death, but this was for his proving to be a true prophet of the Most High God down to the end. (Deuteronomy 18:15-22; Acts 3:13-23) His violent death caused a short-time scattering of his disciples who were loyal to him. The true prophet Zechariah was used to foretell this, for God went on to say to him: "'O sword, awake against my shepherd, even against the able-bodied man who is my associate,' is the utterance of Jehovah of armies. 'Strike the shepherd, and let

25. This course of supreme loyalty to Jehovah has been adopted by whom and since when, and how has this affected their spiritual "land"? 26. (a) As a prophet, Jesus Christ was struck and wounded for what reason? (b) How did Jehovah foretell this through the prophet Zechariah?

116

reliable promises. It is a peace and security that we can enjoy only in association with his visible organization on earth.

15 It would be out of line with the plain teachings of the Scriptures to believe that God does not have an organization, an organized people, that he exclusively recognizes. Jesus Christ recognized that his heavenly Father had a visible organization. Until Pentecost 33 C.E., it was the Jewish organization in covenant relationship with Jehovah God under the Law of Moses.—Luke 16:16.

16 Just as the ancient nation of Israel was in a covenant relationship with Jehovah God through the mediator Moses, so the nation of spiritual Israel, "the Israel of God," has a covenant relationship through a mediator. (Galatians 6:16) It is as the apostle Paul wrote to his Christian fellow worker: "There is one God, and one mediator between God and men, a man, Christ Jesus." (1 Timothy 2:5) Was Moses the mediator between Jehovah God and mankind in general? No, he was the mediator between the God of Abraham, Isaac, and Jacob and the nation of their fleshly descendants. Likewise, the Greater Moses, Jesus Christ, is not the Mediator between Jehovah God and all mankind. He is the Mediator between his heavenly Father, Jehovah God, and the nation of spiritual Israel, which is limited to only 144,000 members.

15. Is it unreasonable to think that God has an organization, and what did Jesus Christ recognize?
16. (a) Between whom was Moses the mediator? (b) Between whom is the Greater Moses, Jesus Christ, the Mediator?

This spiritual nation is like a little flock of Jehovah's sheeplike ones.—Romans 9:6; Revelation 7:4.

Shepherd Over More Than the "Little Flock"

17 In Psalm 23:1, King David of ancient Israel was inspired to say: "Jehovah is my Shepherd. I shall lack nothing." Jehovah, the Supreme Shepherd, has assigned Jesus Christ to be "the fine shepherd." (John 10:11) At Luke 12:32, Jesus addressed himself to those of whom he is the Fine Shepherd: "Have no fear, little flock, because your Father has approved of giving you the kingdom."

18 In ancient times, there were non-Jews, such as the Nethinim and the sons of non-Israelite servants of Solomon, who were associated with the nation of Israel. (Ezra 2:43-58; 8:17-20) Similarly today, there are men and women who are wholly dedicated to God through Jesus Christ but who are not spiritual Israelites. They are, however, associated with the remnant of spiritual Israel because of dedicating themselves to Jehovah God through Jesus Christ, "who gave himself a corresponding ransom for all." (1 Timothy 2:6) Today, these far outnumber the 144,000 spiritual Israelites, who are to inherit the heavenly Kingdom.

17. (a) What has Jehovah God assigned Jesus Christ to be? (b) What did Jesus say to those who are to inherit the heavenly Kingdom?
18. (a) Who today correspond to the Nethinim and the sons of non-Israelite servants of Solomon? (b) With whom are they closely associated?

117

ABOUT THE AUTHOR

Christina Darlington is the Director of Witnesses for Jesus, a ministry to Jehovah's Witnesses and Latter-day Saints (Mormons). As a devoted Christian, her passion is to alert the Christian community to the doctrines of these groups and to train and equip Christians to be effective witnesses to those ensnared by these counterfeit religions.

Jehovah God is the God of truth, and truth does not fear examination. If a religious organization or church cannot stand up under examination, it is not "the Truth," but is rather a counterfeit, and LOYALTY to a counterfeit is DISLOYALTY to Jehovah God. The ministry of Witnesses for Jesus was born out of a deep love and concern for Jehovah's Witnesses who have committed their lives to a counterfeit faith.

> "But I am afraid, lest as the serpent deceived Eve by his craftiness, your minds should be **led astray** from the **simplicity** and **purity** of **devotion to Christ**. For if one comes and preaches **another Jesus** whom we have not preached … you bear this beautifully."
> —2 Corinthians 11:3-4 [24]

> "Test yourselves to see if you are in the faith; examine yourselves! Or do you not recognize this about yourselves, that **Jesus Christ is in you-unless indeed you fail the test?**"
> —2 Corinthians 13:5

Exclusive religions like Jehovah's Witnesses often refer to their religious faiths as being the ultimate "truth." Because the

---

[24] All Scripture citations in this section of the book are from the *New American Standard Bible.*

147

members of these groups are taught that the only way to God is through their particular faith, each person's identity and security is wrapped up in his or her religious faith. Thus, as is the case with Jehovah's Witnesses, when one Jehovah's Witness meets another, he or she will often ask the other person, "How long have you been in THE TRUTH?"

Real truth, however, is not found in identifying with a particular religious faith or denomination, but in a personal relationship with Jesus, for He proclaims that He is THE TRUTH: "and you shall **know the truth**, and the truth shall make you free ... If therefore the Son shall make you free, you shall be free indeed ... I am the way, and **the truth**, and the life; no one comes to the Father, but through Me." —John 8:32, 36; 14:6

> "And the witness is this, that God has **given us eternal life**, and this life is in His Son. He who **has the Son has the life**; he who does not have the Son of God does not have the life. These things I have written to you who believe in the name of the Son of God, in order that **you may know** that you have eternal life." —1 John 5:11-13

WITNESSES FOR JESUS INC
POBOX 50911
COLORADO SPRINGS, CO 80949 USA

4WITNESS.ORG * 4JEHOVAH.ORG